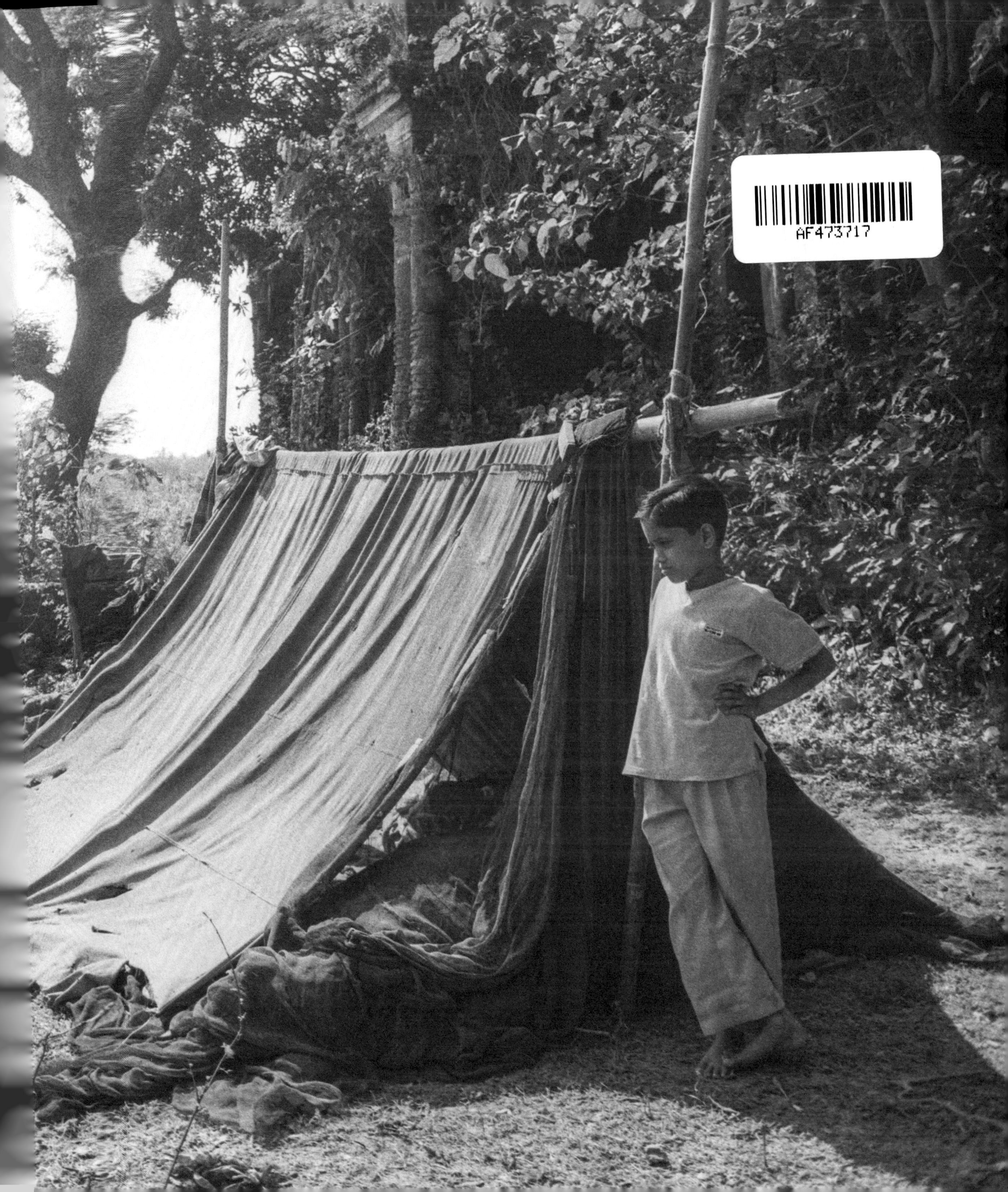

Homage to Bangladesh

'Just think of your camera as a flame-thrower... It's a lot more effective than bullets.'

Henri Cartier-Bresson, in a postcard to Patrick Zachmann, fellow Magnum photographer, in February 1990. Zachmann was in hospital after being shot by the police as he photographed Nelson Mandela on his release from prison.

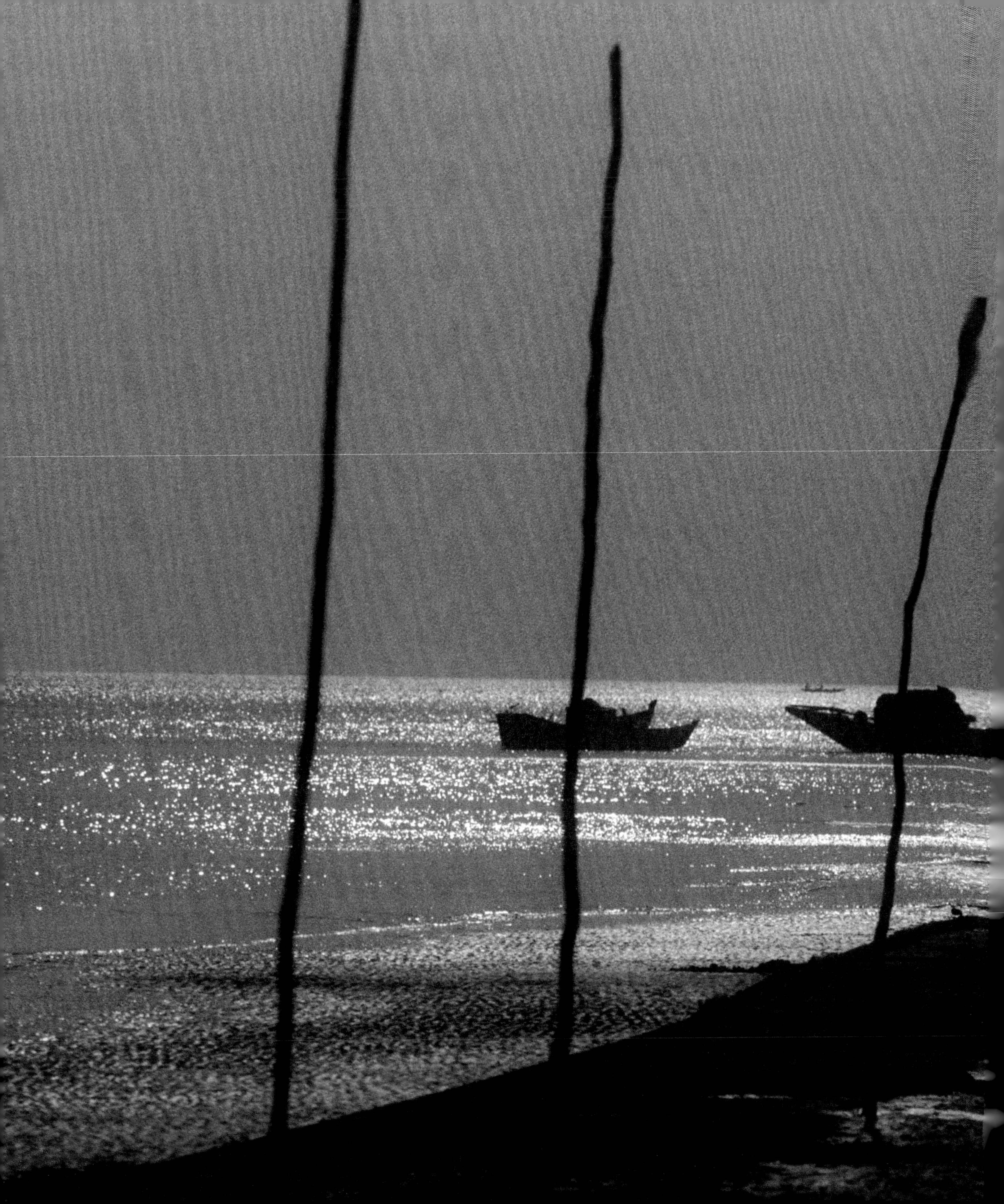

Homage to Bangladesh

A Memoir of a Time and a Place

RUPERT GREY

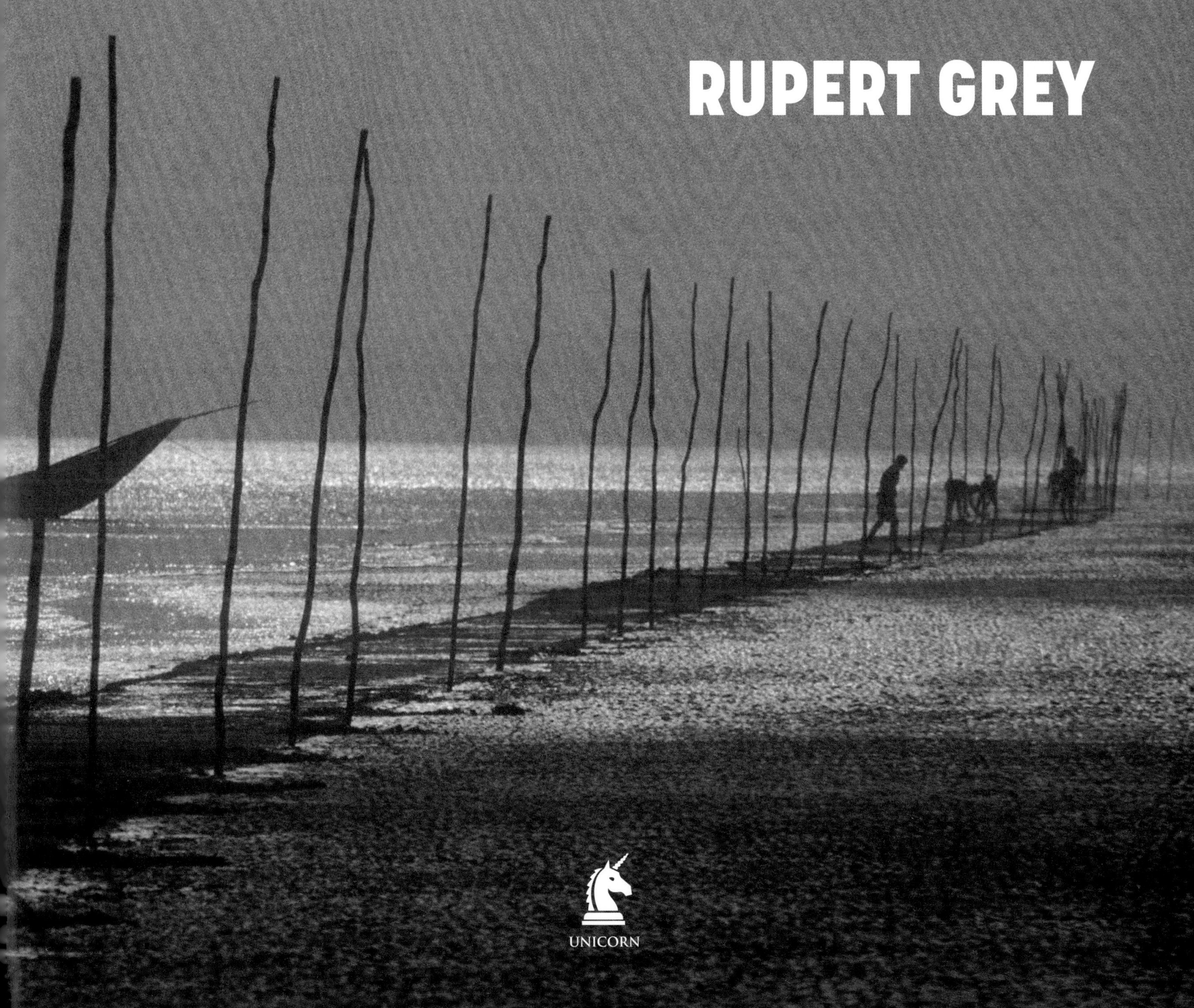

UNICORN

To Jan, the Navigator

Front endpaper
A family of water gypsies in Old Sonargaon in 2004

Back endpaper
The Buriganga, near Sodherghat, and the port of Old Dhaka

Previous page
One of many tributaries of the Ganges as it flows through the Sundarbans into the Bay of Bengal towards the Swatch of No Ground. In the foreground are seine nets, which catch fish as the tide flows out.

Published in 2023 by Unicorn
an imprint of Unicorn Publishing Group LLP
Charleston Studio
Meadow Business Centre
Lewes BN8 5RW
www.unicornpublishing.org

ISBN 978-1-911397-39-7

10 9 8 7 6 5 4 3 2 1

Designed by Guy Callaby
Printed by Fine Tone Ltd

Contents

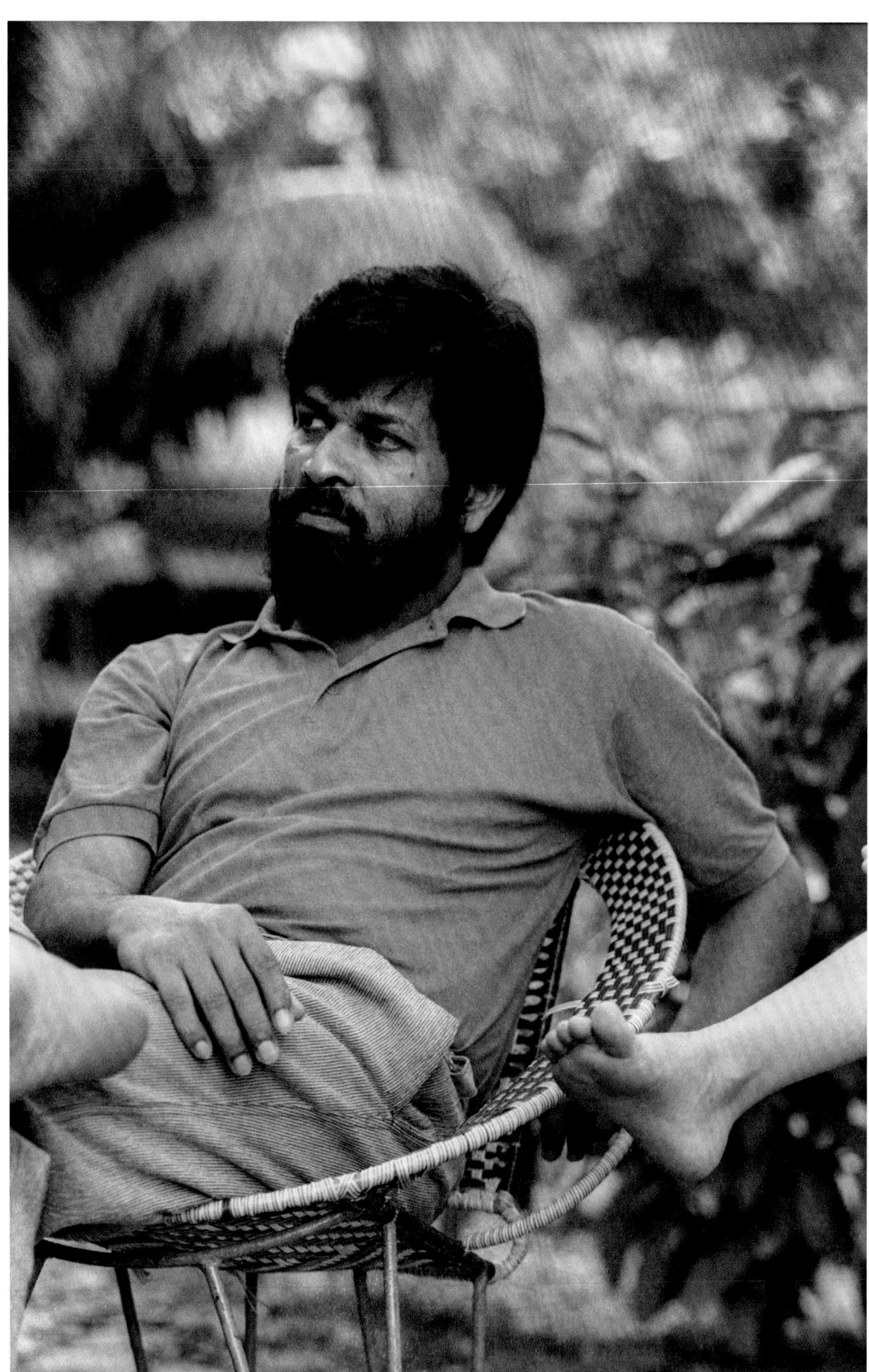

Dr Shahidul Alam, aged 37, in the Sundarbans

'During that week, eating hot curries with our fingers under dome-shaped umbrellas fending off the rains, he spoke of the camera's power to shape opinion and influence events, both in and beyond Bangladesh. His vision of the future of photography struck a chord. I wanted to be a part of it, both as a photographer and a lawyer.'

Journal, 20 July 1992

Foreword

Breeches, Rolls-Royce and Earl Grey tea aren't the associations one would normally make with a Bangladeshi activist, fiercely critical of imperialism. We were worlds apart and made an odd couple, but despite the eccentricities and upper-class roots of Rupert Grey, we gelled. Photography was one glue. My interest in copyright was another, but it was the twinkle in his eye, his insistence on fair play, his passion for adventure and the sheer audacity with which he threw himself into the wind that endeared me to this remarkable man. He has also been there, steady and loyal, when I went against the bigger fish. Through Rupert, we sued and got compensated by the BBC, and while no such outcome is likely in the case of the Bangladesh government, Rupert was there along with others, drenched in the rain outside the Bangladesh High Commission in London, in the debating room in Oxford, and in the parliament building in Westminster, making sure that elected representatives of the British people, and bureaucrats propping up a repressive regime in Bangladesh, knew they were being watched.

His colourful life and range of encounters is enviable, but it is his ability to weave a tale that sets him apart. Equally at ease in a roadside tea shop in Old Dhaka, as he is in the Travellers Club in Pall Mall, Rupert can hold court on a deserted island and give African griots a run for their money. The fact that he never takes himself too seriously and has a wry sense of humour helps. He clearly relishes being at the receiving end of my partner Rahnuma's jokes about monarchy and how blood can be 'blue'.

I've spent much of my professional career questioning the monopoly of Western photographers (predominately male and white) to be telling our stories. Here is a male photographer, as white as they get, doing exactly that. It was never my idea that others should not tell my story. All singular stories should be questioned, including my own. It is the singularity of the Western depiction of majority world cultures that I've questioned. That is where Rupert's story becomes important. We all carry baggage, but Rupert has made a conscious effort to shed his, though there still is a long way to go. This is not a fly-by-night photographer parachuting in, but a concerned and curious photographer, trying to understand, embracing a culture very different from his own. He is prepared to be laughed at, and laughs at himself. The Rolls and the breeches get muddied. With clay between his toes and the whiff of teargas in his nostrils, he momentarily, albeit safely, tastes the vulnerability that his privilege denies him and in the process emerges less white than he was. ■

Shahidul Alam

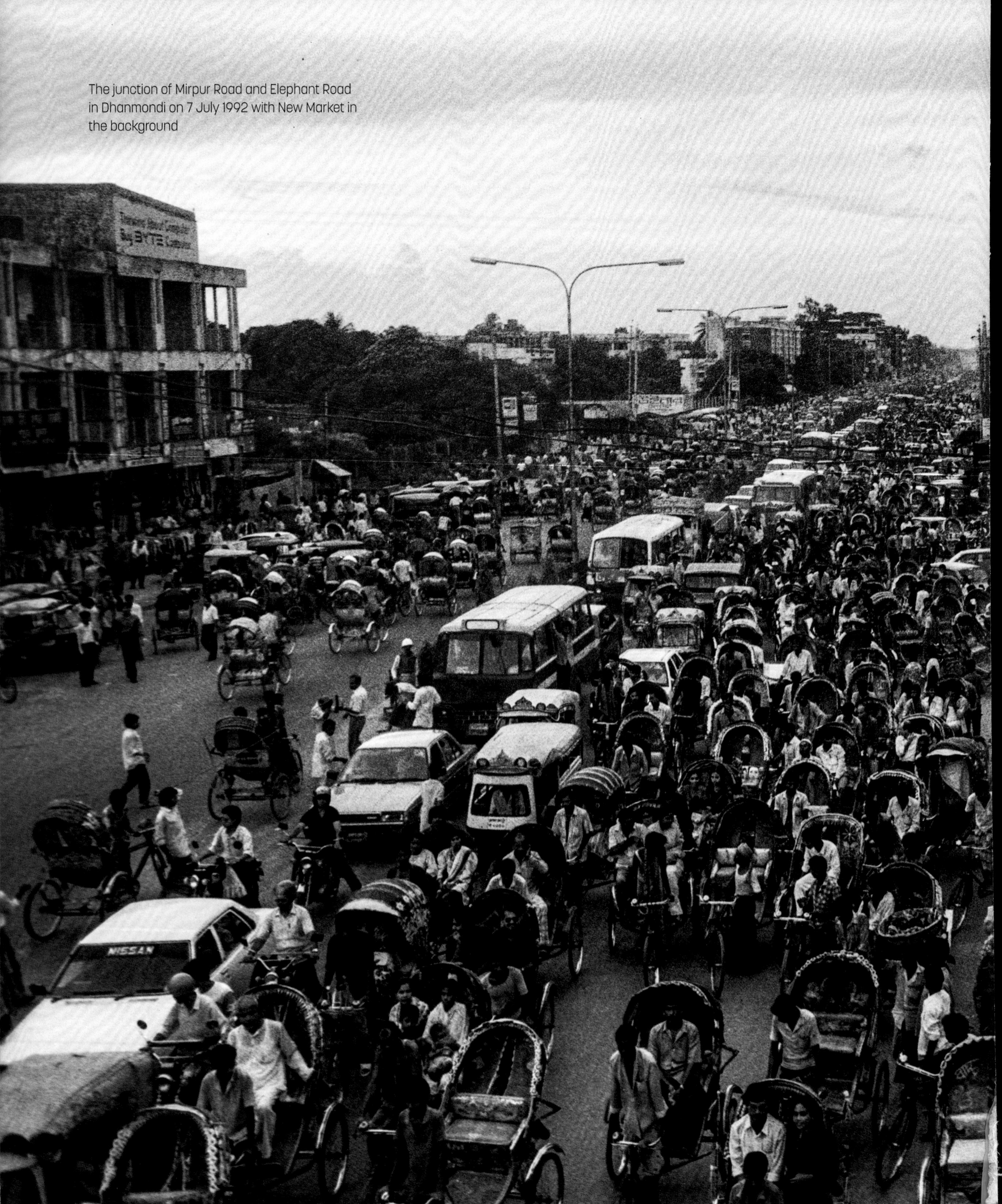

The junction of Mirpur Road and Elephant Road in Dhanmondi on 7 July 1992 with New Market in the background

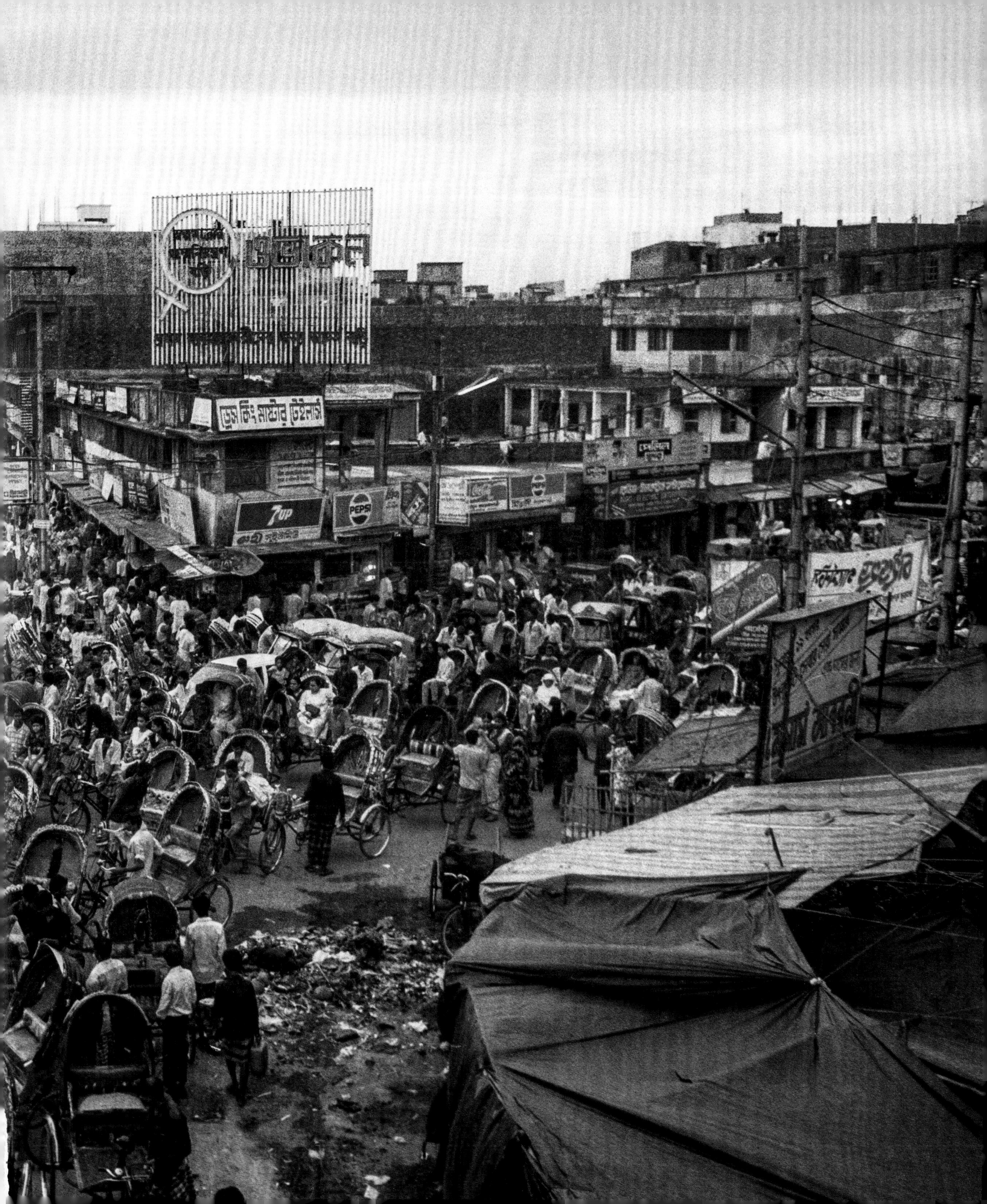
7UP
PEPSI

Preface

'... this amazing little brown box ...'

It is now a more or less accepted convention of social documentary and journalistic practice that photographs of developing countries should be taken by photographers from developing countries. This is an appropriate convention but it is one with which this book does not comply. Its author is an Englishman.

The first time I came to Bangladesh, in 1992, was as a traveller, the second as a lawyer, and the third and subsequent times as a photographer increasingly preoccupied with what the camera was for and what it could do. As a practising lawyer I was acutely aware that the ownership of an image is the bedrock of copyright law, but it was in Bangladesh that I came to understand its actual and potential power.

At that time, Bangladesh was a young nation with a venerable past and profound culture; to me, as a traveller, it had the excitement of the unknown. As a lawyer I became increasingly aware that, like all nation-states, there were injustices which need to be challenged. As a photographer I learned that the camera is an instrument for doing so: as Magnum photographer Philip Jones Griffiths, whose lawyer I once was, presciently observed in the 1980s, 'with this amazing little brown box round your neck you could change the world'.[1]

I can see all that now, but of course I didn't realize it at the time. What I did realize was that I had stumbled upon a remarkable group of people in an infrequently visited corner of South Asia who were bent on doing just that, and that I very much liked their company.

I also relished what they were doing: building the first platform in the developing world to challenge the dominance of international news by Western media. Bangladesh had a voice and they were determined that it be heard. ■

1 Henri Cartier-Bresson, founder of Magnum and doyen of documentary photographers, said of him: 'Not since Goya has anyone portrayed war like Philip Jones Griffiths.'

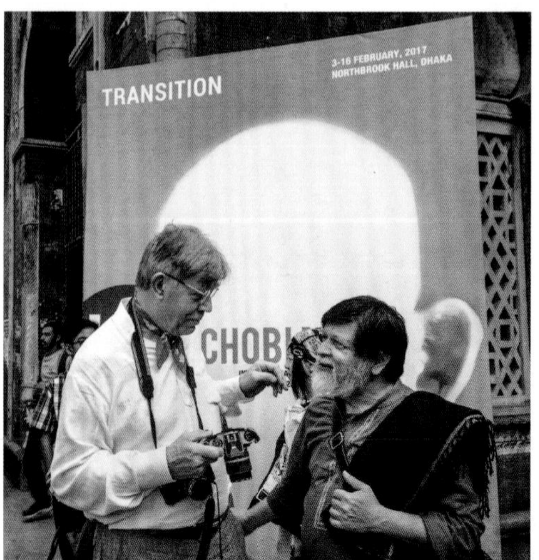

The author and Dr Shahidul Alam in Old Dhaka in 2017

Introduction

'Welcome to Bangladesh before the tourists get here', we were told, in letters writ large above the airport exit in Dhaka. It was midday on 14 August 1992, twenty-one years after Bangladesh was conceived in civil war, born during genocide and coming of age in poverty and conflict. Thirty years later the tourists still haven't got there.

Since then, I have returned many times over the years. My acquaintances have been mystified. They see Bangladesh, as do many of those who have not been there, through the prism of poverty, famine, floods and hopelessness. No doubt they read Henry Kissinger's description of it in 1972 as an international basket case. 'Why Bangladesh?' they asked.

This book is the answer, in photographs and words, as seen through the eyes of a camera-carrying lawyer with one eye open for adversity and the other for magic. Bangladesh has more than its fair share of both.

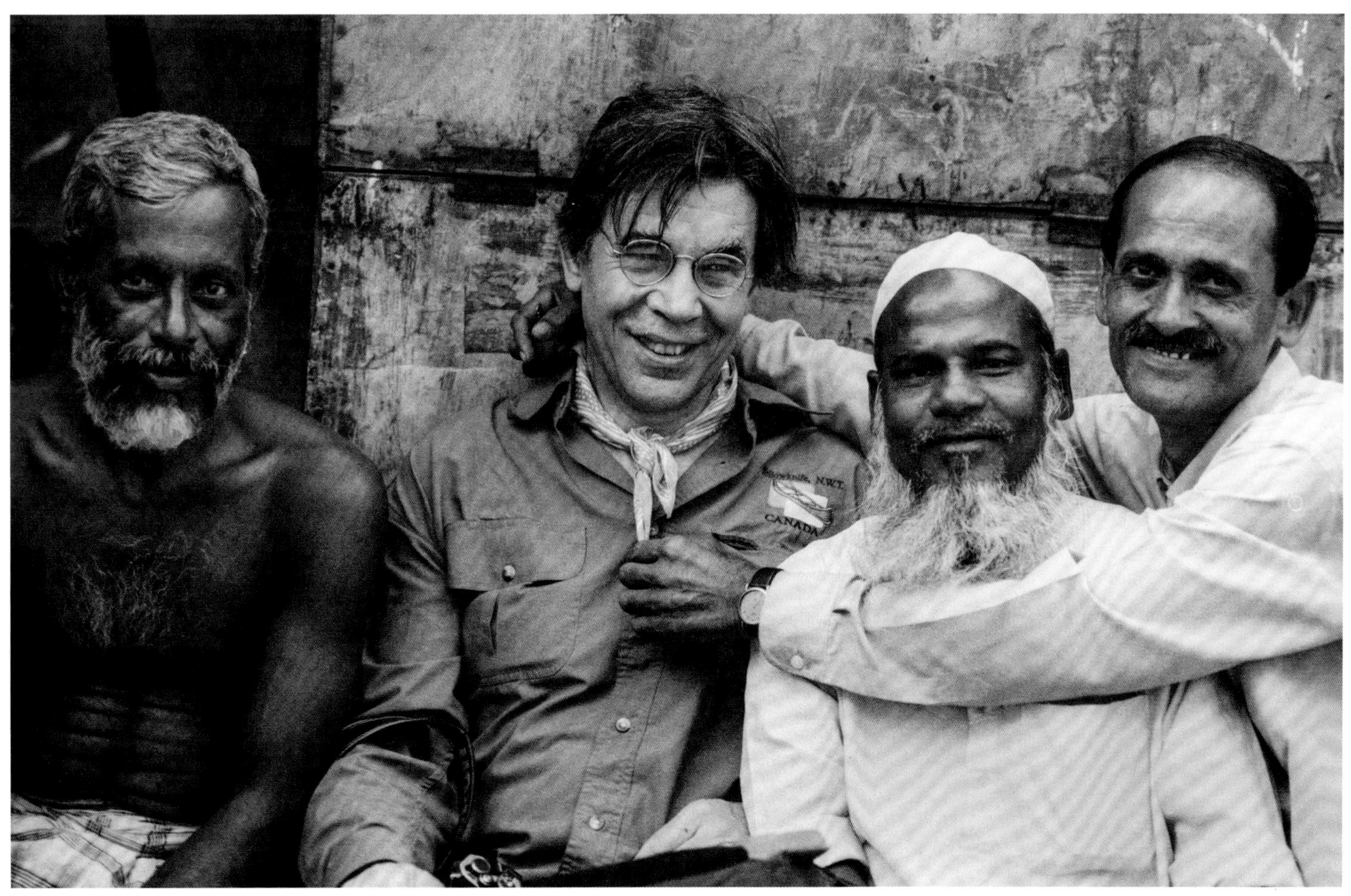

The author on the wharf at the Sadharghat in 2004

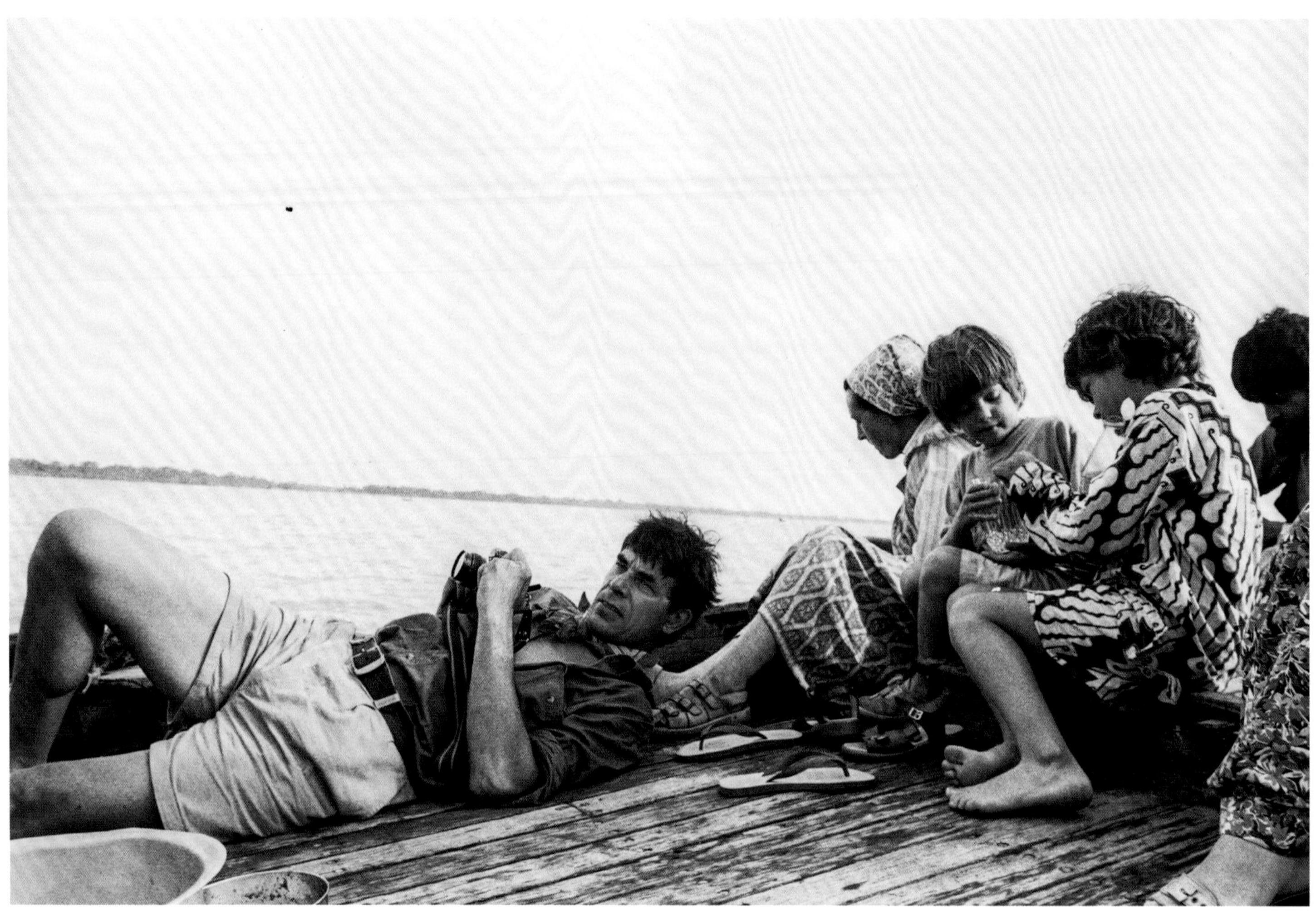

The author with his wife Jan and daughters Rose and Carmody crossing the Bay of Bengal in 1992; Shahidul Alam in the background.

'The Children, all six of them, lie on the deck half asleep. An orange sun is falling slowly into the mangrove forests, and the world will shortly be shrouded in darkness. We have crossed the open sea [when this picture was taken] and are now in a narrow tributary of the Ganges; small boats glide past like ghosts in the night, dimly lit by wick-lamps which cast dark shadows on the deck. Occasionally dwellings can be seen on the banks, large bats fly silently overhead and dark clouds gather in the night sky ahead of us.'

Journal, 27 July 1992

It was not an easy beginning. There were five of us at the airport. Jan, our three daughters aged five, eight and eleven, and me. Waiting for us beyond the glass doors of the airport building, and for anyone wealthy enough to travel by air, were the poor of Bangladesh, dense crowds of desperate people. To them we were the best chance of a temporary alleviation of hunger; to Jan and I they were the human face of Kissinger's basket case. To our three daughters they were frightening.

Bangladesh was the sixth country we had visited in the previous six months. Our sabbatical was timed to coincide with that short window in children's lives when the bonds of childhood and hunger for knowledge were roughly in balance, before exams cast their shadow on the teenage landscape and other allegiances beckoned. During those months we drifted downstream on bamboo rafts across islands in the South Pacific and rode horses along steep-rocked canyons in Arizona. Nights were spent in rain-forest shelters, on the hard decks of riverboats and occasionally on soft beds in grand palaces . Away from school, the children's education continued in the context of unfamiliar food, language, lifestyle and values. Experienced though they were, Bangladesh added another layer.

During the thirty years since that unforgettable moment I have touched the collective life force embedded in this so-called basket case and come away much moved and a little wiser. Each time I return I derive a particular satisfaction from realising how wrong Kissinger was. Bangladesh may not be perfect, but it is not and never was a basket case.

Kissinger was right in one sense. Bangladesh may have been a nation on paper, but on the ground it was little more than a hope. The reality, after the War of Liberation from Pakistan in 1971, was widespread destruction, 10 million refugees, no infrastructure of government administration, no parliament and no schools. The department of education consisted of one room with one table, a chair and one telephone. This was not so much a country starting from scratch as one that had to fashion the tools to make one.

In other senses he was wrong. Nations are founded on and sustained by a strong cultural identity. The province of Bengal has for centuries been the cradle of the Indian subcontinent, the gathering place for artists and musicians, intellectuals and poets. The boundary between East Pakistan and India, created twenty-four years before the war of liberation by a British barrister who had never visited the subcontinent, divided Bengal politically. But it had no effect on the intellectual and cultural legacy of the centuries, which remained vibrant. The 1971 war, sparked by a dispute over language – up with Urdu the Bengalis[2] refused to put – gave birth to Bangladesh, albeit at devastating cost in lives, but the Bengali culture remained vibrant.

The vigour of the performing and creative arts, and photography in particular – coupled with the determination to preserve political and artistic freedom – was and remains the magnet which draws me back. Artists play a critically important role in shaping political and societal change at a time when politics and business are tainted by incompetence and corruption. This is as true in Europe as it is in Bangladesh.

The five of us were the only foreigners off the plane that morning in 1992. We fought our way through the crowds in the hope of finding Zaman, the driver our friends in Dhaka had arranged to collect us from the airport. The heat was sudden and violent. So was the impact on our children, as their Bangla peers touched their arms and asked for baksheesh.[3] Rose, five years old with a shock of blond hair, perched on my shoulders. Katherine and Carmody, likewise of a fair countenance, clung tightly to Jan for protection.

Zaman bundled us into his vehicle and drove to Dhanmondi through a bedlam of buses, trucks and rickshaws, their drivers oblivious to the exhaust fumes, the deafening cacophony of hooters and the beggars at the windows. The children's reaction was a blend of bewilderment and excitement. The vibrancy was infectious, the poverty challenged everything they believed in, the heat and the dust exhausted them, the food rearranged their tastes and the monsoon redefined the meaning of rain. It was as if they had opened the door in the back of C.S. Lewis' wardrobe and found themselves in a world where nothing was quite the same; the rules had to re-learned and risks were measured by different yardsticks.

We spent a month in Bangladesh, mostly in the Sundarbans, where we met Dr Shahidul Alam, who thirty years later was to write the foreword to this book. Our friendship was to have a profound influence – long before the contemporary re-appraisal of colonial history – on my perception of the legacy of empire and the relationship between the West and the majority world.[4]

2 Bengal is English usage. Bangal is the correct name for the province and bangalis for its citizens. Bangladesh means the 'Land of the Bangalis'.

3 The strict meaning is a tip or bribe, but baksheesh is commonly used by beggars to ask for money.

4 It also had an impact on the children: Carmody used the photograph on pages 27 and 28 to introduce a lecture she gave at the Royal Geographical Society in 2022 entitled, 'So what's philosophy got to do with it?' ('it' being climate change). It was, she said, during these early expeditions that her thinking as a philosopher was conceived.

During the next decade Shahidul founded Drik, Bangladesh's first photo and news agency, followed by Pathshala, now the leading school of photography in Asia, and Chobi Mela, a world-renowned festival of photography. This was at a time when the business of photojournalism was changing radically, driven by the compelling need to address socio-political issues and tell the human stories which gave them meaning. Bangladesh played and continues to play an important part in these changes. It was that to which I was drawn. While my role as copyright lawyer was useful to young Bangladeshi photographers whose images attracted the attention of the Western media, the real driver was the excitement of knowing that these images, taken from their perspective, really might, as Philip Jones Griffiths hoped, change the world.

During the many times I returned to Bangladesh over the next thirty years, always with my three Nikon FM2s,[5] I took the photographs in this book. They record what I saw, what spoke to me of Bangladesh, what warmed my heart and informed my understanding. The captions in italics are taken from journals I kept at the time.

On Documentary Photography

'Above all, I craved to seize the whole essence, in the confines of one single photograph, of some situation that was in the process of unrolling itself before my eyes.'

Henri Cartier-Bresson

A photograph is a mirror of the world. The photographer creates an image and the person who sees the image and absorbs it in turn becomes the publisher.

The viewer is also, of course, absorbing the photographer's background, experience and personality. These dictate, or at least influence, how and when a photograph is taken, and of whom. The resulting images do not qualify as objective truth, for the camera is never neutral, but if integrity attends upon the photographer's choices the images will be the photographer's truth.

The truth I seek is the aspects of our human-ness which are revealed by a sudden movement, a poise, the flash of understanding when eyes met or wind blew, when the relationship between humans became, like lightning, visible for a split second. It is such revelations to which I respond most strongly and which inform what I choose to photograph. By their nature such images are captured on the spur of the moment.

Their selection, however, permits time to reflect and compare, to search for those which reveal the threads which lie behind the form: companionship and separation, adversity and resilience, despair and joy, action and contemplation.

Since 1992, when the earliest images in this collection were taken, the function and role of documentary photography has changed. A practice which institutions had regarded as a legitimate and valuable record of the lives, occupations and culture of those photographed is now viewed as a tool for the exercise of power.

5 35 ml cameras using black and white film.

This awakening, enhanced by the internet, has put documentary photographers in the spotlight. A photographer's agenda, subconscious or otherwise, is rightly perceived as being generated by, or at the very least linked to, their nationality and background. These and related factors will shape their truth.

The photographic community in Bangladesh, led by Shahidul Alam, has been at the heart of, and to an extent driven by, this change. It has also become, as touched on in Chapter 2, an international gathering place for photographers from every continent, each one bringing their own values, their own truths, their own pasts and, importantly, their own questions. The answers, so far as they can be defined, are the photographs they take. Hence (bearing in mind the potential of the little brown box) I include images of rock miners and brick workers earning a pittance and an early death.

They images are also an aesthetic tribute to a people whose courage and humour and companionship have enormously enriched my interior landscape and heightened my awareness over the last three decades. As Henry Miller remarked of those who take journeys, one's destination is never a place; it's a new way of seeing things. ■

Rickshaw-drivers are on a par with Olympic athletes when it comes to physical output, but without the diet

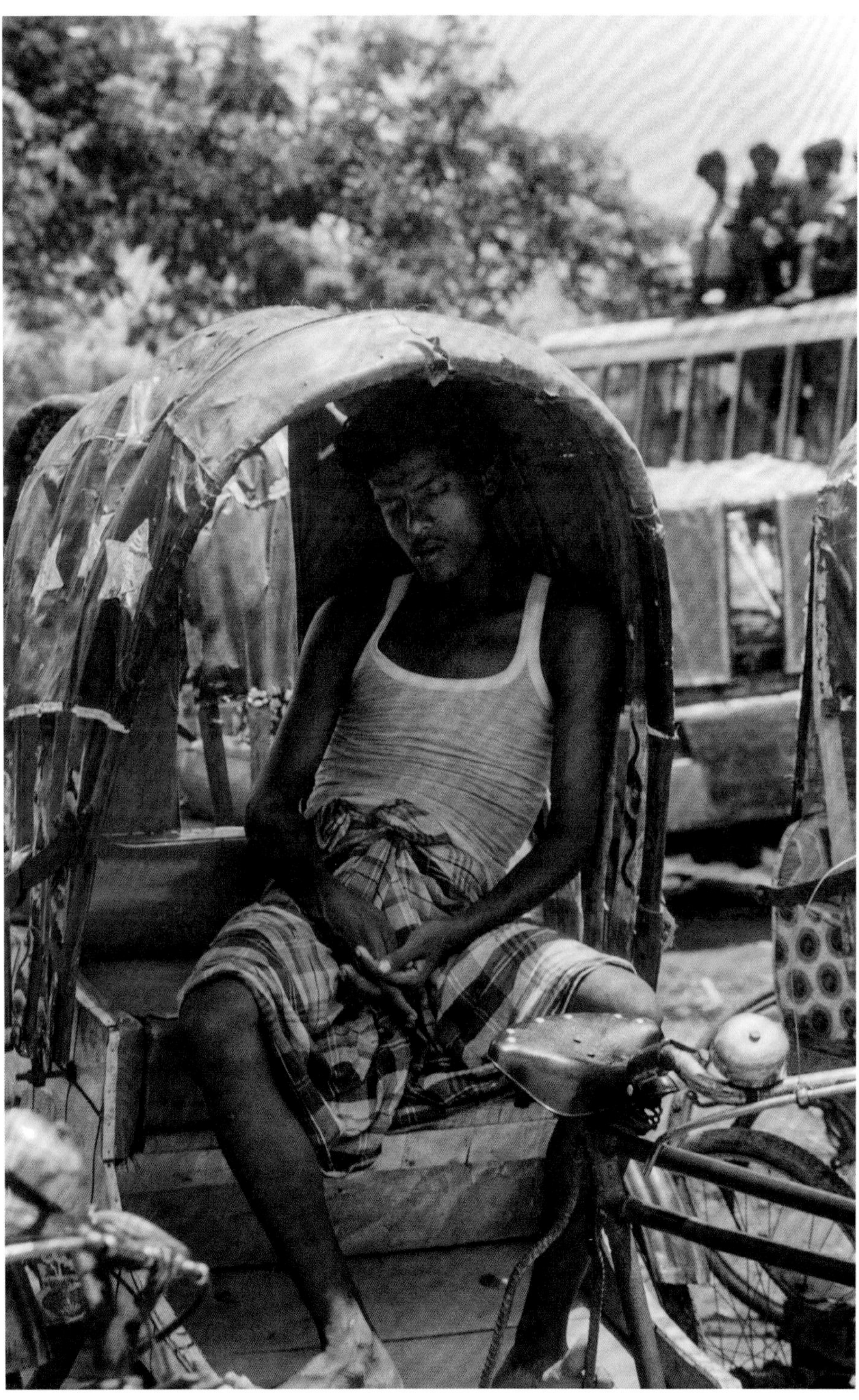

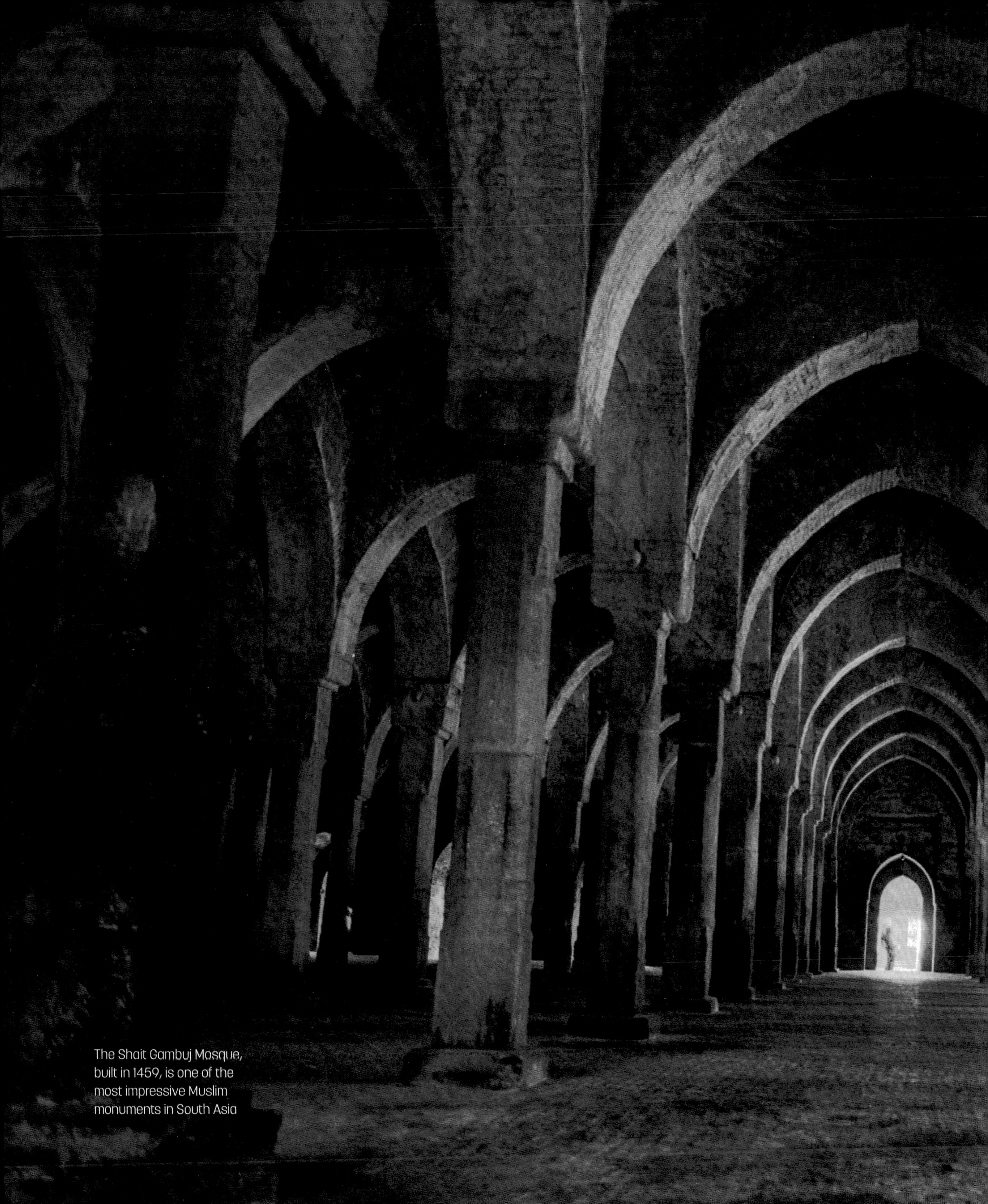

The Shait Gambuj Mosque, built in 1459, is one of the most impressive Muslim monuments in South Asia

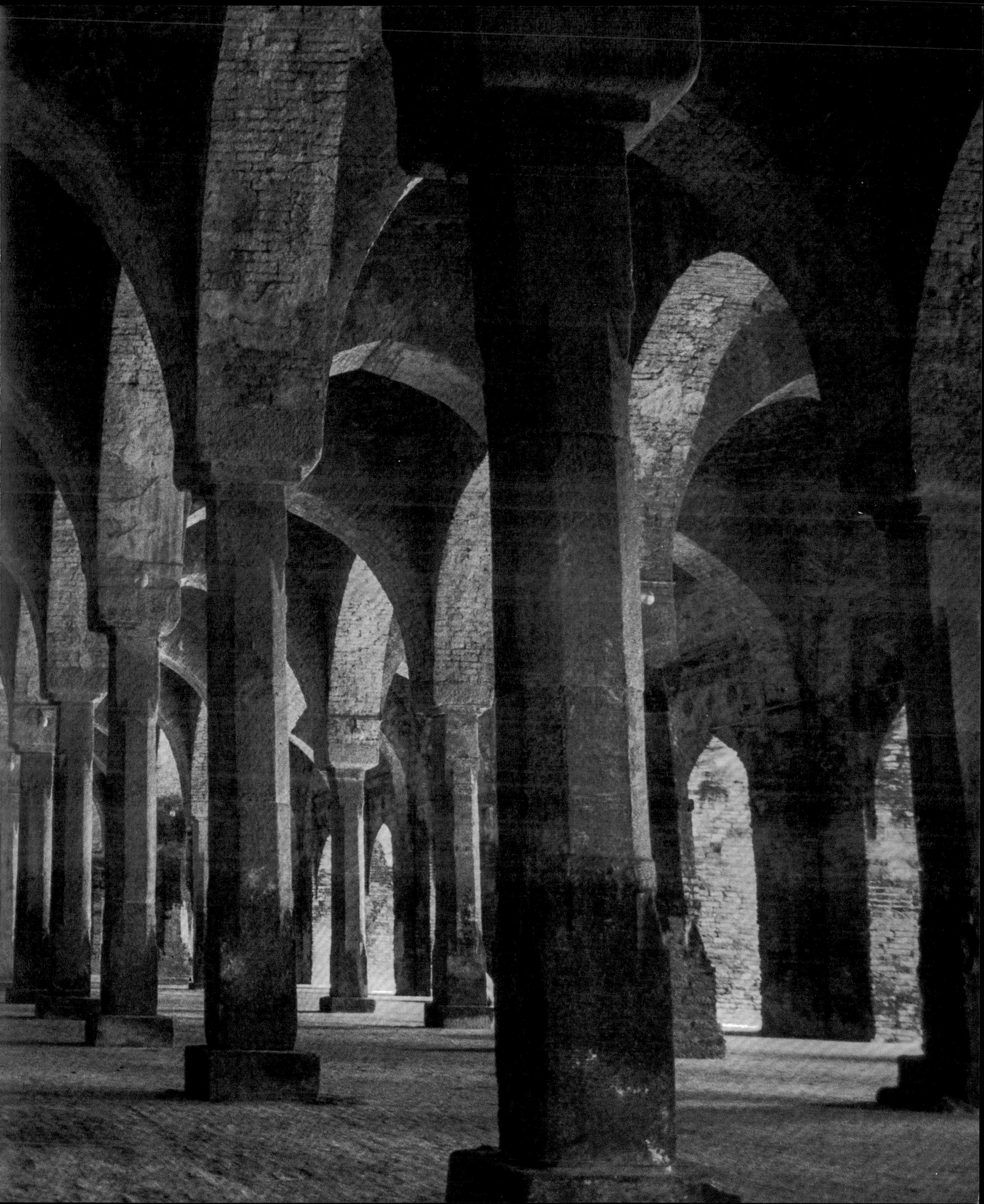

Patchwork Sails and Pirates, 1992

The Buriganga River flows slowly, for Bangladesh is a flat land. As it meanders into the mangrove forests of the Sundarbans, it divides into narrow channels where mud-crabs and crocodiles live, and flows on to the Swatch of No Ground[6] in the Bay of Bengal.

Slowly, too, flowed the river traffic in 1992. We emerged from our cabins on the ferry boat at first light to see a host of sampans, patchwork sails hanging listlessly in the windless dawn, and cargo boats stacked high with bricks, so low in the water they seemed barely a whisker from foundering. Weaving between them as they crossed from bank to bank were flat-topped taxi-dinghis on which there stood passengers packed like vertical sardines.

We docked at Borishal that afternoon and reached the Sundarbans the following day. We were a party of fifteen: six children, two aid-workers,[7] an activist photographer, a social worker, a libel lawyer and a king. The other three were men with guns whose task it was, we gathered, to protect us from the pirates.[8]

The King was actually a major who had deserted the Pakistani Army to fight in the War of Liberation in 1971. Major Ziauddin formed his own regiment of freedom fighters in the Sundarbans and became known as *Mukuthin Samrat* – the emperor without a crown. Twenty years later, after a period in exile, he was standing for parliament. Our boat, built of mighty timbers and powered by an ancient two-stroke engine, was the headquarters for his election campaign.

For a week we motored through the largest mangrove forest in South Asia, ate hot curries on hot decks, slept in candle-lit villages and sheltered from the monsoon rains under sturdy black umbrellas. We stood by while the King, as we called him, made speeches from the deck to villagers on crowded sandbanks, accompanied him and the gunmen on wet paths through dense mangrove forests and joined him in the evenings as villagers gathered round.

One night we lodged in a government rest-house. We arrived in the dark on rickshaws with wick lamps for headlights. The rest-house was locked and a cow blocked the door. As a place to lay our exhausted children's heads it looked distinctly unpromising. Eventually a man in a clean white kurta appeared and opened the door, revealing dark musty rooms with dusty concrete floors, a bed and a mattress. 'Major Zia will have the top floor,' he announced, 'he is less likely to be assassinated up there.' The six children were asleep on the first floor within twenty minutes, strewn about the room with rucksacks for pillows and mosquito nets for blankets.

That night the villagers came to pay homage to their war leader. They queued in the darkness, on the stairs and in the upstairs room. As they passed they bent down to touch the hem of his garments, as is the way in the subcontinent. Amongst them were men who had fought alongside him.[9] A year before these people had gone to the polls to vote on their country's constitution; what we saw that night was the frontline of a newly established democracy.

The activist photographer was Shahidul. He had a jet-black beard, wore a dark green kurta and sat at the back of the boat with three black Nikons round his neck. The children warmed to him and so did we. Sitting on that scrubbed deck aged by tropical suns, he spoke of the camera's power to shape opinion, influence events and record what was important: cameras in deft hands, he said, are more powerful than guns. His vision for the future was to enable Bangladeshi photographers to play a part in the exercise of that power.

A few years earlier, Shahidul had turned his bedroom into a darkroom; in due course his home became the first agency to represent photographers in South Asia. Drik[10] was to become the platform for his role as a human rights activist. Twenty-five years later, when reviewing one of his books in an academic journal, I was to describe Shahidul as an activist who has used photography to chronicle his nation's anguish.

For me, as a media lawyer[11] who represented photo agencies and newspapers, Shahidul's approach to photography had a particular resonance. Some days later, back in Dhaka, I gave a talk on copyright to the Bangladesh Photographic Society, of which Shahidul was president.[12] This was the beginning of my involvement at many levels with photographers and lawyers in Bangladesh, and of a friendship with Shahidul and his partner Rahnuma which has lasted these thirty years.

The photographs in this chapter were taken during that first month in Bangladesh. ■

Next page
The gangway to the ferry boats at Sodherghat

'There we beheld a scene of magnificent chaos, boats of all sizes and methods of propulsion going in every direction, giant ferry boats vying for a mooring by simply shoving each other out of the way.

The only note of sanity was the rolling out of prayer mats on rooves and decks right across the river, and men bowing towards Mecca, just about due west of Dhaka towards the setting sun.'

Journal, 14 July 1992

6 A 14 km-deep underwater trench, home to globally threatened species of marine animals, including dolphins and whales. In 2014 it became the first marine protected area declared by the Bangladeshi Government.

7 Clare Blenkinsop and Richard Holloway are old friends who lived in Dhaka, with whom we had previously undertaken expeditions with our respective children.

8 Piracy is rife in the Sundarbans. Twenty years later, the King was severely wounded in a pitched battle with pirates. He died in 2013.

9 Zia also mentioned, Shahidul told me later, how important the British support to the freedom fighters had been during the war.

10 The word Drik is derived from the Sanskrit dr., meaning to see, or vision.

11 In 1992 I was senior partner of William Charles Crocker, a law firm in Fleet Street.

12 Halfway through there was a power cut, a routine event in Dhaka at that time. With the slide projector out of action, I recounted into the darkness stories of cases I or others had won or lost, duly translated by a High Court judge and presided over by Shahidul.

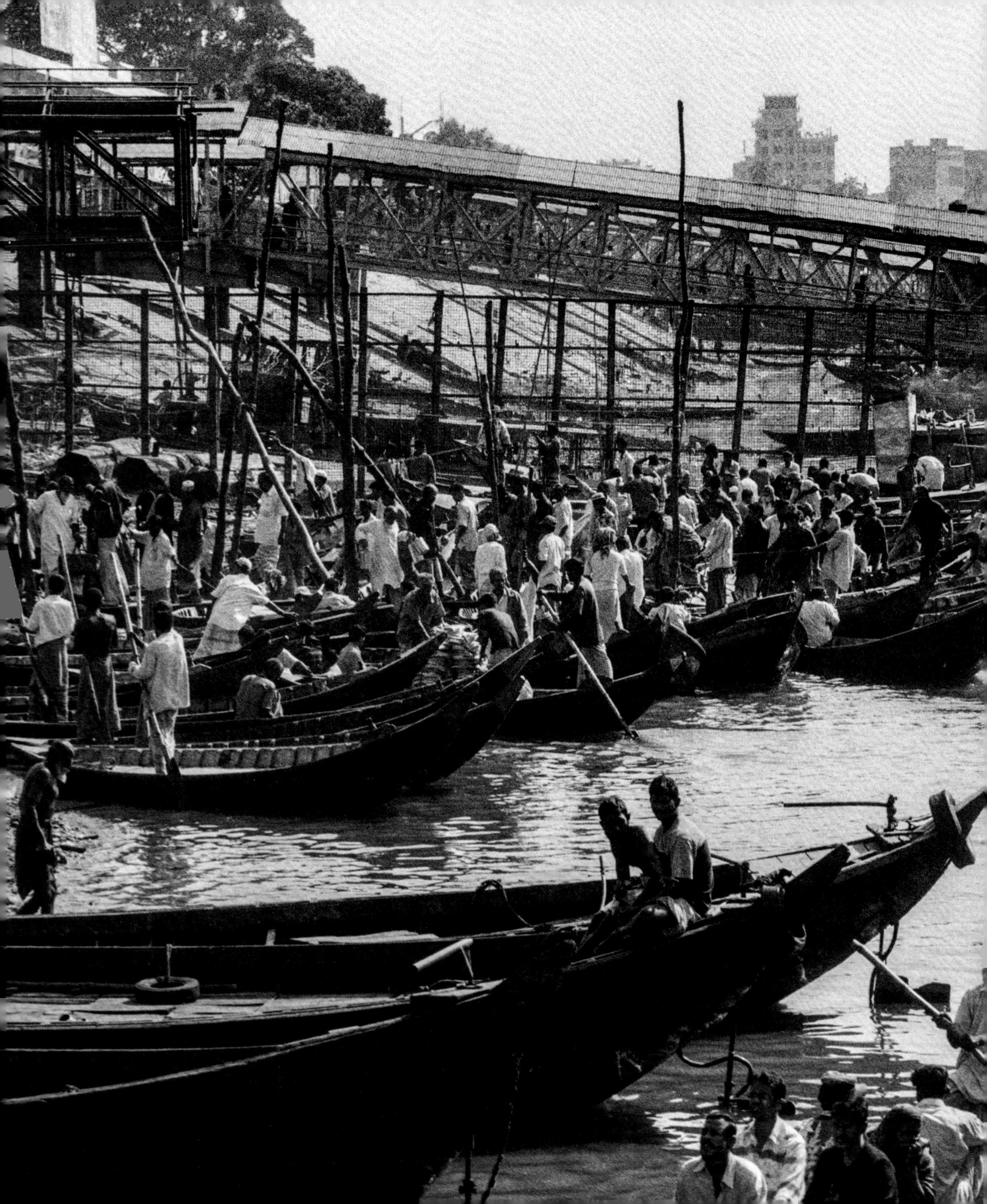

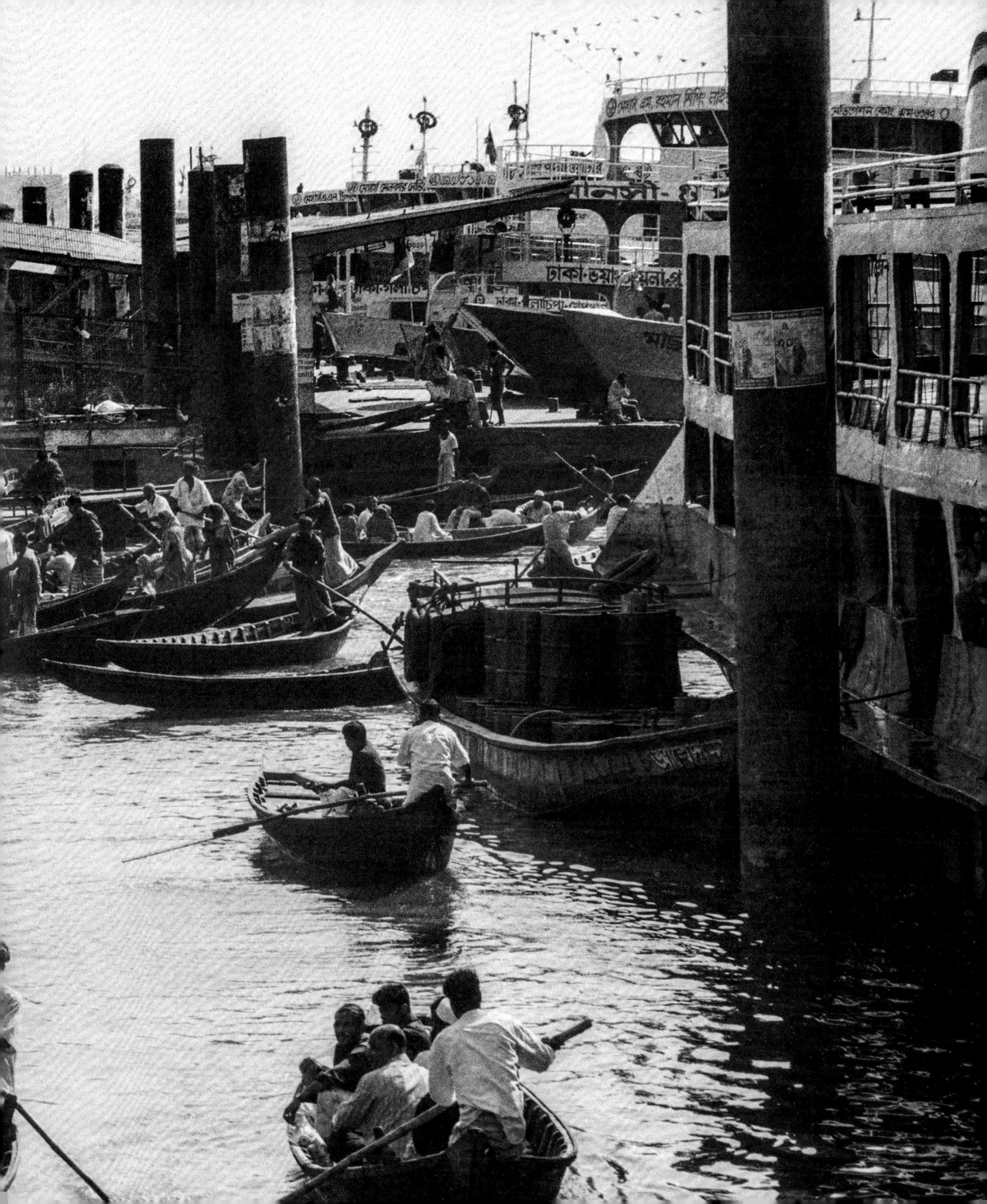

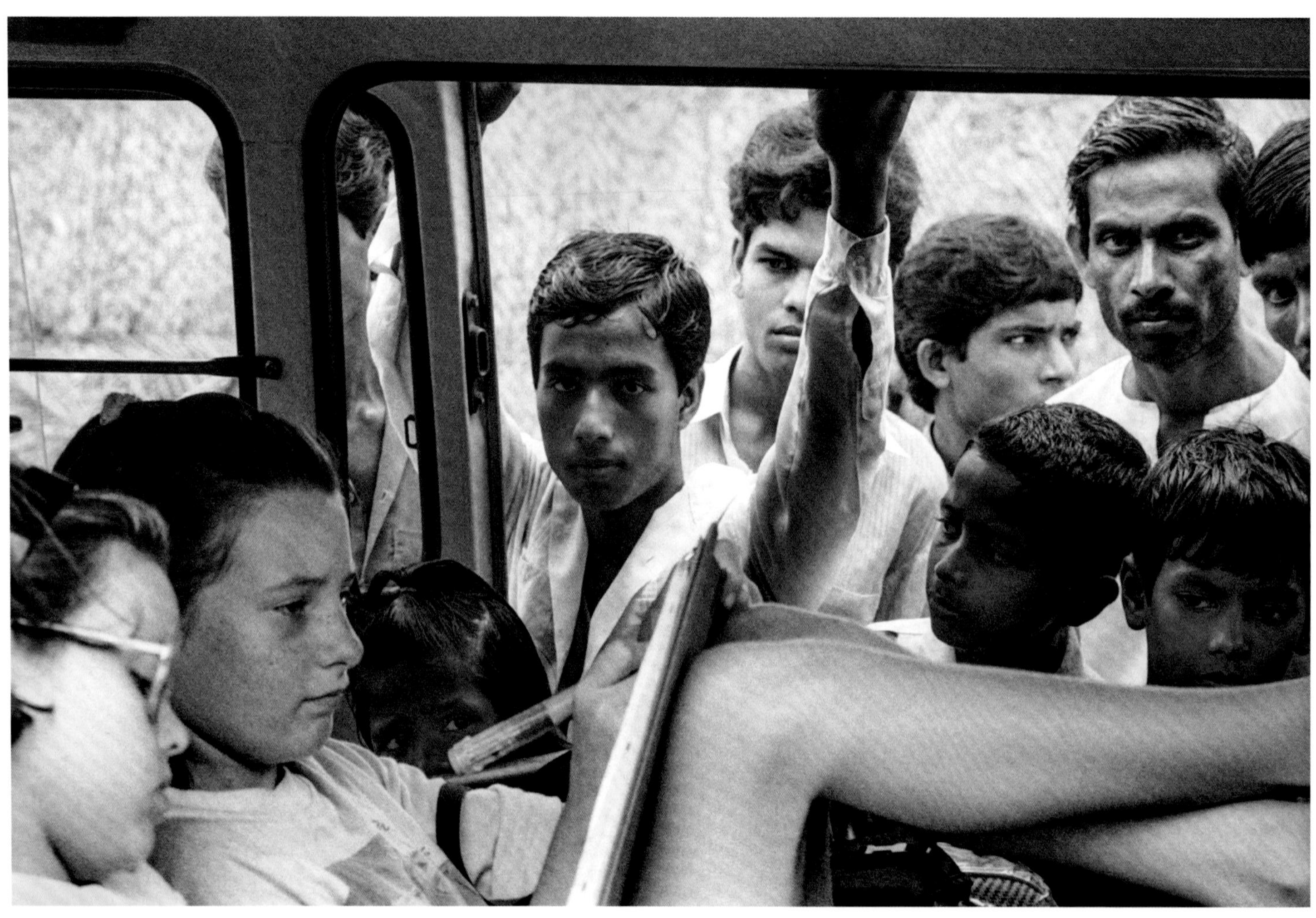

Heron Holloway and Katherine Grey
both aged 11, on arrival in Borishal

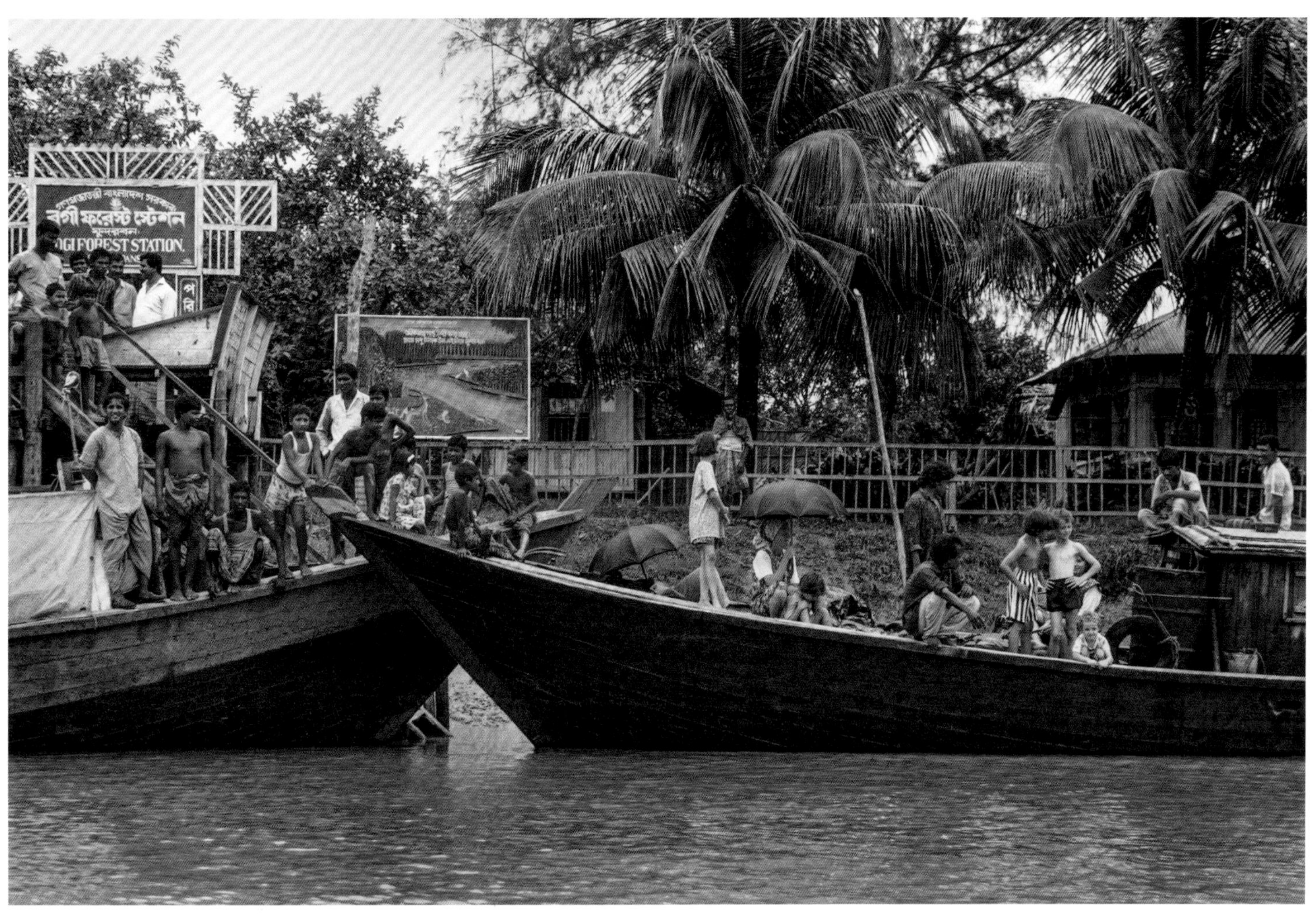

'The boat we occupy is a magnificent local fishing boat, with a high prow, a cabin which is all engine, a campfire and lavatory at the stern (through which you can see the sea racing past below, much to Rose's amazement). Zia's men sit on the roof of the cabin with rifles at the ready, for pirates, tigers or crocs – Zia is in a permanent state of war with the pirates; they seized one of his boats, full of fish, yesterday. Zia sleeps on deck and occasionally sits cross-legged with his Webley revolver beside him. It's like a scene from African Queen.'.

Journal, July 1992

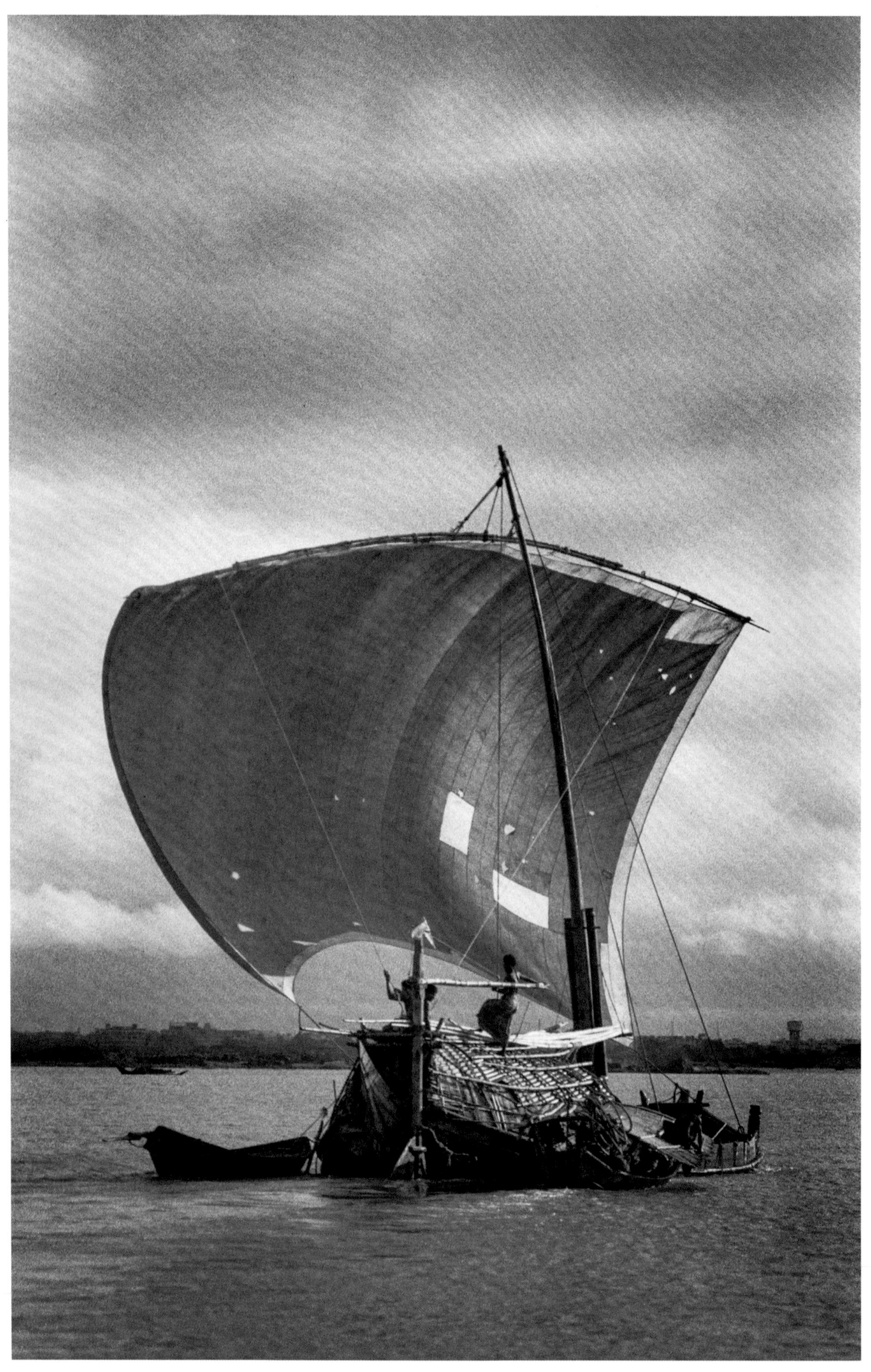

A barge offloads for delivery to the market

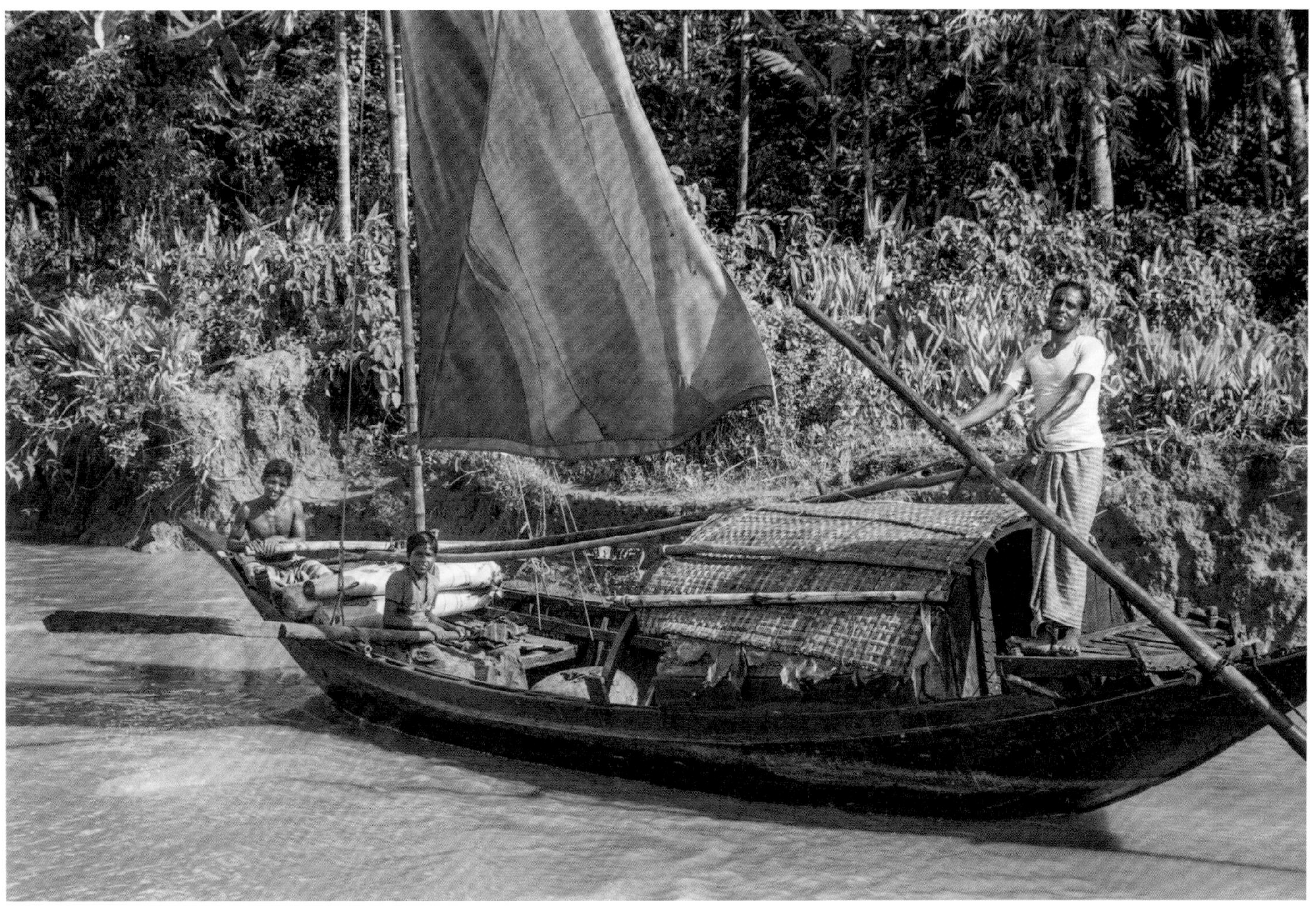

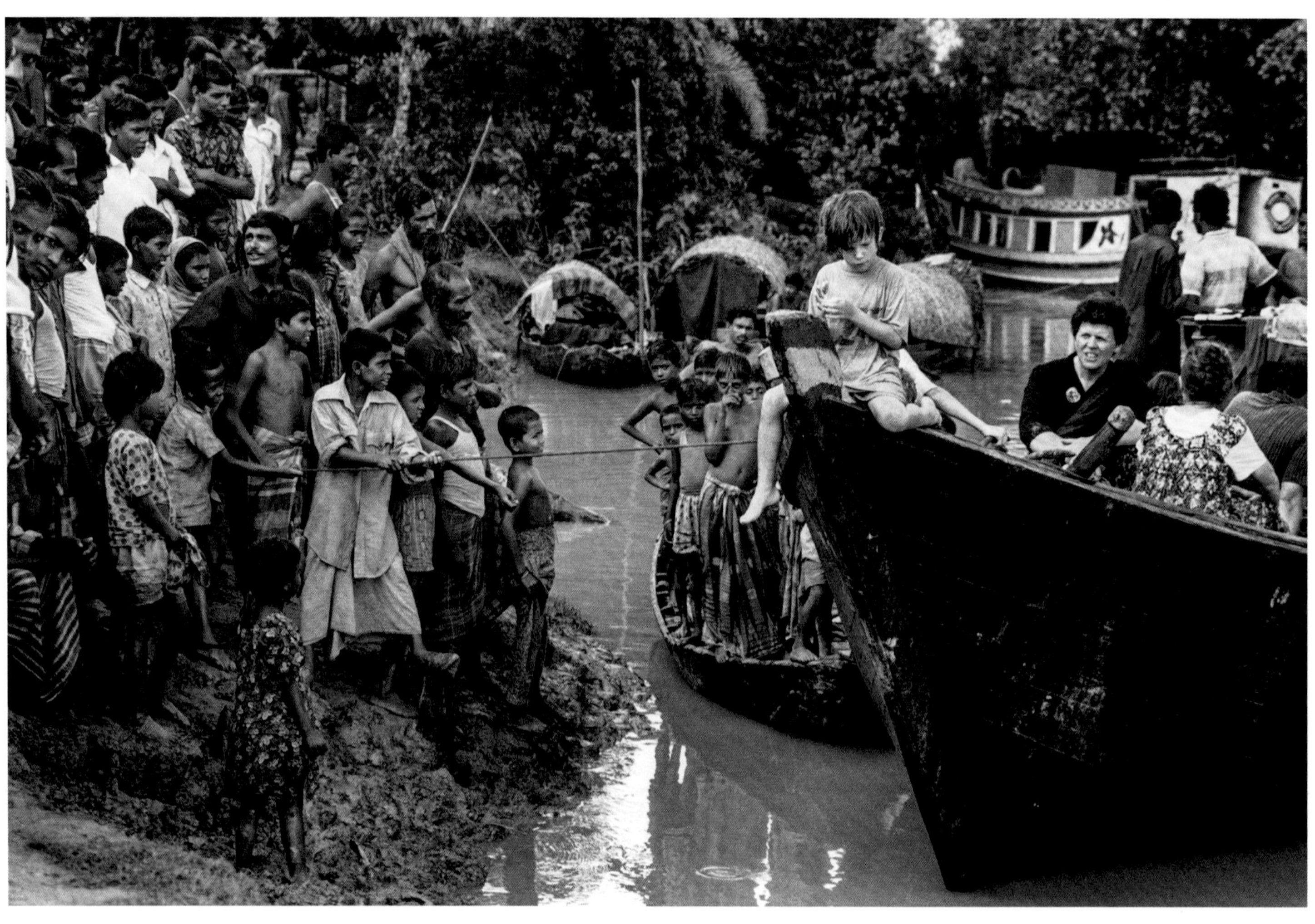

Arrival at a village
in the Sundarbans

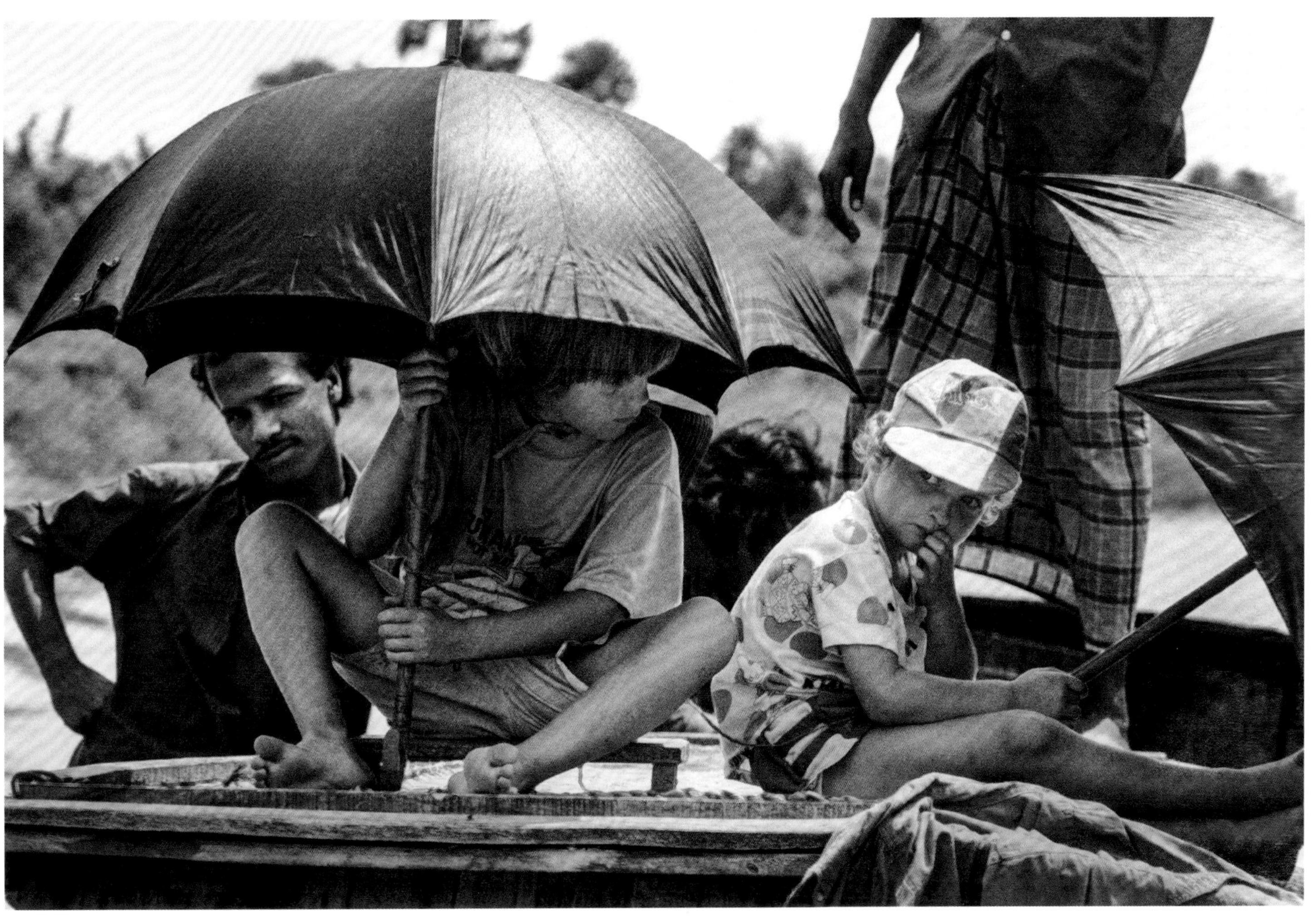

Rose Grey, aged 5,
and Guy Holloway

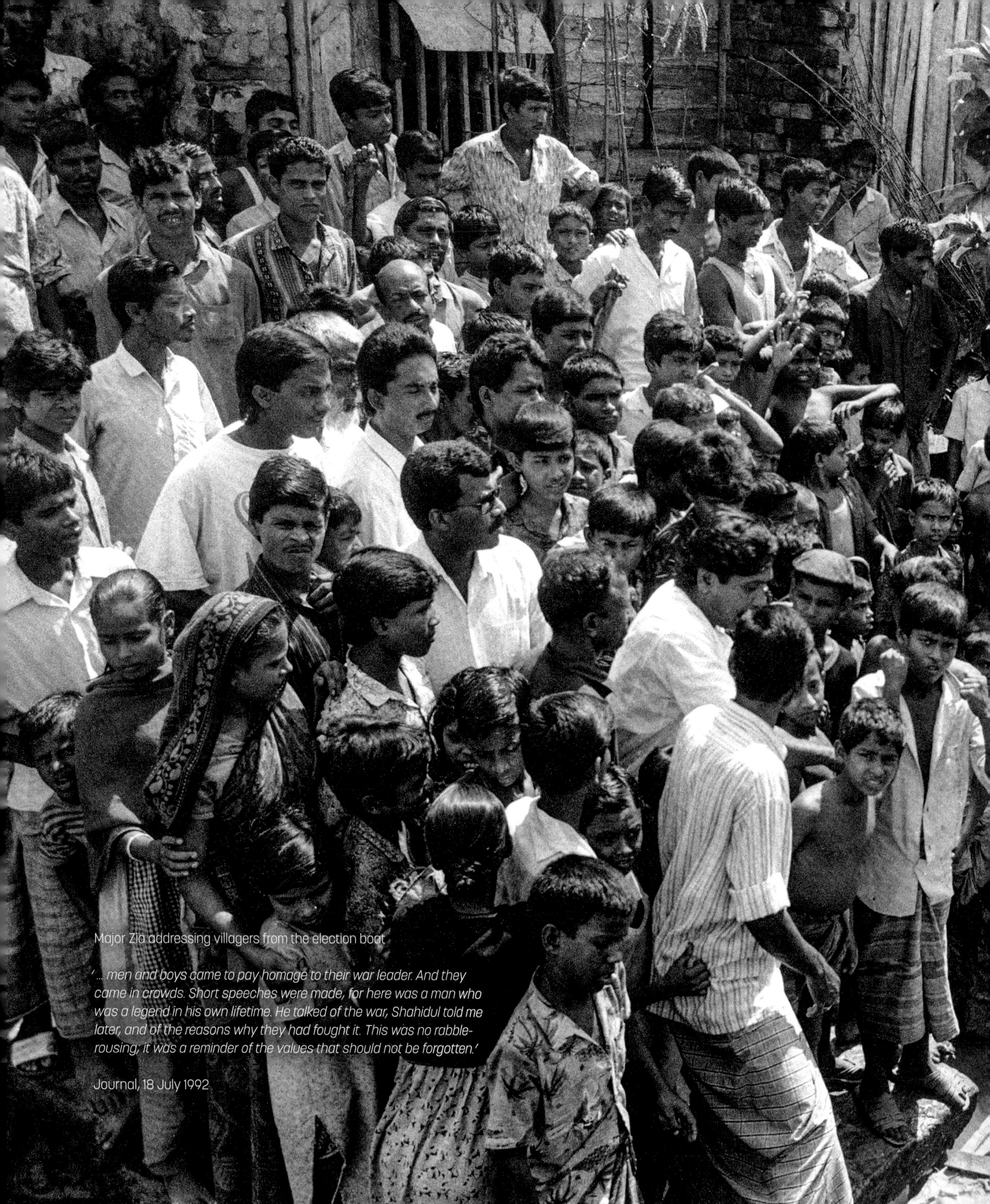

Major Zia addressing villagers from the election boat

'… men and boys came to pay homage to their war leader. And they came in crowds. Short speeches were made, for here was a man who was a legend in his own lifetime. He talked of the war, Shahidul told me later, and of the reasons why they had fought it. This was no rabble-rousing; it was a reminder of the values that should not be forgotten.'

Journal, 18 July 1992

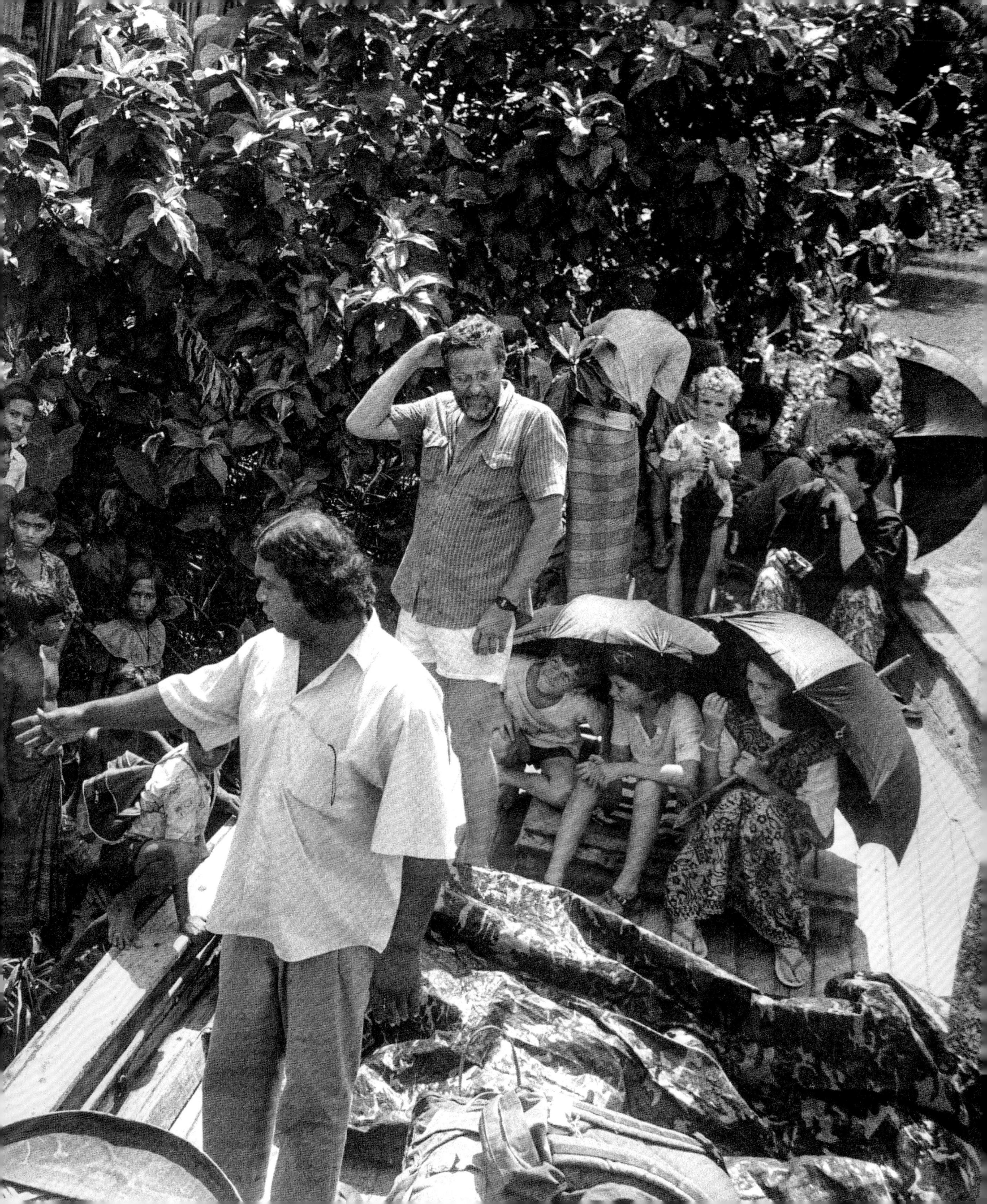

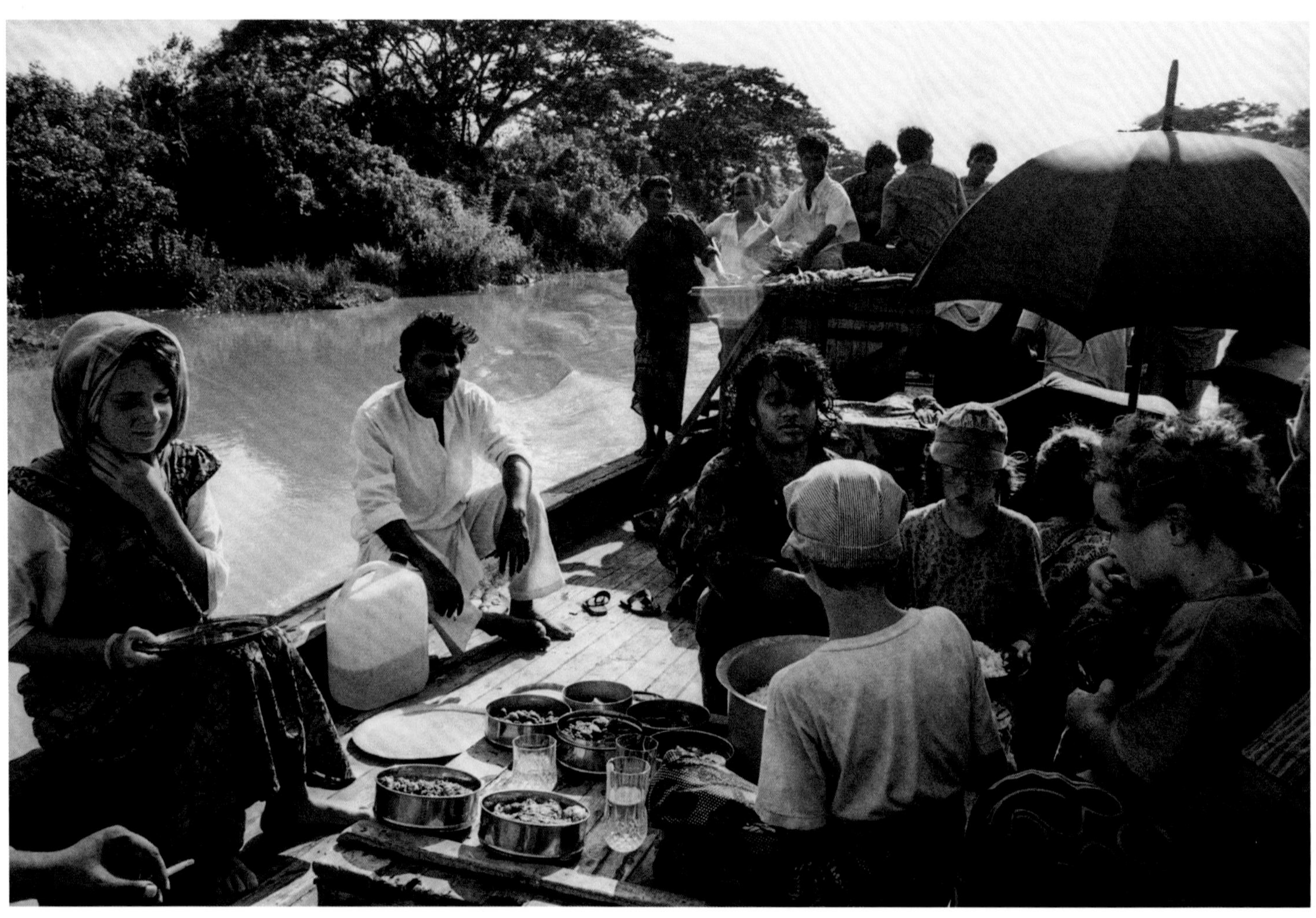

'We moved on to a small village where our lunch was being prepared. Once again Zia was given a royal welcome and, more to the point, a hero's lunch: king prawns and fish, lamb, chicken with a variety of vegetables and rice, all heavily spiced and curried; the children, hungry and now warm again, tucked in with gusto.'

Journal, 19 July 1992

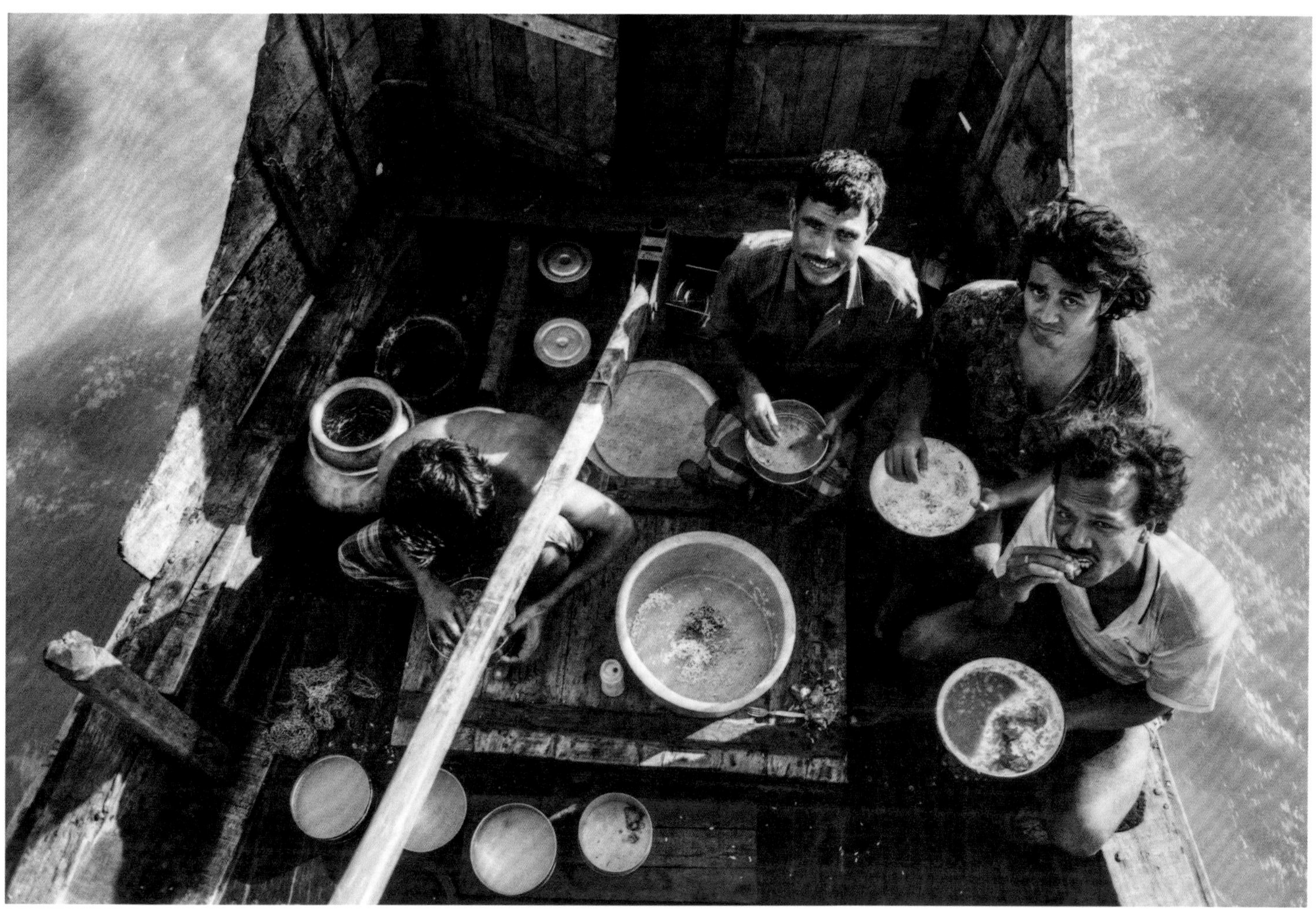

The cookhouse on the election boat

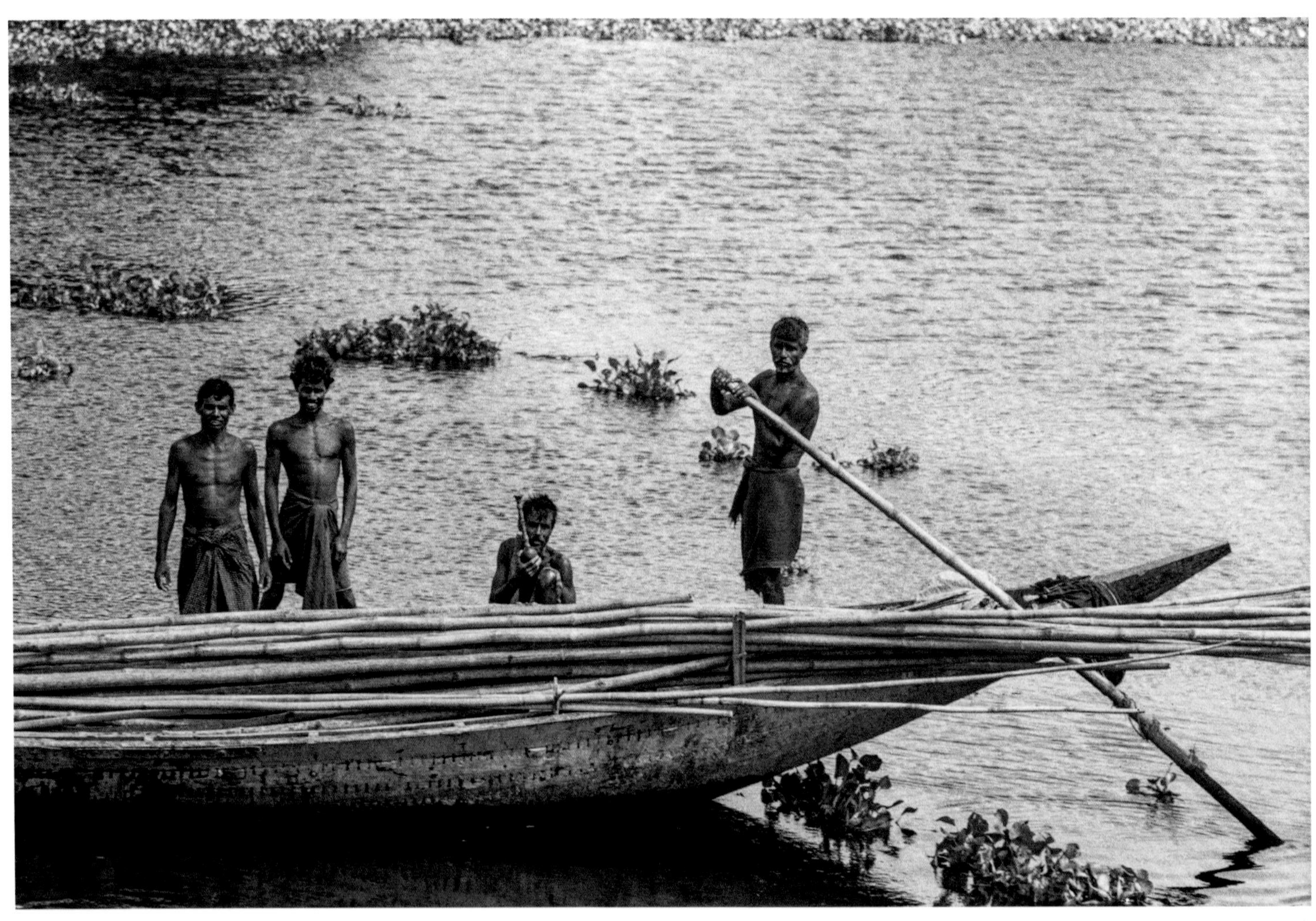

Fit men and long bamboos on the Buriganga

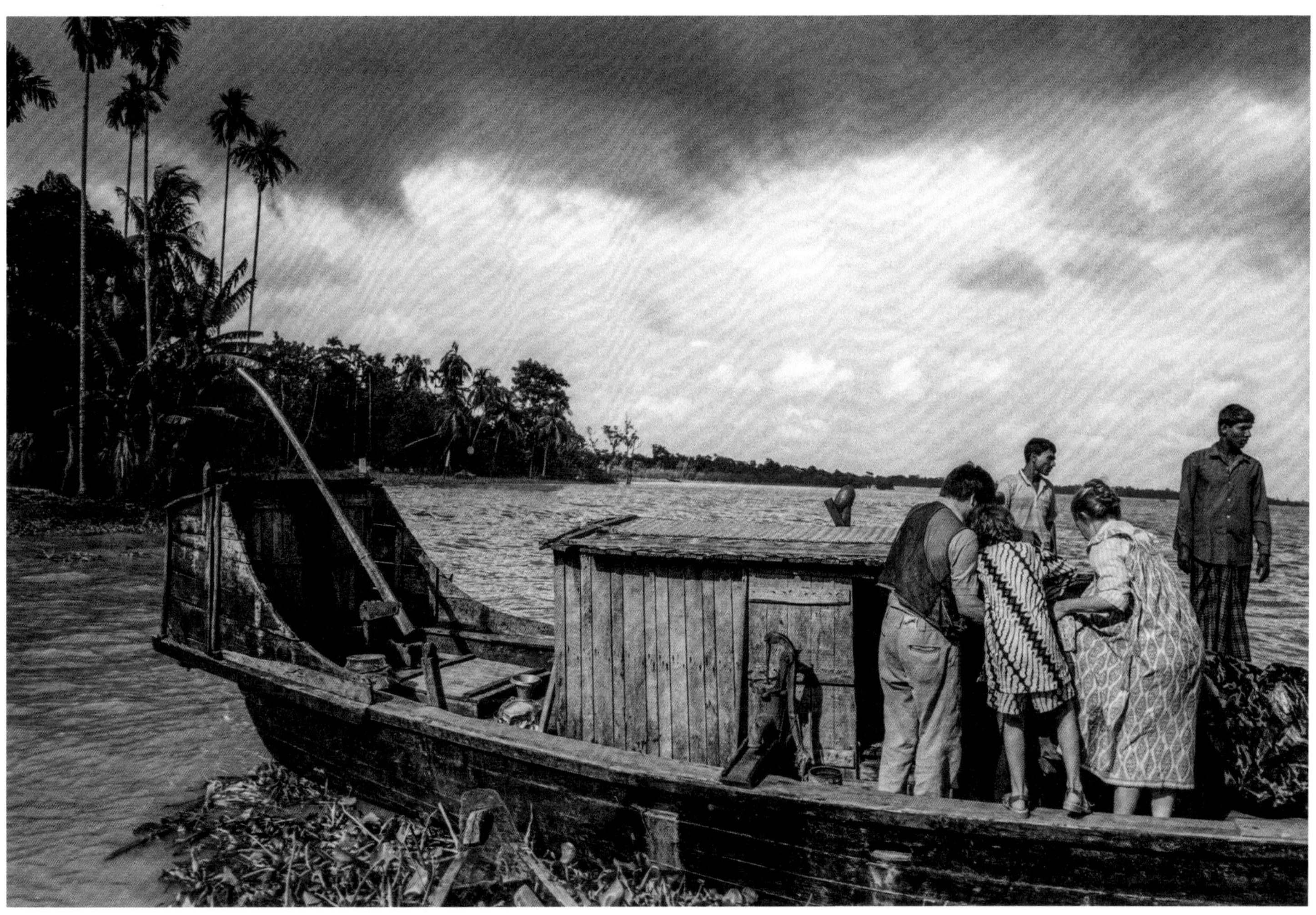

Unwrapping the tarp before the rains

'Shortly it begins to rain, suddenly and heavily. We stand in front of the engine-house wrapped in the tarp we bought 4 months ago in LA, the children at our feet with torches and hugely excited by the drama and unknown-ness of it all. Except for Rose, who was, not surprisingly, exhausted, having been up since 5 and it now being 7, and no supper. With immaculate timing the rain stopped and the first fireflies flashed their tiny lights from the jungle all around us, creating the perfect diversion for a tired little person who had not seen them before; so the situation was saved.'

Journal, 17 July 1992

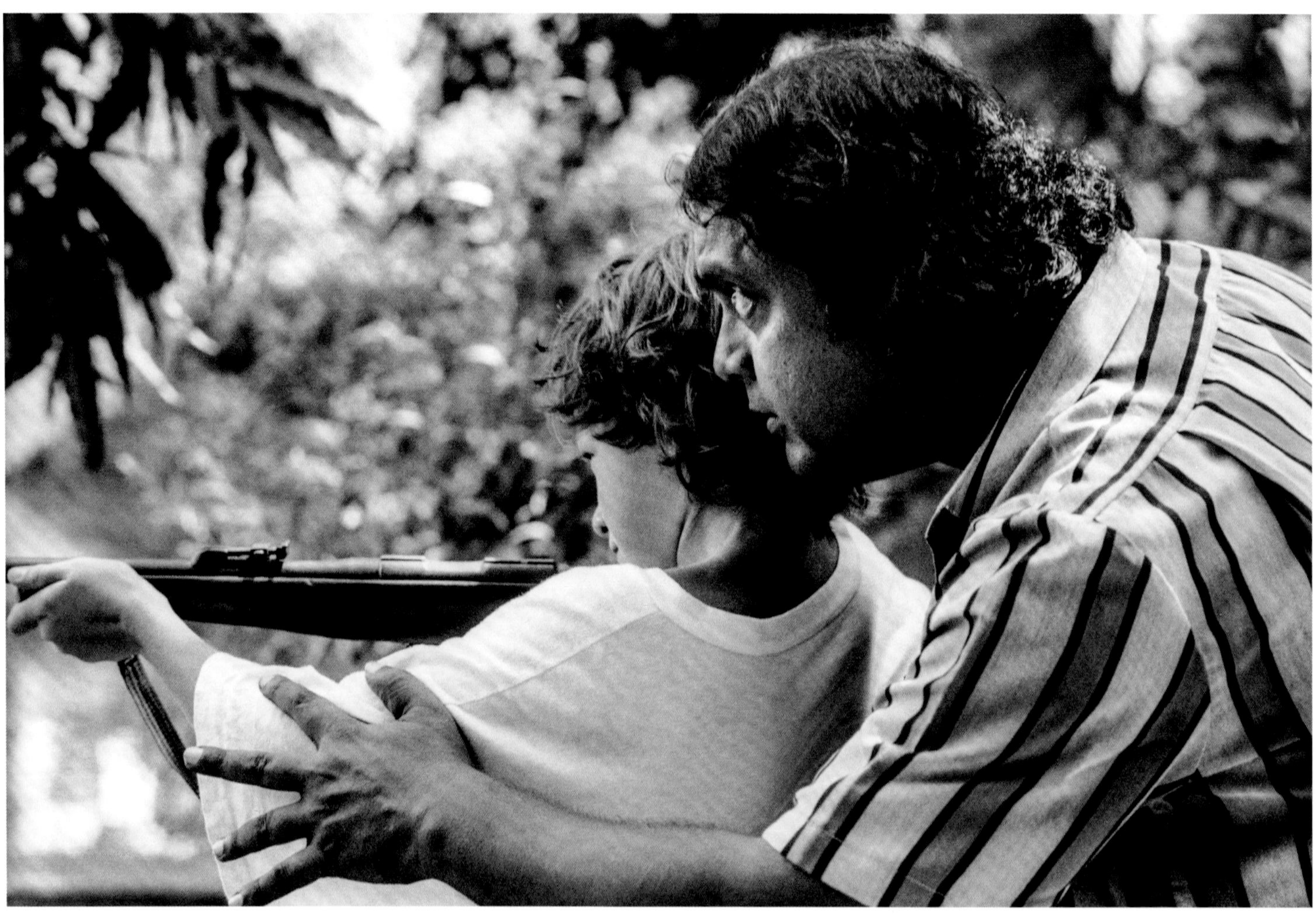

Carmody Grey, aged 8,
with Major Zia

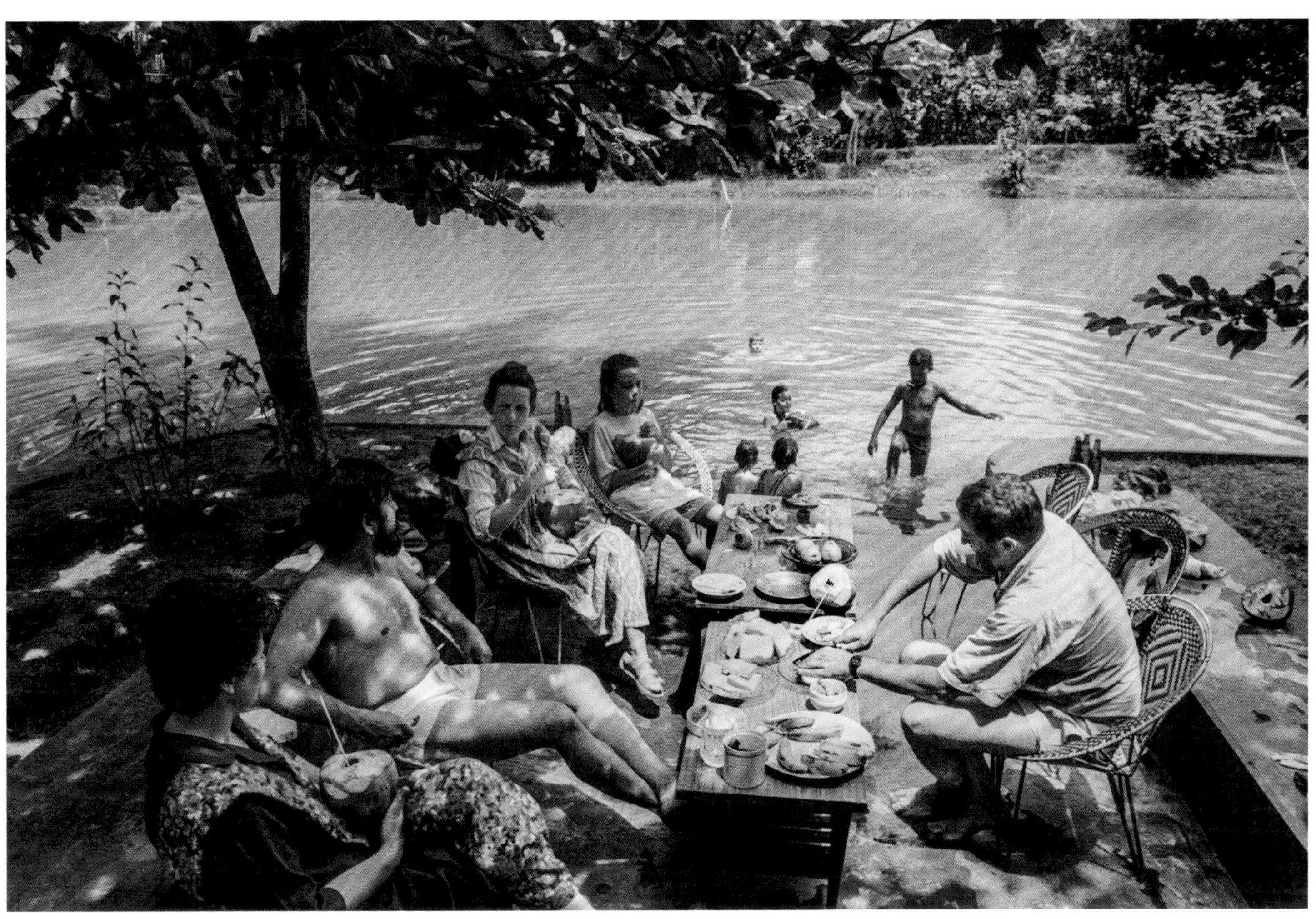

Clare Blenkinsop, Shahidul Alam, Jan Grey and Richard Holloway at lunch by the tank at the back of major Zia's house. Tanks in the Sundarbans were excavated to obtain earth for building house-mounds for protection during floods. This one was full of large long-whiskered catfish, which frightened me but not the children.

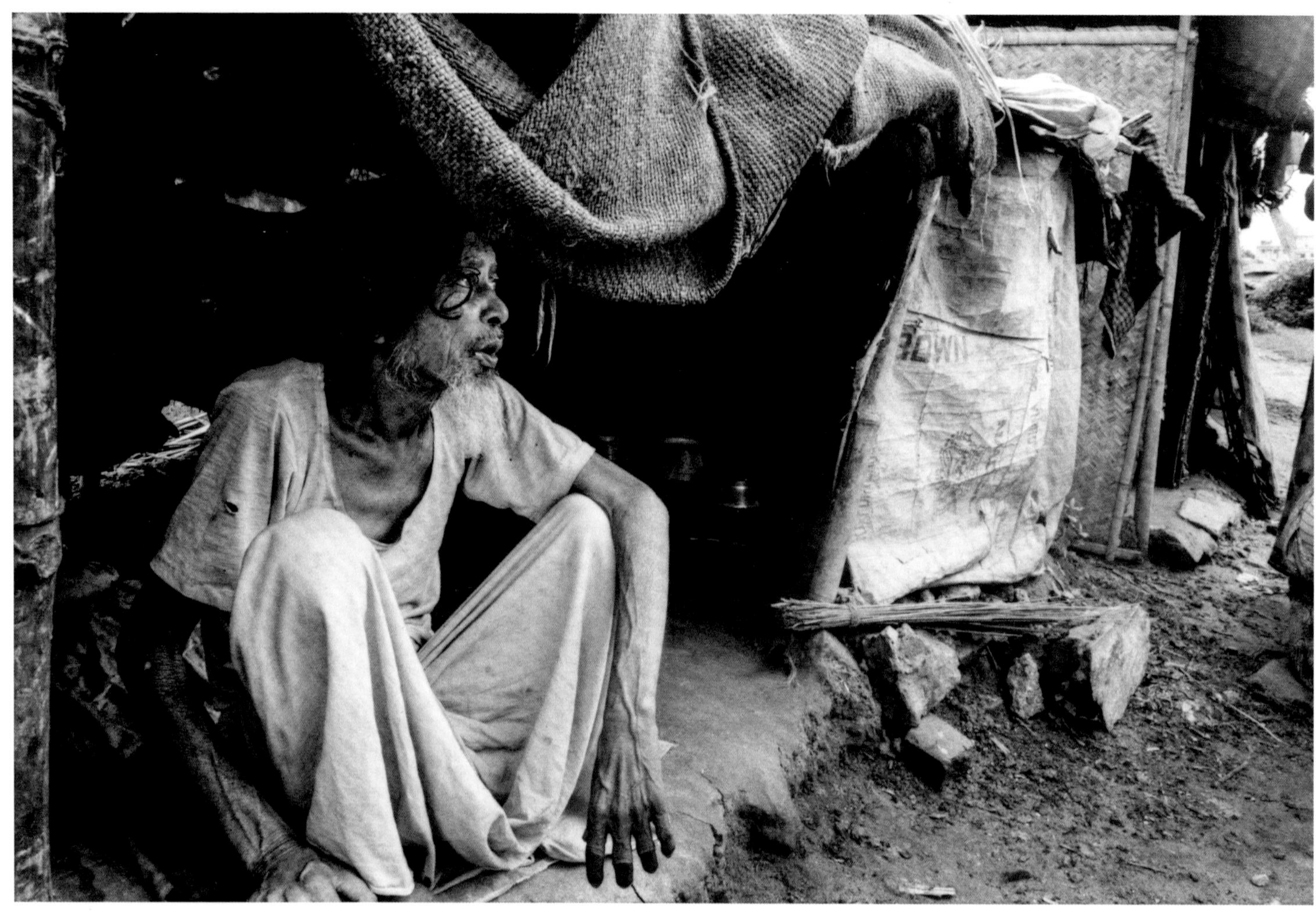

'The other aspect of Bangladesh that has made a deep impression on the children, and provoked a lot of questions, is poverty and the number of beggars. Their existence deeply offends their well-developed sense of fairness. The 3 of them have strong views on what we should give and to whom.'

Journal, 20 July 1992

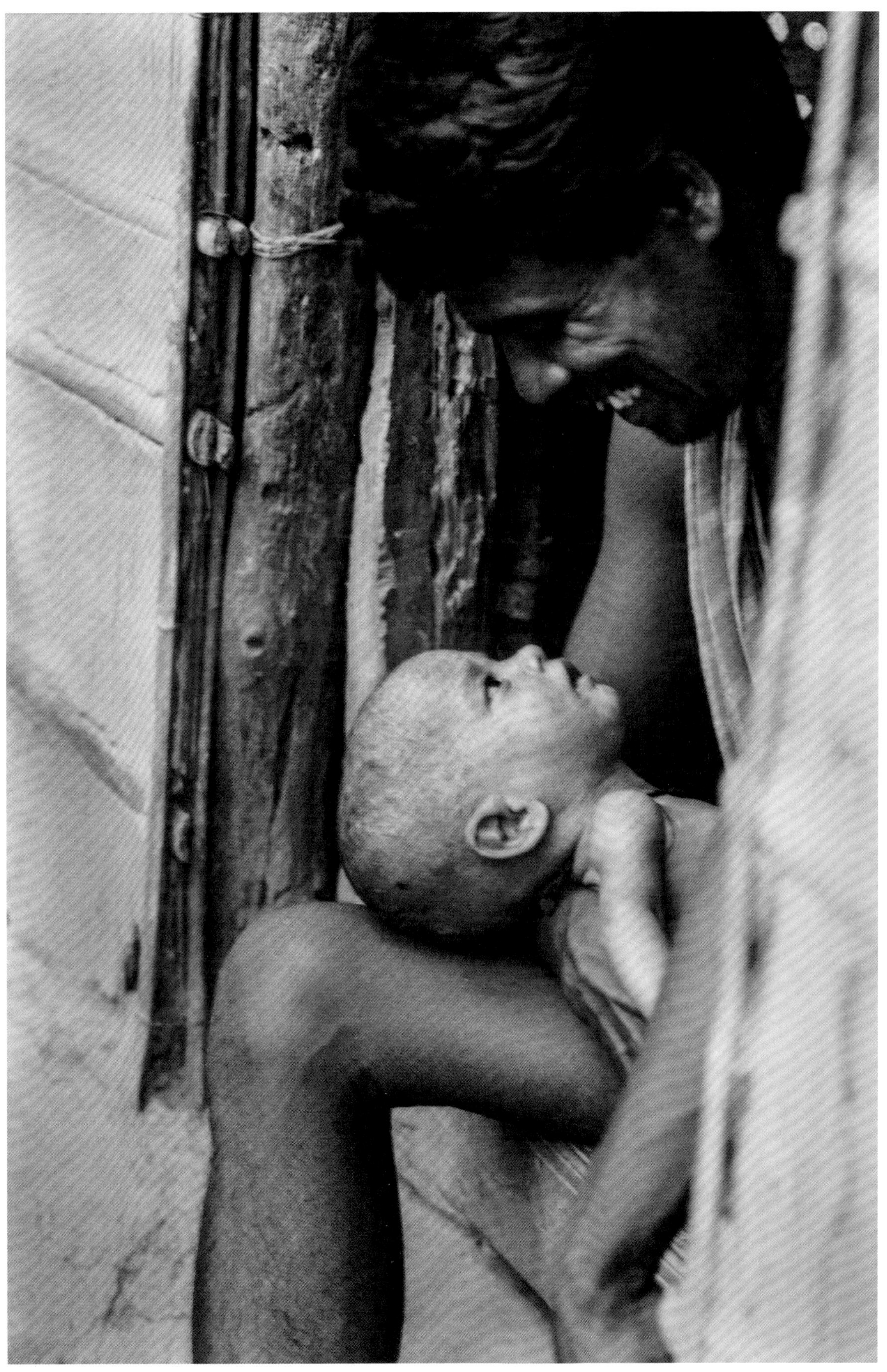

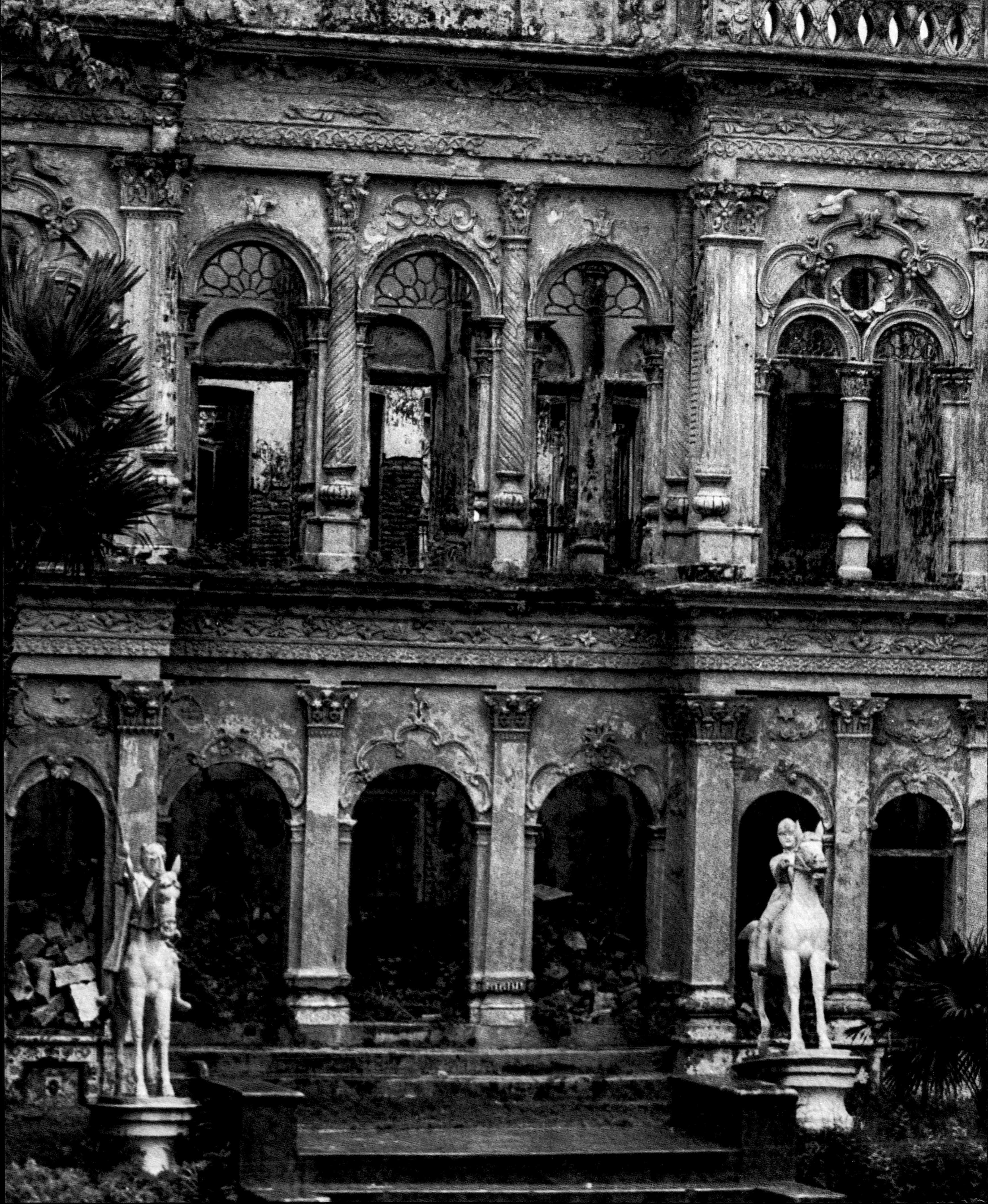

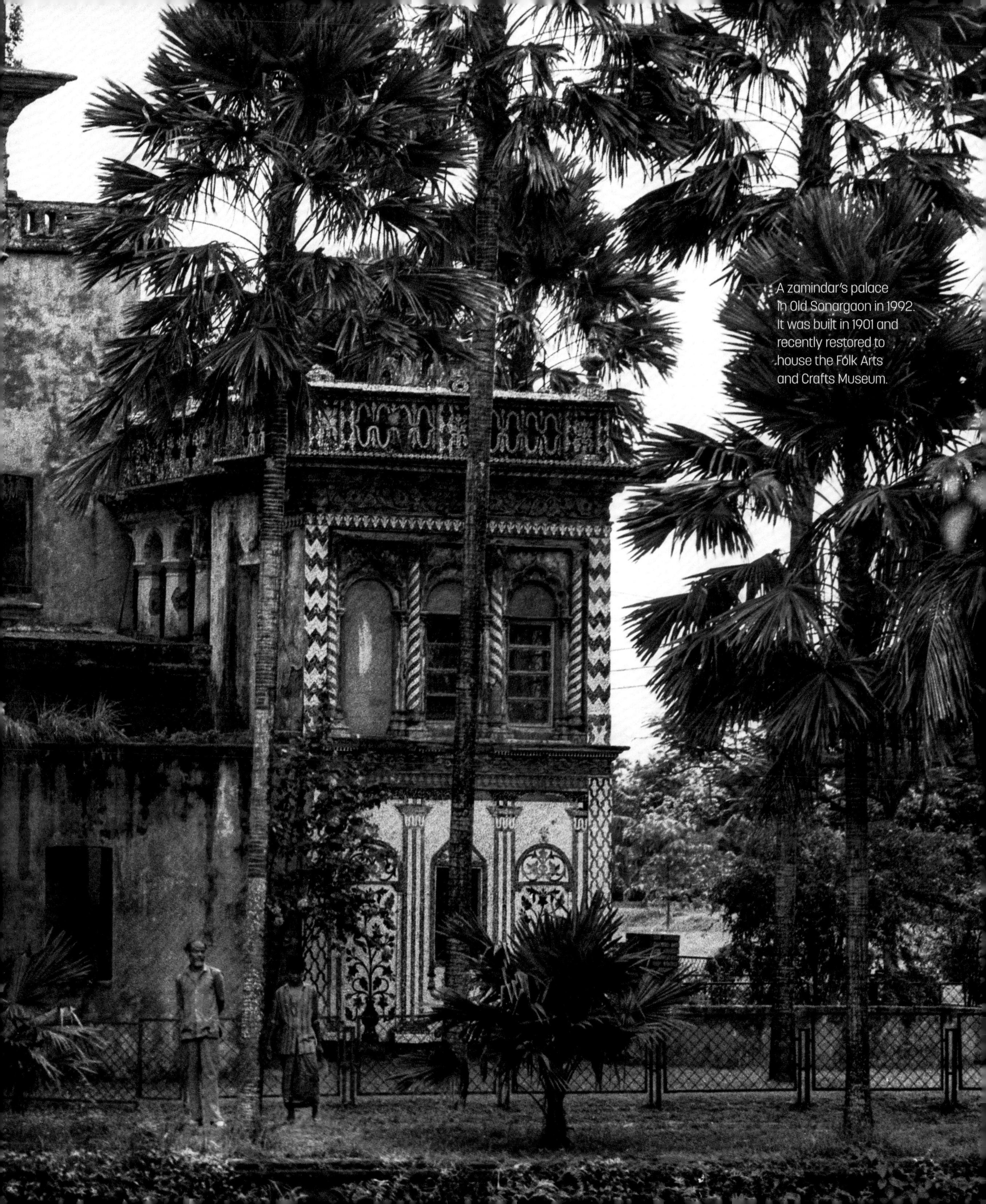

A zamindar's palace in Old Sonargaon in 1992. It was built in 1901 and recently restored to house the Folk Arts and Crafts Museum.

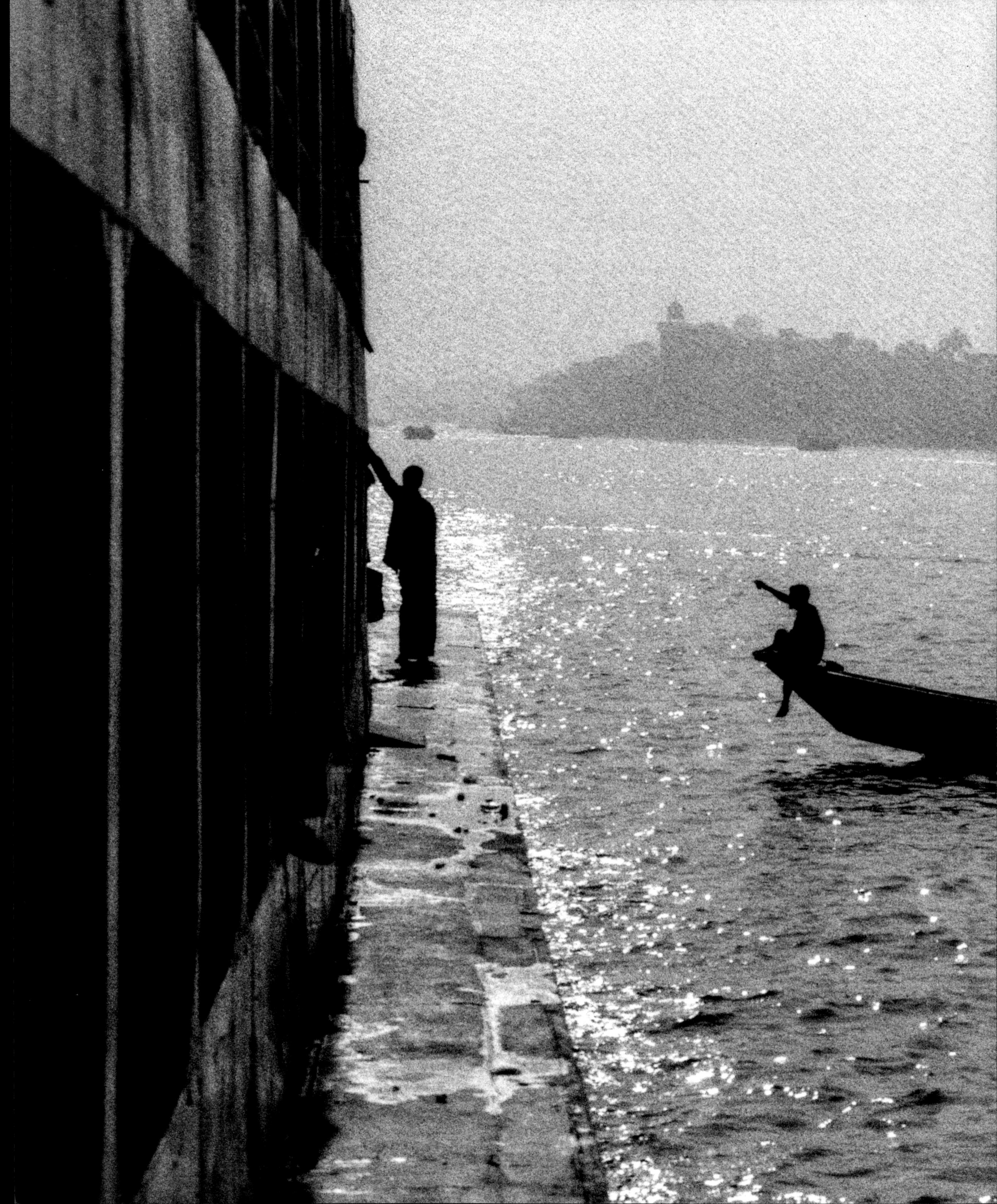

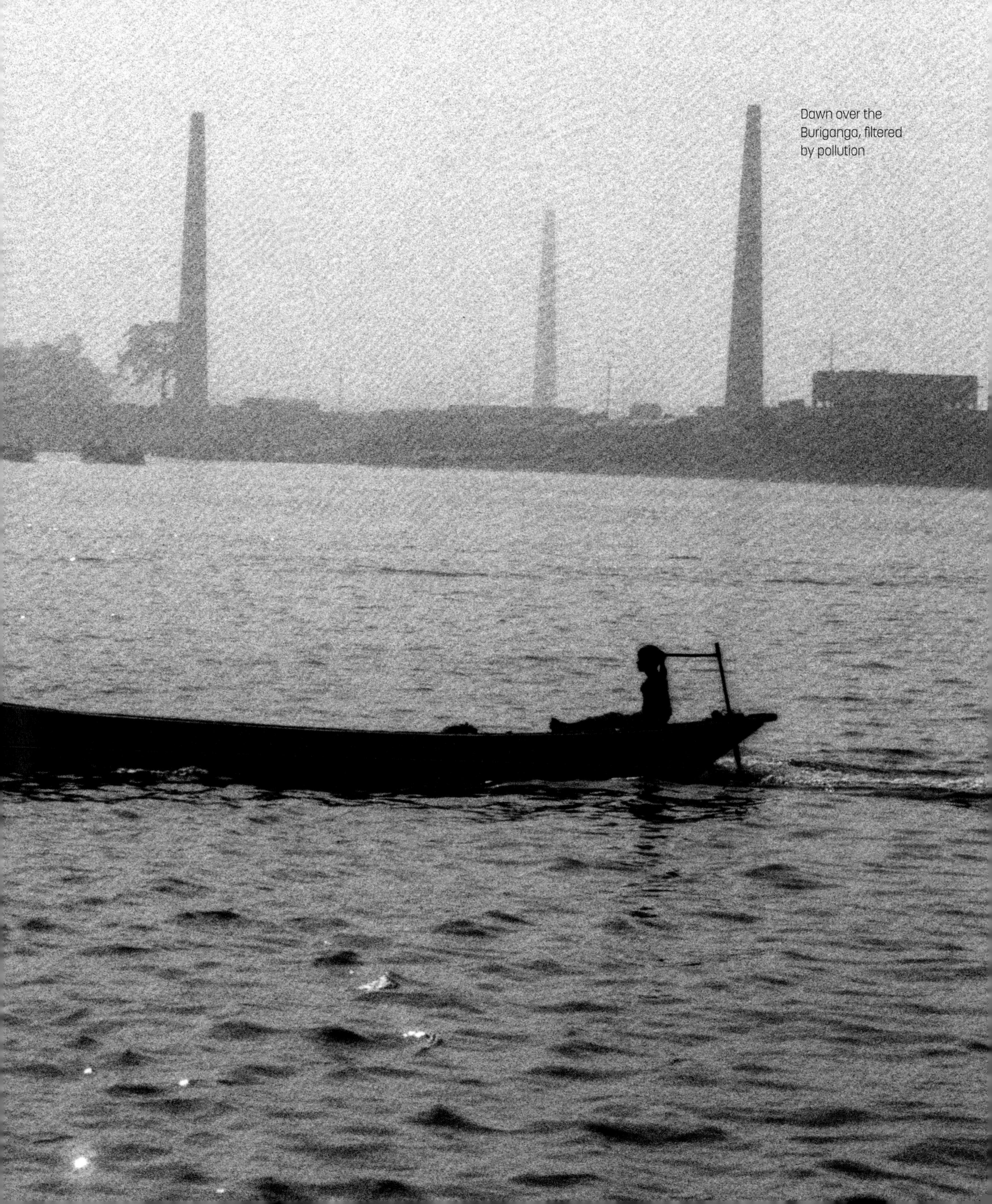

Dawn over the Buriganga, filtered by pollution

Chobi Mela, 2004–19

I arrived in Dhaka at midnight on 5 December 2004 and spent the rest of the night hanging a photographic exhibition which the authorities had tried to close down. It was a fitting introduction to a festival of photography, the theme that year being 'Resistance'. The gallery, in the National Museum, was packed with young photographers in a state of excitement – as was I. The images, curated by Robert Pledge,[13] were groundbreaking and moving. By breakfast – roti and chilli omelettes at a street stall at dawn – I realised that Chobi Mela was not just a festival, it was a campaign for freedom of speech, human rights and the righting of wrongs.

From there to the streets for the opening rally. Crowds gathered behind Chobi Mela banners: drummers and trumpeters drowned the noise of traffic, students sporting headbands danced and shouted. Here was an exuberance with serious intent, and at the head was Shahidul, who I had last seen twelve years before. It dawned on me that Chobi Mela was no mere campaign. It was a movement to change the landscape of photojournalism.

The question at the heart of the festival was what a camera is for. It is not simply a device for taking photographs. It is a non-violent and highly effective weapon for portraying injustice, recording oppression and changing public opinion. In the right hands the camera could be a flamethrower.[14] Rather like a good lawyer, it occurred to me.

At that time I was a senior partner at one of Britain's most prominent law firms.[15] My area of practice was media law, and it was in that capacity that I had been invited to Bangladesh by the British Council to give a public lecture on international copyright. I did not expect to find myself at the barricades in support of an unfamiliar but agreeably radical revolution. That moment was a turning point. After a week of copyright workshops and street-stall chats with students, I realised I was witnessing at close quarters the gradual transformation of a community of young photojournalists in a country which was barely on the map into an internationally recognised force for change.

The opening rally of Chobi Mela in 2004. 'Chobi' is an Urdu word meaning 'picture'. 'Mela' is a Sanskrit word meaning 'gathering' or 'to meet'. Holding a Mela to celebrate photography was new. From left to right: Dr Shahidul Alam, Morten Krogvold and Philippe Tarbouchier

As, many years later, I write this piece, the World Press Photo Exhibition 2022, hosted by the world's most prestigious institution of Photography, is opening in Dhaka. Tanzim Wahab, who chaired the Asian jury, is the third Bangladeshi to do so, following in the footsteps of Shahidul, Munem Wasif and Abir Abdullah. In 2003 Shahidul was the first person of colour to Chair the International Jury of the World Press.

All four are from Pathshala,[16] the photography school founded by Shahidul and his colleagues and referred to in the introduction, alongside Drik, the first platform in the developing world to challenge the dominance of Western media in the selection, interpretation and dissemination of international news. The plan was that Bangladesh would no longer be portrayed as a series of catastrophes, but as a nation with a rich past, a distinctive present

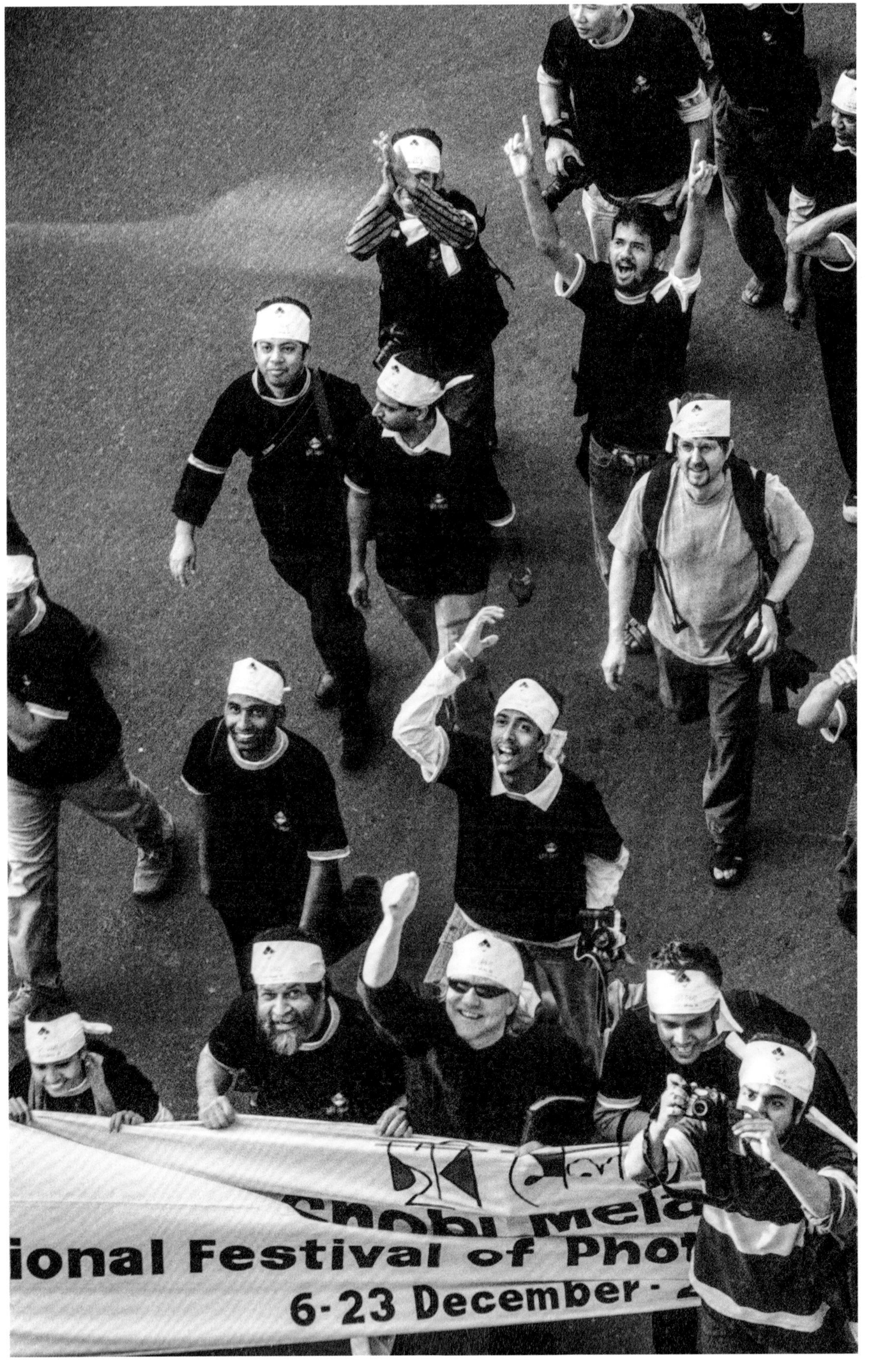
ional Festival of Phot
6-23 December -

and its own future. Drik had become a hub for these young camera-wielding changemakers.

Over the next few years most of the world's foremost curators and photojournalists came to see what was going on, drawn by new voices heralding changes in their field. They recognised, as did I, that the power of the Western gatekeepers was slipping away with the arrival of digital technology. The West's monopoly over storytelling was being challenged, both in the choice of photographer and control over dissemination.

Drik is always the first port of call when I arrive for Chobi Mela. It is the hub for exhibiting photographers just arrived in town wanting to know about their prints, for lecturers like me needing to know the programme, for filmmakers hoping to use the recording studio and for journalists sensing the eclectic magic of Chobi Mela, looking for a touchstone to ignite a story. It looks like chaos, but it is a chaos you want to be a part of, and out of it emerges powerful and coherent storytelling. It is this tension that marks Chobi Mela out from other festivals.

There is another critical distinction: it is no coincidence that political protest and the fight against injustice have been the underlying themes of Chobi Mela since it started in 2000. Freedom of speech is alive and more or less well in Bangladesh, but it has to be fought for. Overt criticism of the government is high risk and there are fears, referred to in a recent report by the *Financial Times*, that Bangladesh is becoming an increasingly repressive environment.[17]

The opening rally of Chobi Mela in 2006. Munem Wasif, now a prominent international photographer represented by Agence VU, a teacher at Patshala and a Director of Chobi Mela, is in the centre of the image.

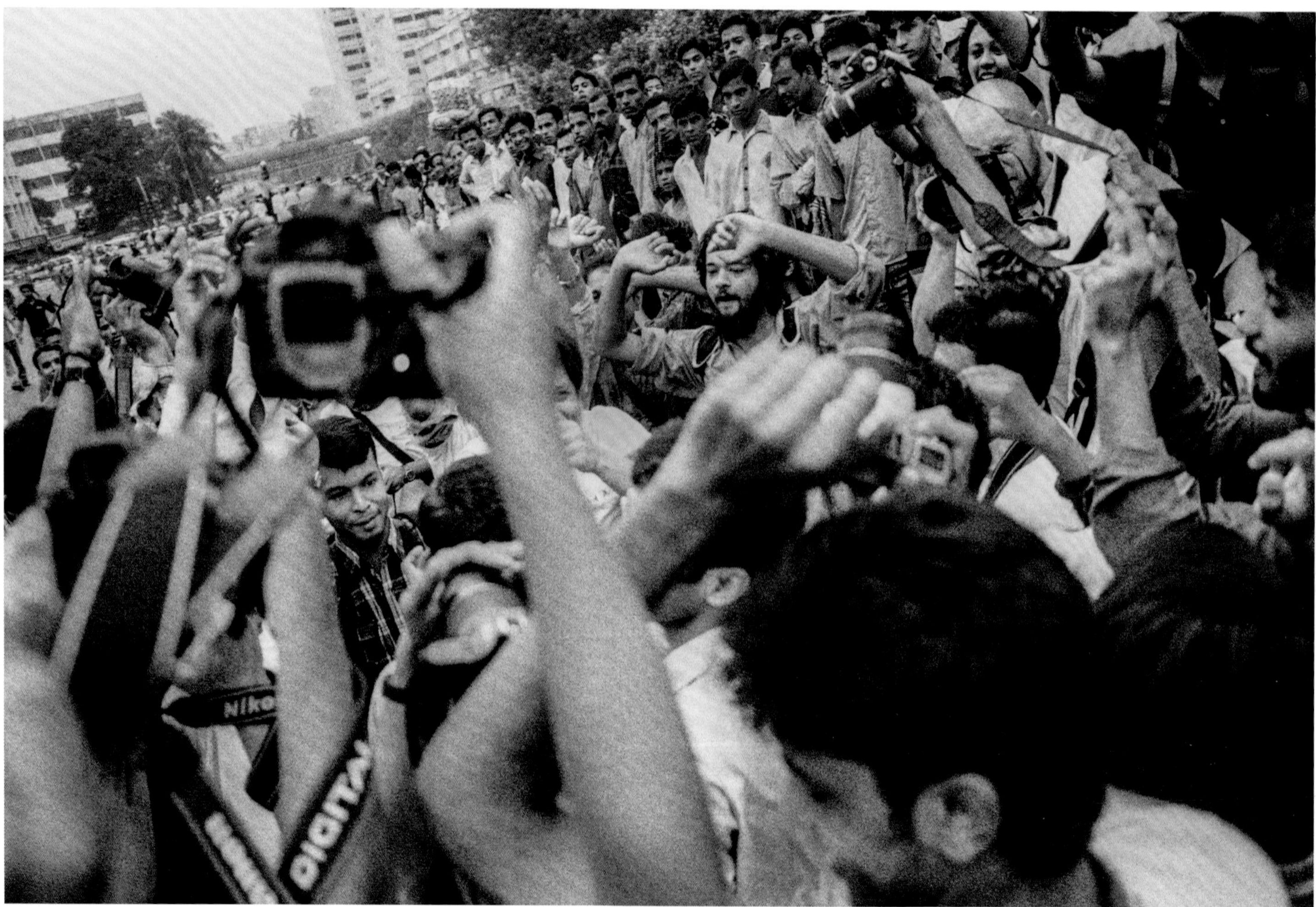

Exhibitions have been closed, dissenters silenced and public speakers cancelled. In 2019, activist and author Arundhati Roy was cancelled twice. At the third attempt six thousand people attended.

The second port of call is Pathshala, the place of learning founded by Drik twenty-five years ago and now the foremost photography school in Asia. It attracts students and teachers from widely different backgrounds and countries.[18] There, as at Drik, you might meet members of the Out of Focus group, whose foundations were laid, in a literal sense, at the traffic lights of Dhaka where street kids sold flowers to drivers. I first heard about this group in 2004 while driving to Old Dhaka with Shahidul. A girl came to the window while we were waiting at the lights. Shahidul bought the flowers and they carried on talking as they waited for the lights to change. I couldn't follow the conversation, but it was clear they were acquainted. I remarked on this as we drove on and the story unfolded.

Back in the 1990s, during the dying moments of the analogue era, Shahidul gave a couple of kids point-and-shoot cameras with one roll of film while he waited for the lights to turn green. The catch was that they had to come to his darkroom to develop the film. It caught on. He set up a darkroom nearby, gave them a regular supply of film, took them on outings and paid for their schooling. Some of those street kids, male and female, are now leading international photographers.

In 2011, I spent a morning with Shahidul in Pathshala interviewing applicants for a scholarship from the Magnum Foundation. On the brick walls of the classroom hung powerful images and statements of purpose, revealing what young Bangladeshis minded about: exposing corruption, and freeing children from slavery and women from violence. We awarded the scholarship to Taslima Akhter, a female student in her last year at Pathshala.

Two years later she took the image which became known as 'a final embrace' after the collapse of the garment factory in Dhaka in which a thousand garment workers died. It won a World Press Photo award and was one of *Time* Magazine's top ten photos of 2013. It also delivered a high voltage worldwide shock to the garment industry.

The vision which Shahidul shared with me on the scrubbed decks of the King's boat in the Sundarbans thirty years ago has become reality. ■

---

13 Founder of Contact Press Images and one of the most highly thought of curators in the field of photojournalism.

14 Cartier-Bresson (see epigram, page 1).

15 Farrer & Co.

16 The pathshala system of education in Bengal dates from early times: ad hoc open-air gatherings at which charismatic teachers taught students of all religions and castes. They had no permanent structure, and each one became known by the name of the teacher who founded and ran it. The system eroded under the education policies of the colonial government in the nineteenth century.

17 Dispatch from Dhaka by John Reed, *FT Weekend* magazine January 14/15 2023.

18 A number of whom are financed by the Sam Banks Memorial Fund in the UK. Sam was a student at Bedales school, who died in 2010.

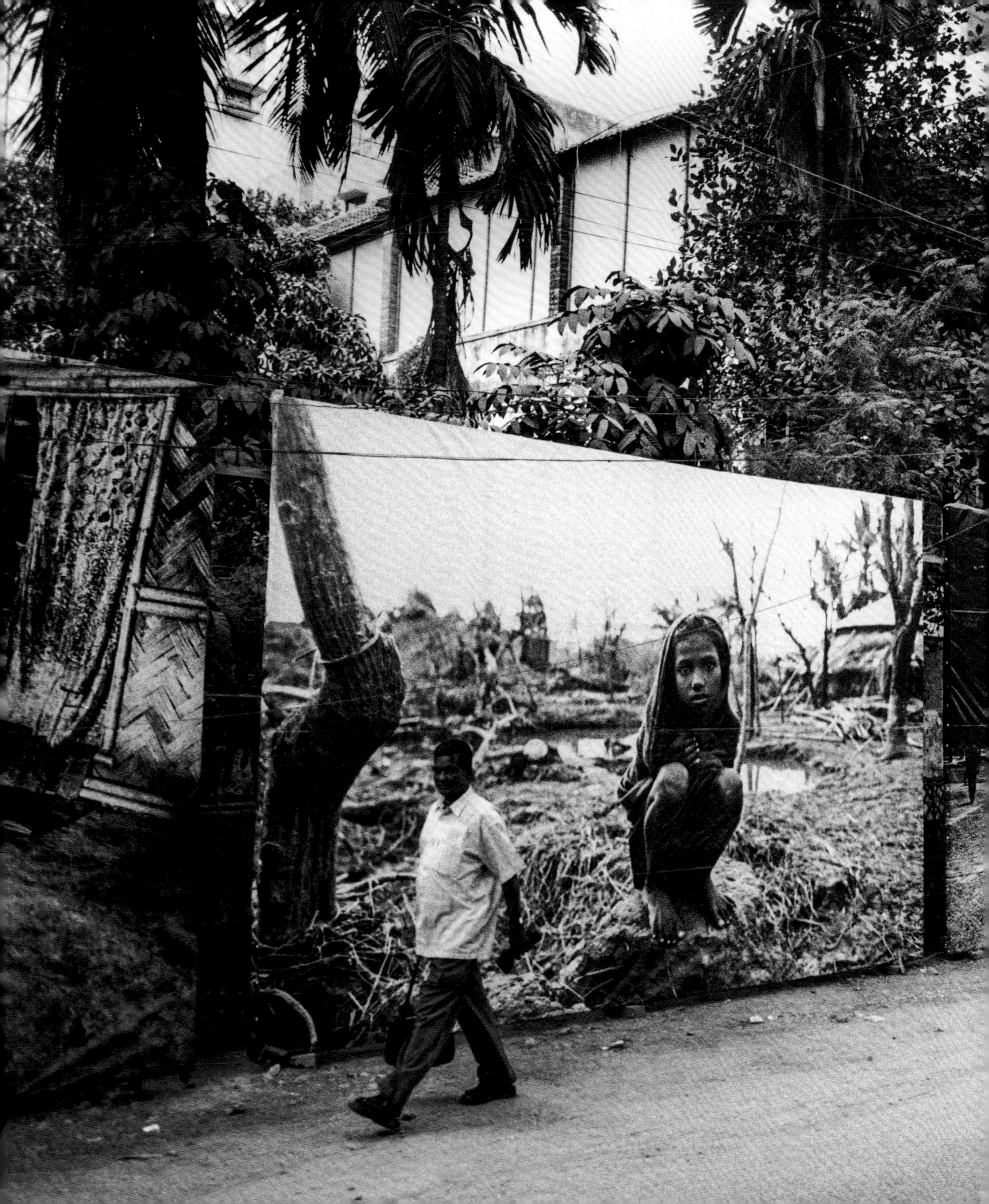

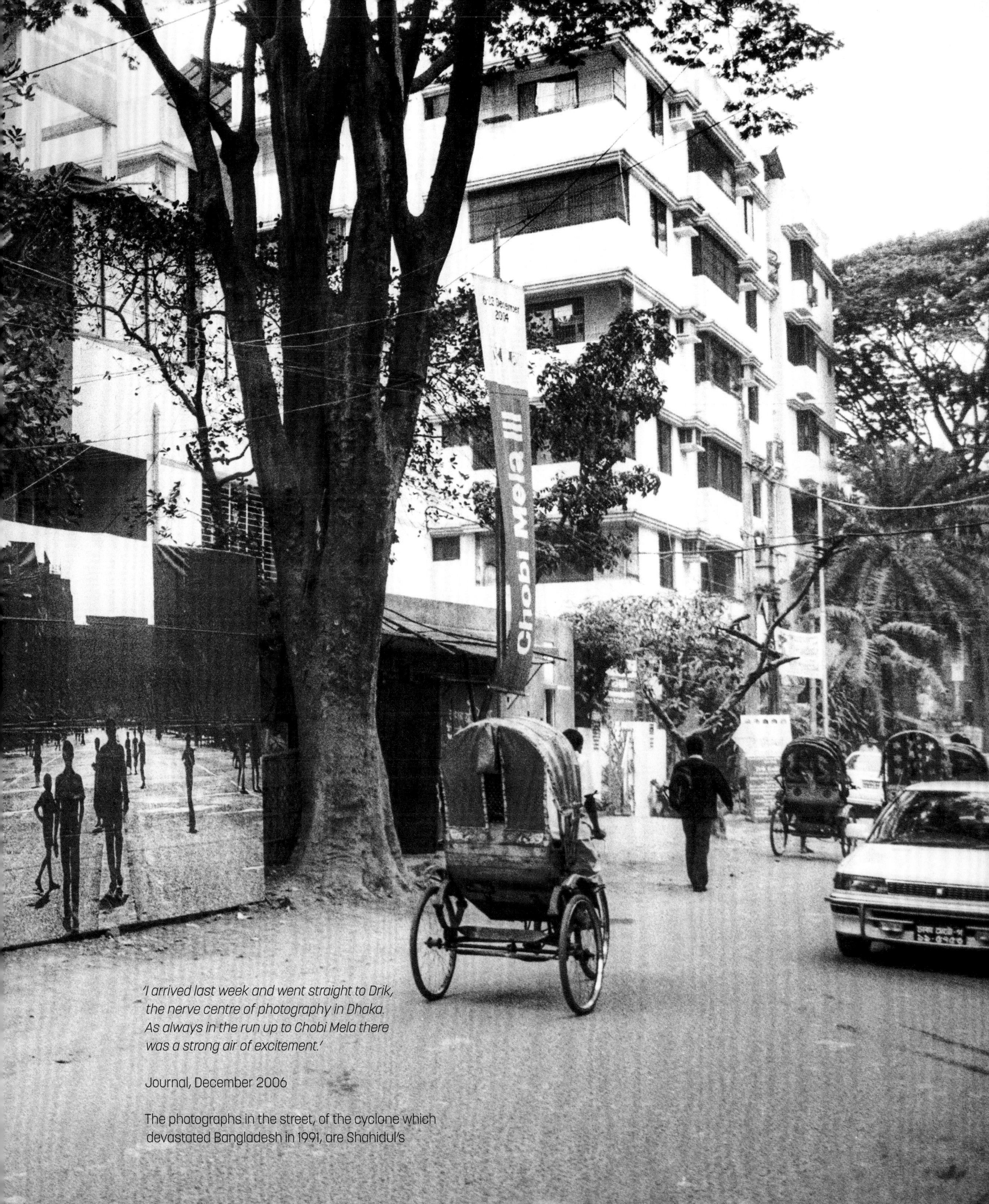

'I arrived last week and went straight to Drik, the nerve centre of photography in Dhaka. As always in the run up to Chobi Mela there was a strong air of excitement.'

Journal, December 2006

The photographs in the street, of the cyclone which devastated Bangladesh in 1991, are Shahidul's

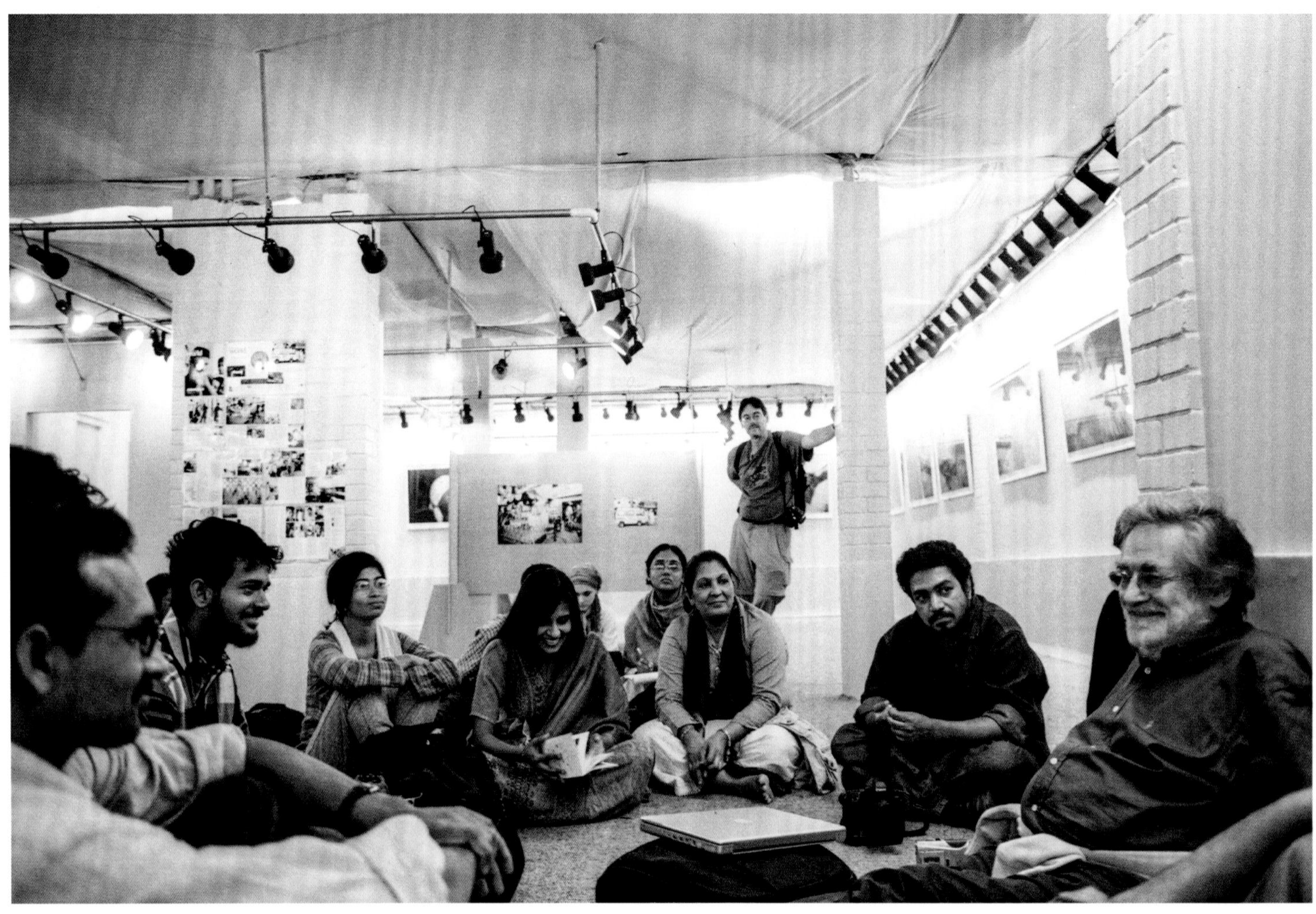

Pedro Meyer, a Spanish photographer based in Mexico and at that time a pioneer of the digital revolution in photography, at a seminar in Drik in 2004. Dick Doughty, an American magazine editor, stands in the background. On the floor are staff and students of Patshala.

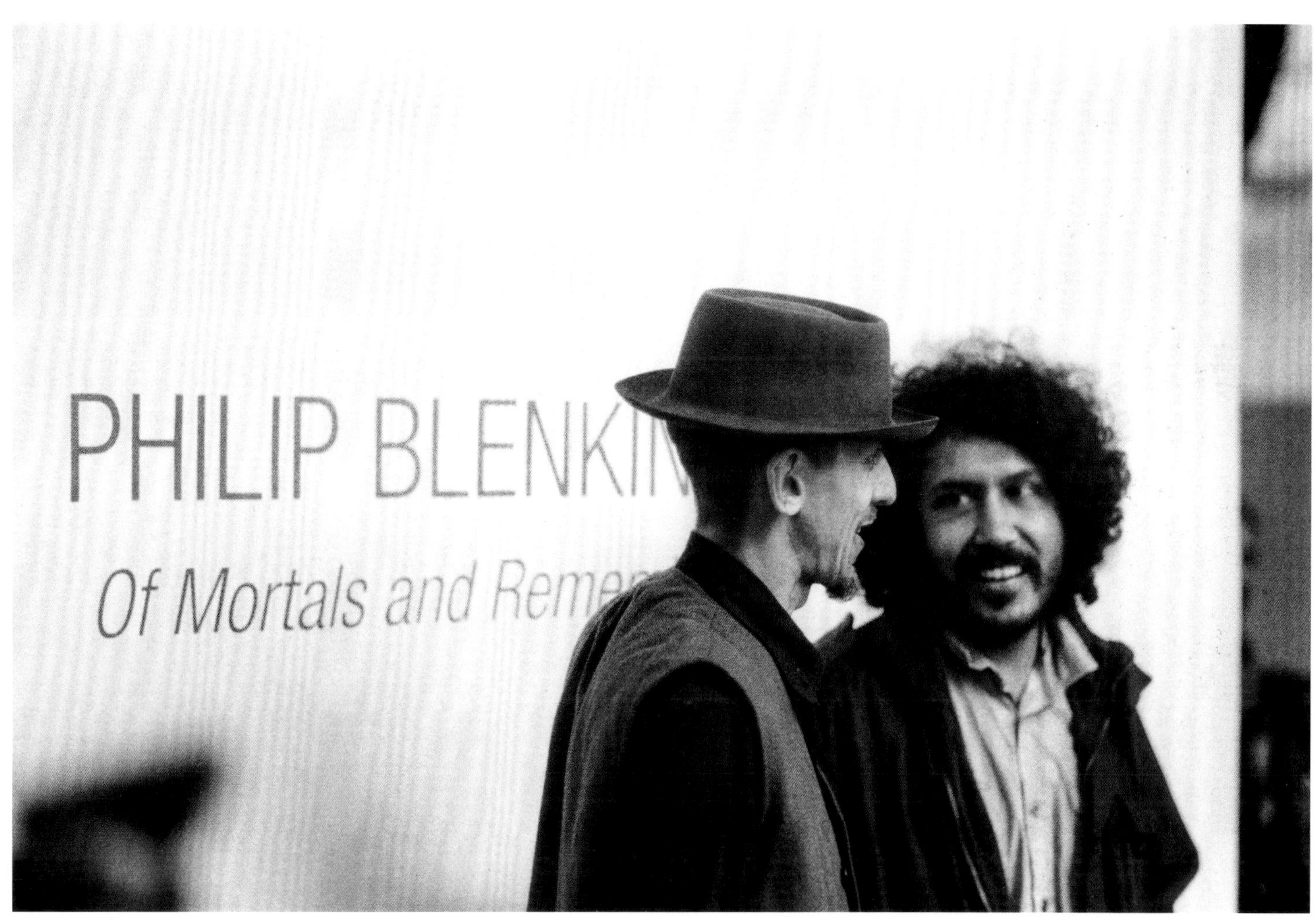

'How to describe the complex threads which Chobi Mela brings together? The stories told on stage by young photographers learning how to present their talents, or established professionals like Philip Blenkinsop speaking to Tanzim [Wahab] of his work, Morten Krogvold teaching students how to select their photographs, Robert Pledge appraising their work, Pedro Meyer leading seminars sitting cross-legged on the floor at the age of seventy. Perhaps it's the passing of knowledge between generations and cultures that touches me.'

Journal, January 2015

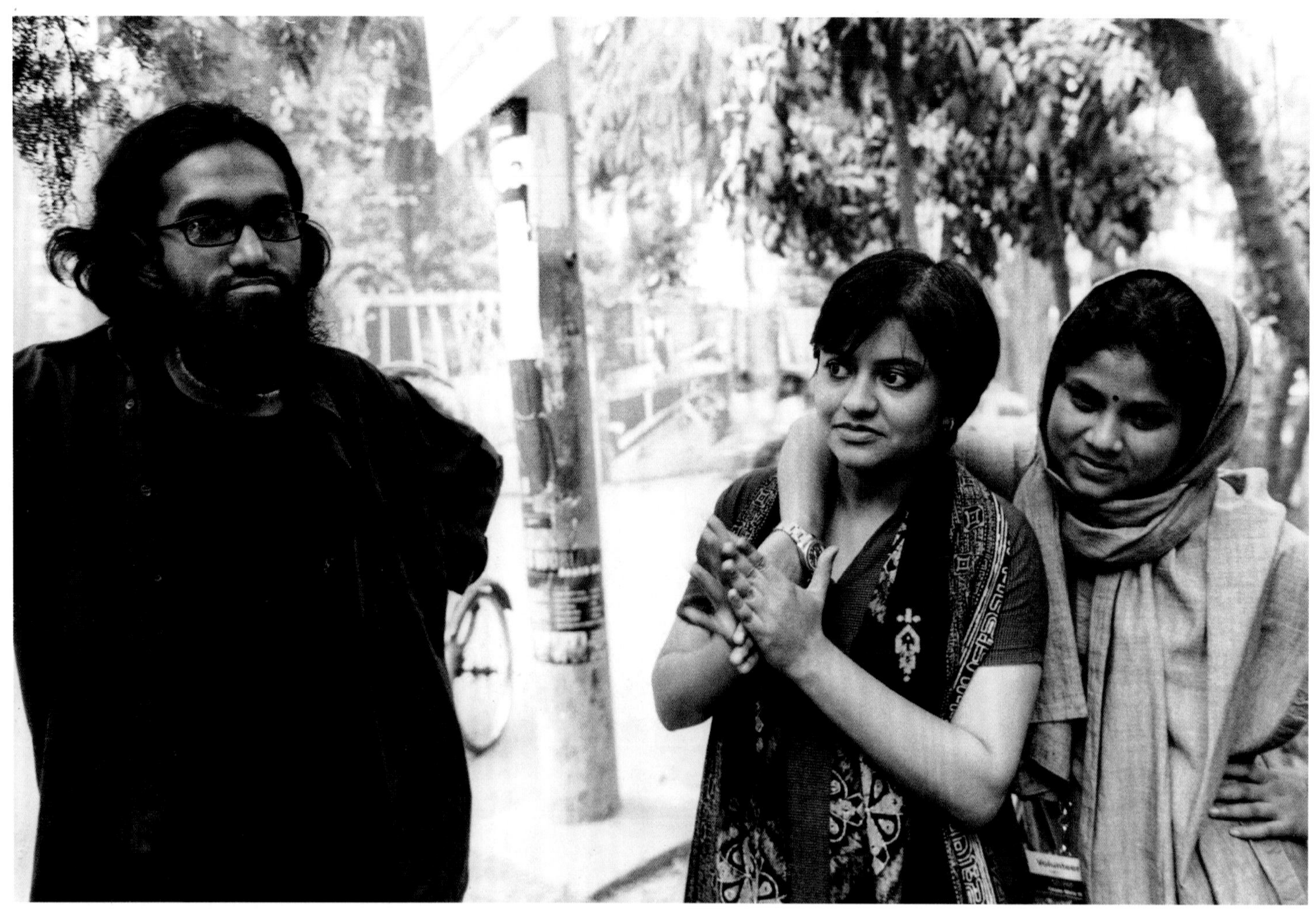

Tanvir Murad Topu, now Head of Photography at Patshala, with two colleagues from Drik in 2004

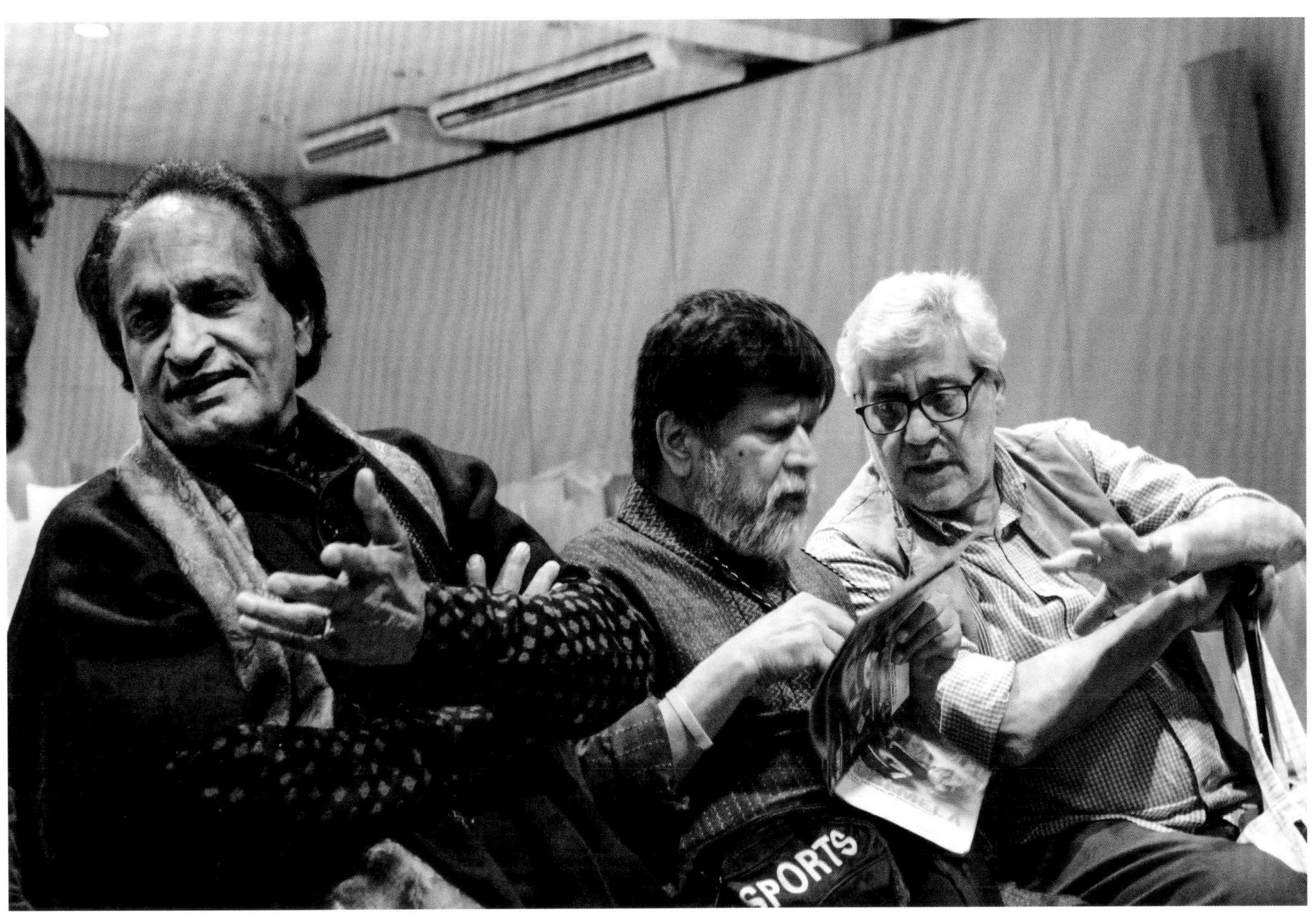

Raghu Rai from India, Shahidul Alam and Robert Pledge from the United States at Chobi Mela X

'Each time I come to Chobi Mela I am moved afresh by stories of young photographers engaging with their world, searching for meaning in their own and other's lives, recording the fragility, the perversity and the magic of the human condition. Alongside them photographers and curators prominent in their fields are showing their work, sharing their perspectives and passions and teaching what they have learned while reporting from the front line on the major issues of our times.'

Journal, February 2019

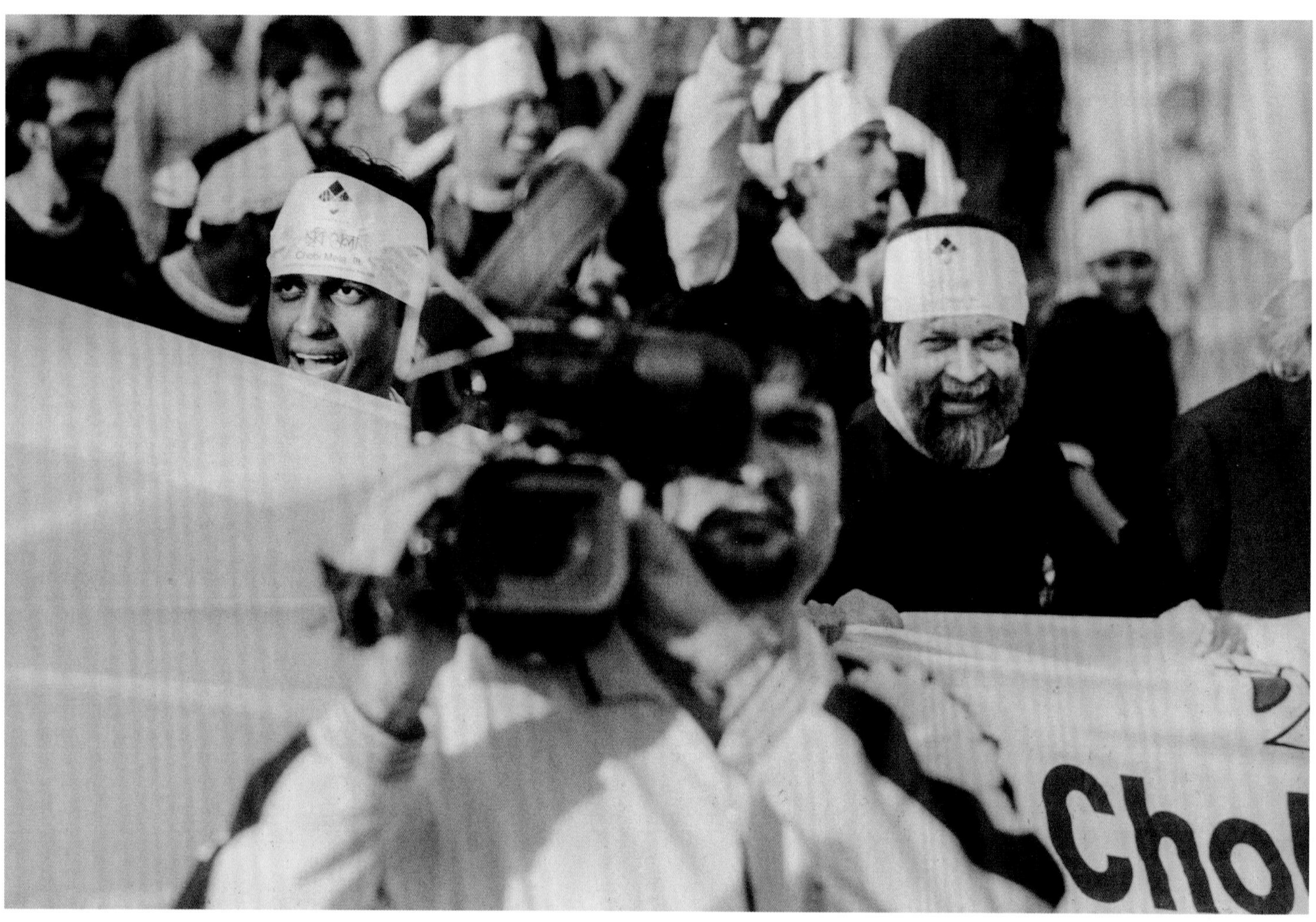

Shahidul Alam holding up the Chobi Mela
banner at the opening celebrations in 2004

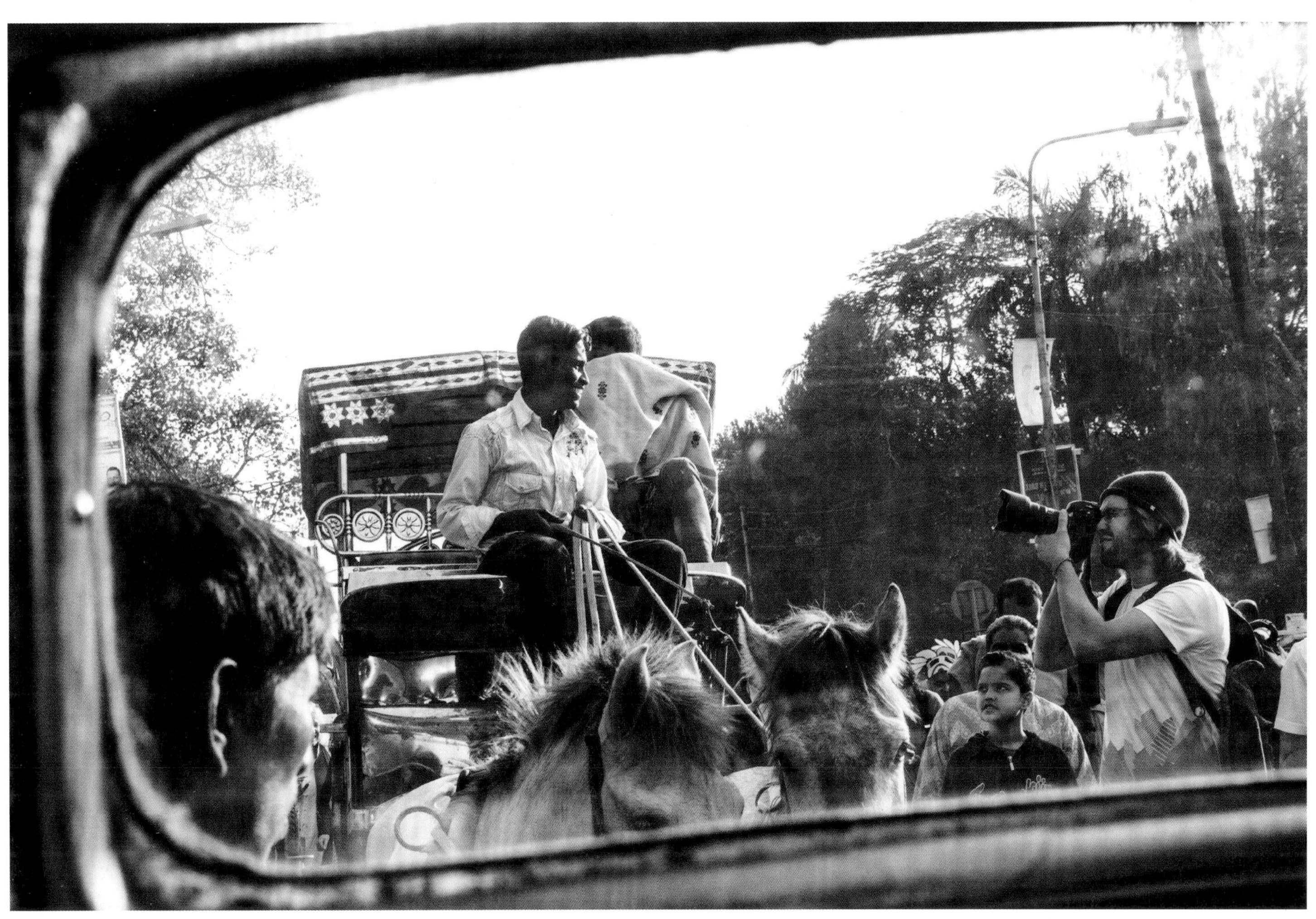

Through the rear window of the Rolls during Chobi Mela VII in 2013

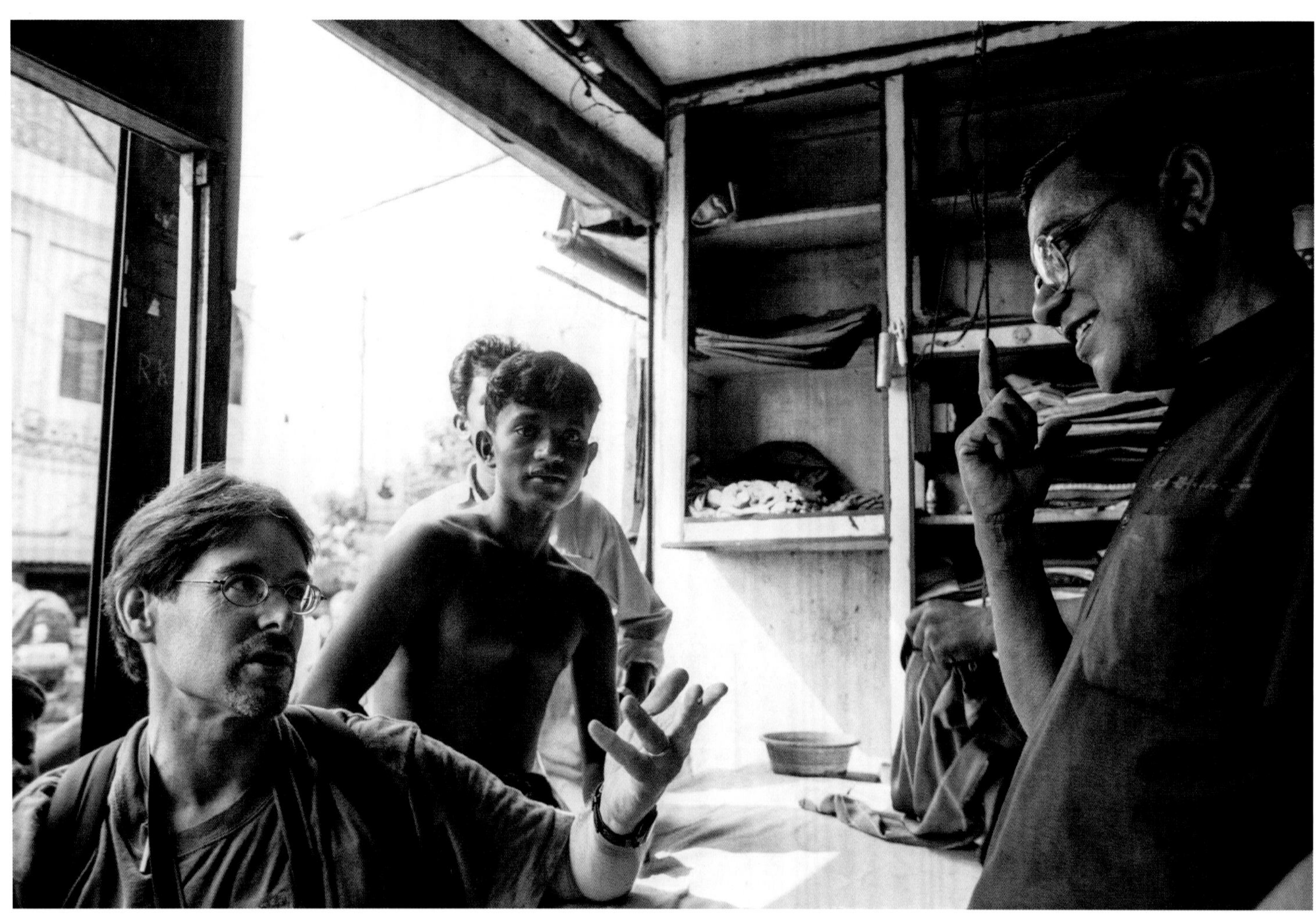

'Dick [Doughty] and I walked through Old Dhaka this morning and drank a liesurely tea with my friend who irons shirts beside the Buriganga. Later we joined Morten Krogvold for lunch. For 2 hours we spoke of the critical issues in contemporary journalism and reportage photography.'

Journal, December 2004

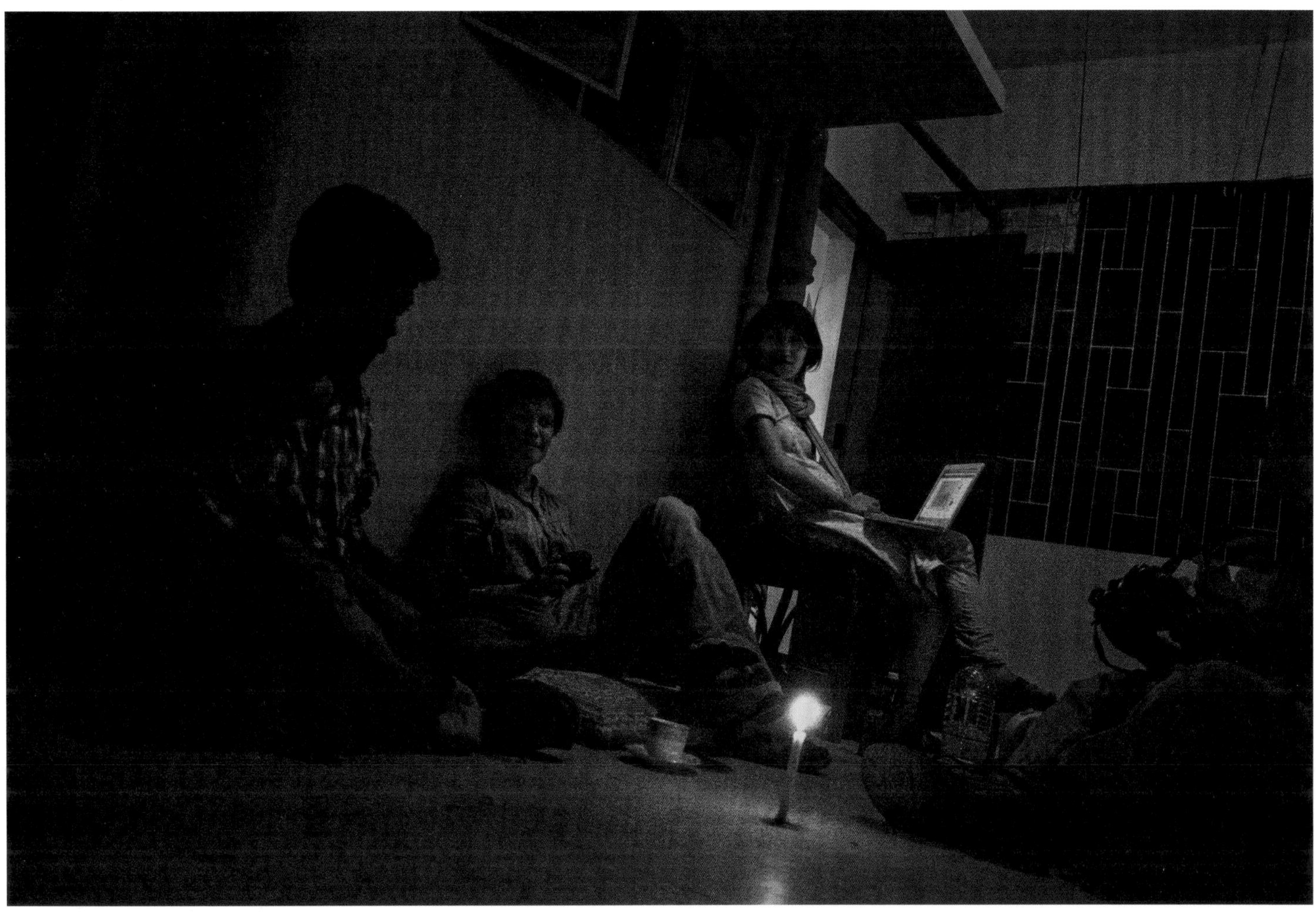

'Midnight. Back from dinner on a dusty balcony overlooking palm trees and pantile rooves stretching into the darkness. There were 4 of us. We had all been at my copyright jam-session at Patshala, and had met each other for the first time during the last 36 hours – save for Schumon, who I last saw some years ago, and were drawn together by the chances and vagaries of our unorthodox lives.

Schumon spoke of the influence of Ian Berry, who he regarded as the last surviving photographer of the golden age of Magnum; Maria from Norway, drawn here by Drik and Patshala and the ideals they represent, and Christina, a Chinese Canadian who has been on the road for two years and believes that art is the way to bring peace to the world.

It was late and the conversation flowed easily. We shared our histories, a little something of our lives and even of our loves, not in an intimate way but after the manner of travellers giving and taking and sharing the passing moment. There was amongst us an understanding that something was stirring here in Bangladesh which drew us in.

Difficult to put a finger on it. It's not Shahidul himself but it is to do with his presence. He has, in Chobi Mela, lit a candle, one of us remarked, and we and others have come to see what it is that he is looking at; having seen it we realise that it is bigger than ourselves and we want to be a part of it.'

Journal, 18 February 2009

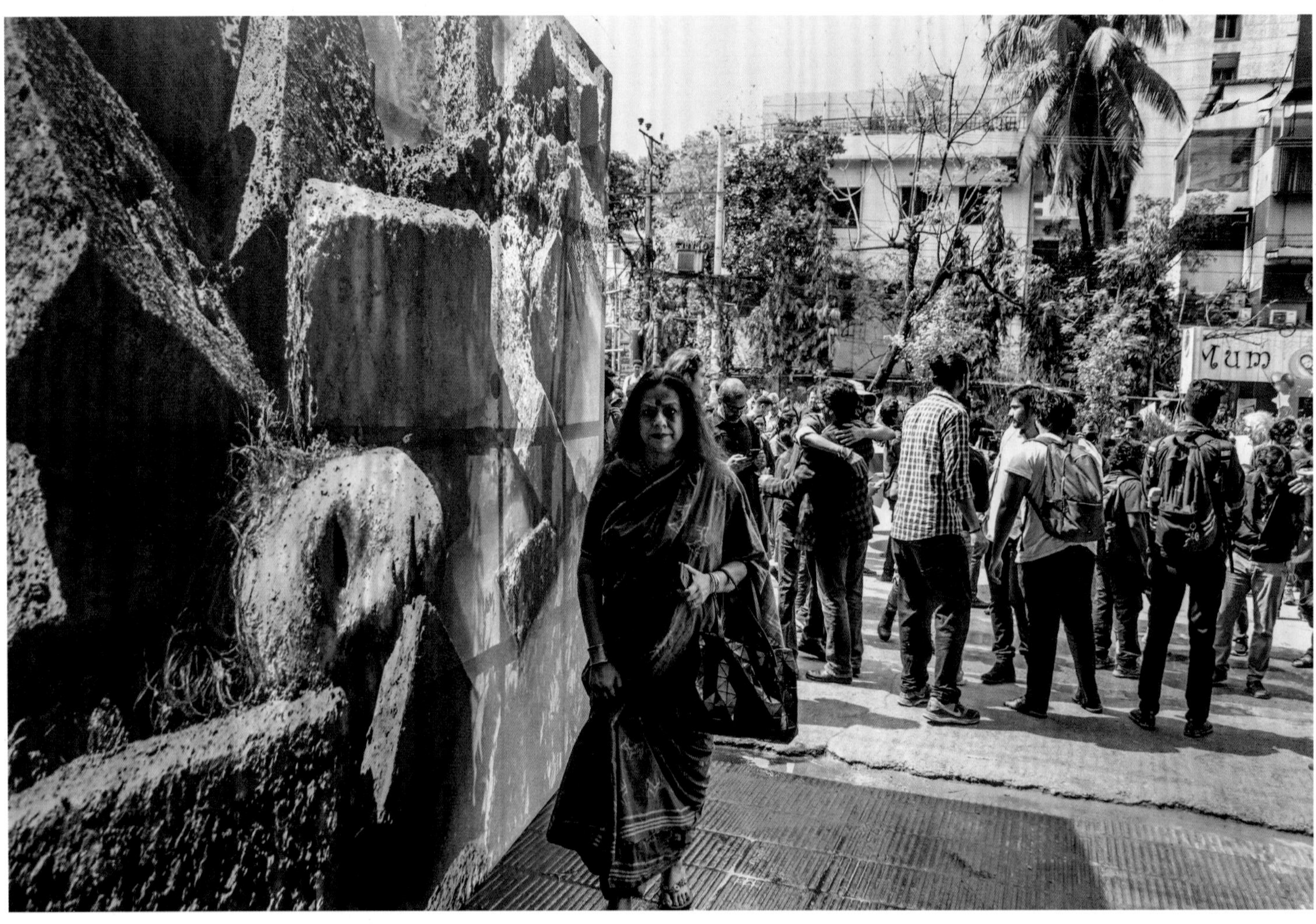
Mum

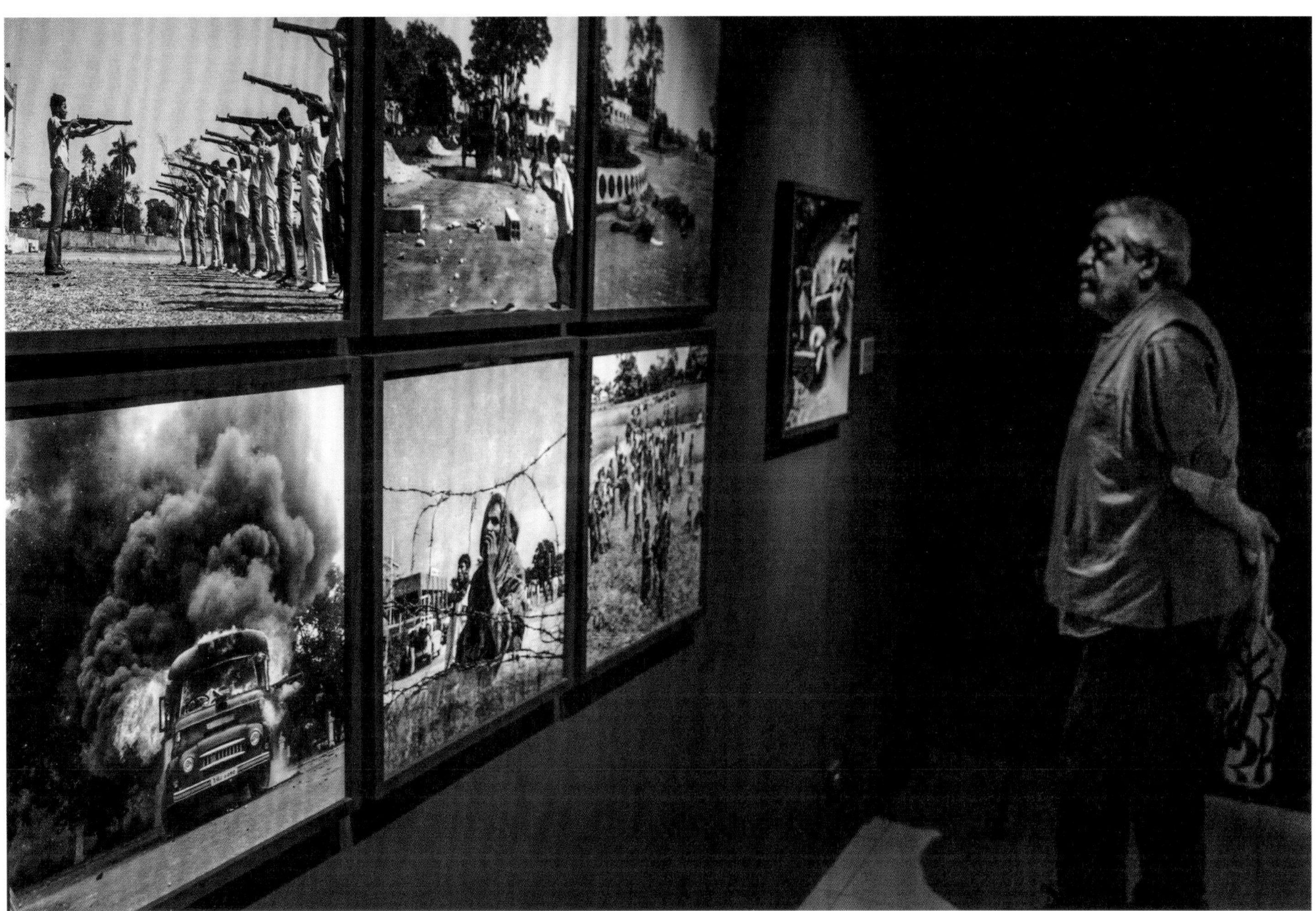

In 2017 Ina Puri, an Indian curator who works in Dhaka with Drik, walks past Rashid Talukder's photograph of a severed head at the killing fields in Dhaka, taken two days after the nation's finest intellectuals were murdered by the Pakistani army on the night of 14th December 1971. Robert Pledge views others inside.

Rashid Talukdar's images of the 1971 War, in which one million Bangladeshis were killed and ten million fled to India, have shaped the political history of Bangladesh. He was relatively unknown until recently, for he kept his images to himself. Publishing them would have revealed the perpetrators, equivalent, as Shahidul put it, to signing his own death warrant. The Western photographers who covered the war had no such handicap. Talukdar is now regarded as the founding father of photography in Bangladesh.

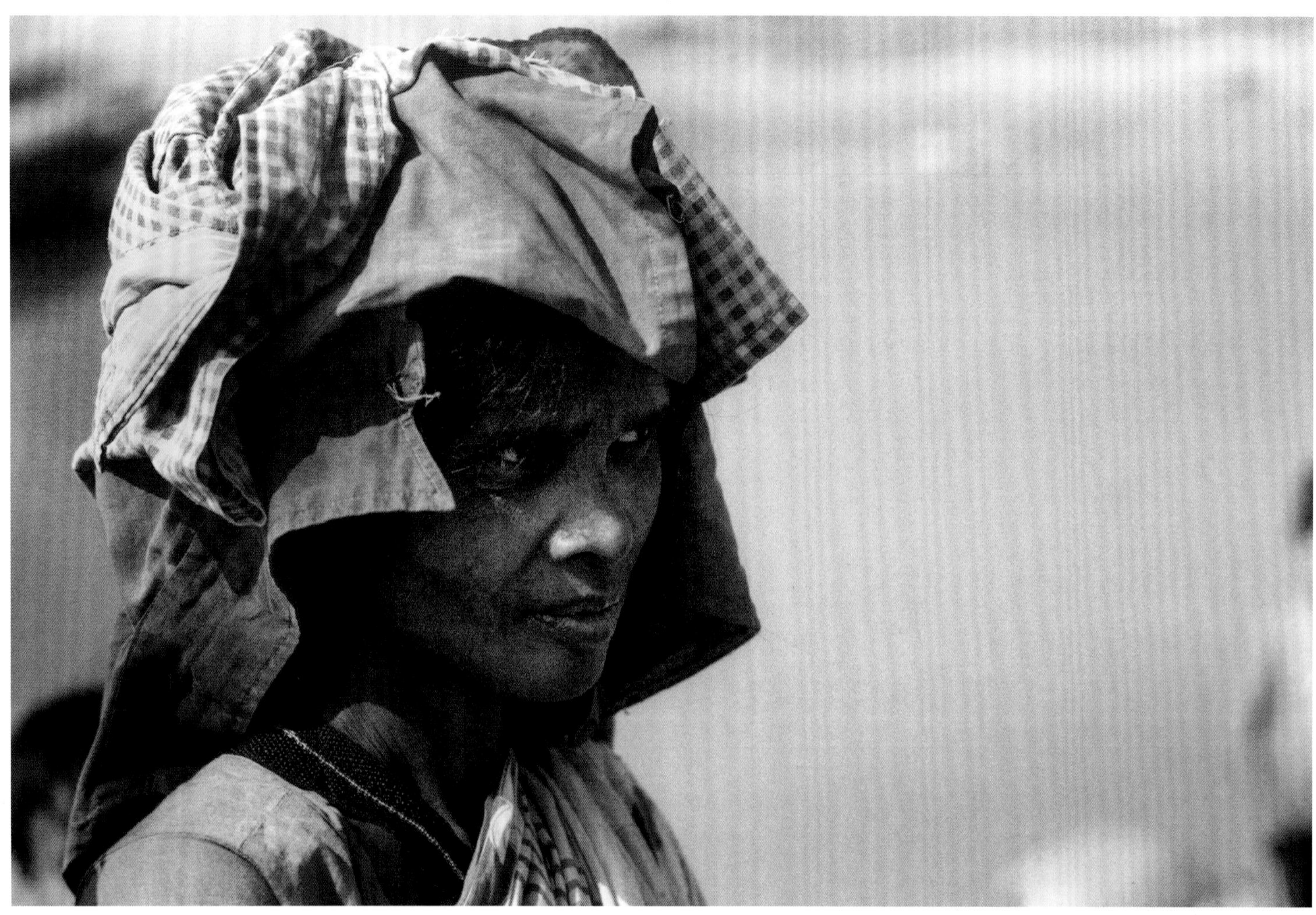

Jaflong, Sylhet

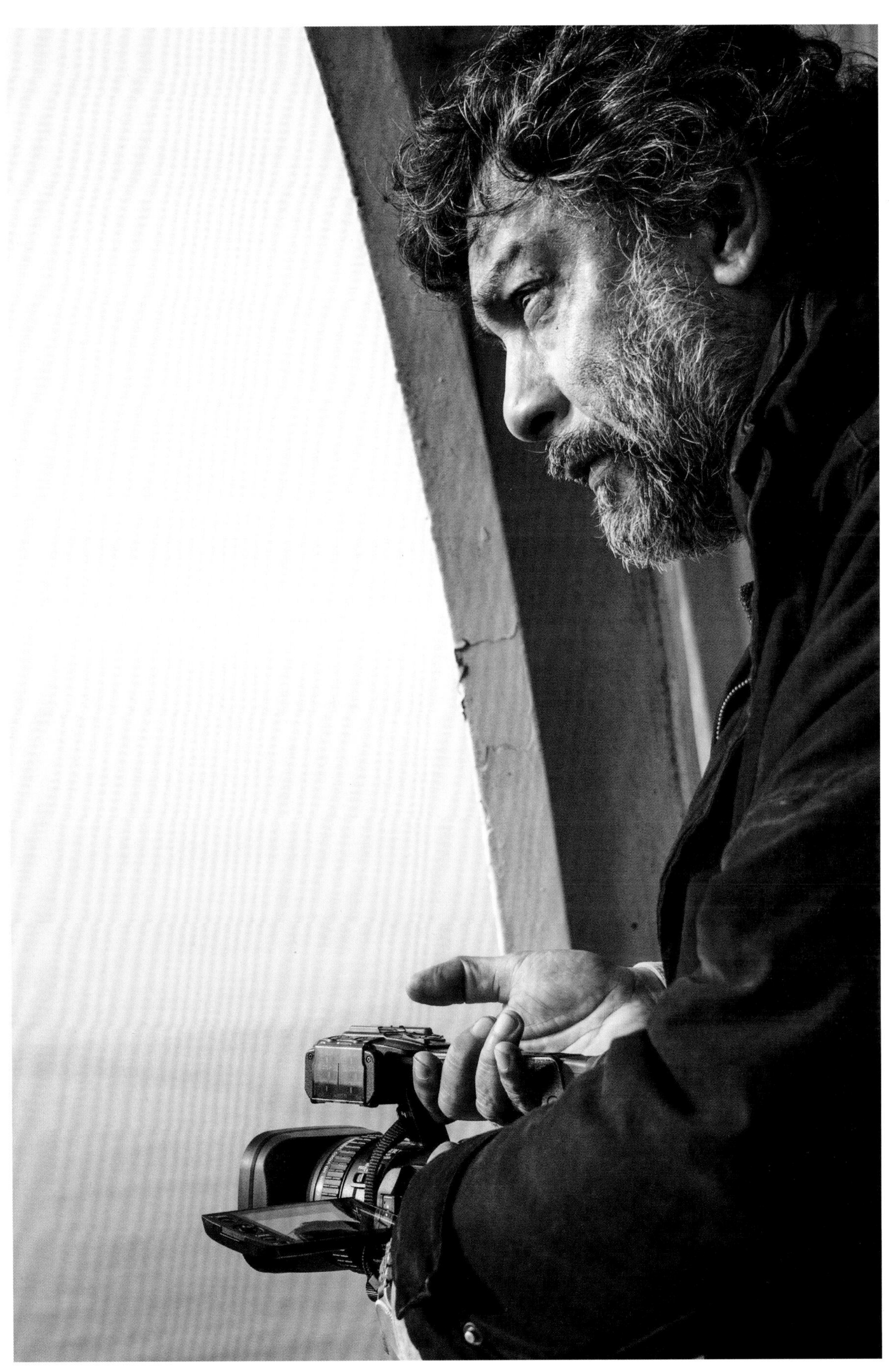

Pablo Bartholomew on the deck of a river ferry at first light on the Buriganga.

'Pablo, whose exhibition Outside In, A Tale of 3 Cities, *opens at Drik Gallery tomorrow, has just emerged from his cabin beside me as I write. Today is the day his Padma Shree – the major award he will receive in March for services to India as a photographer – is made public. With a gruff "good morning" he gets out his camera and focuses on the river boats.'*

Journal, January 2013

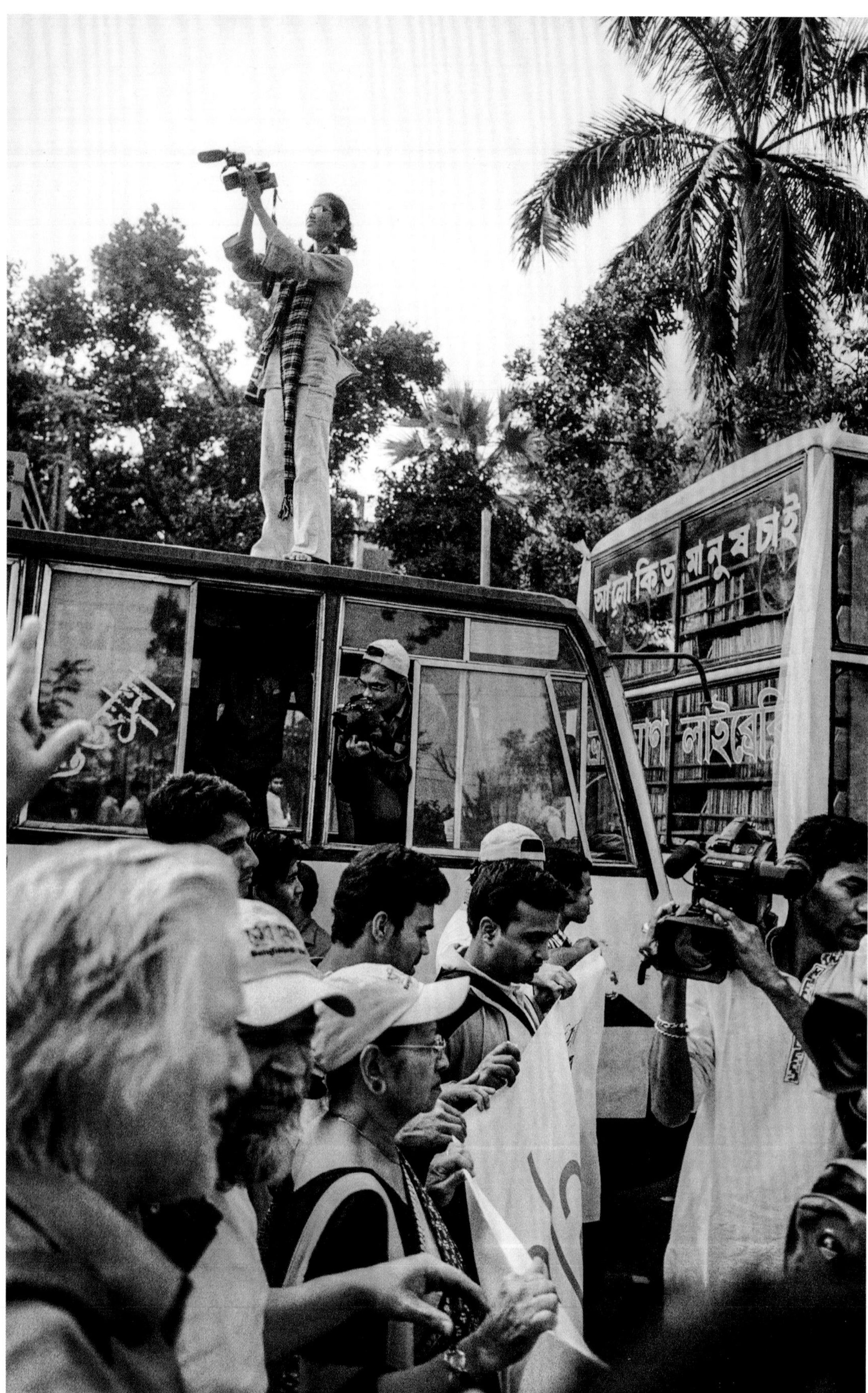

The opening rally of Chobi Mela in 2009. Standing on the bus is Rabeya Sarker Rima, a Patshala student. Morten Krogvold, a much-loved teacher at Patshala, Shahidul and Nurun Nahar Ahmed are holding the banner.

'I went to one of Morten's sessions. Hearing him in action was one of the many seminal moments in this year's festival – striding to and fro across the classroom, gesticulating with gusto to ram his points home, student heads nodding in the darkness. I learned more in that short half hour than in years of looking through my Nikon lenses.'

Journal, January 2013

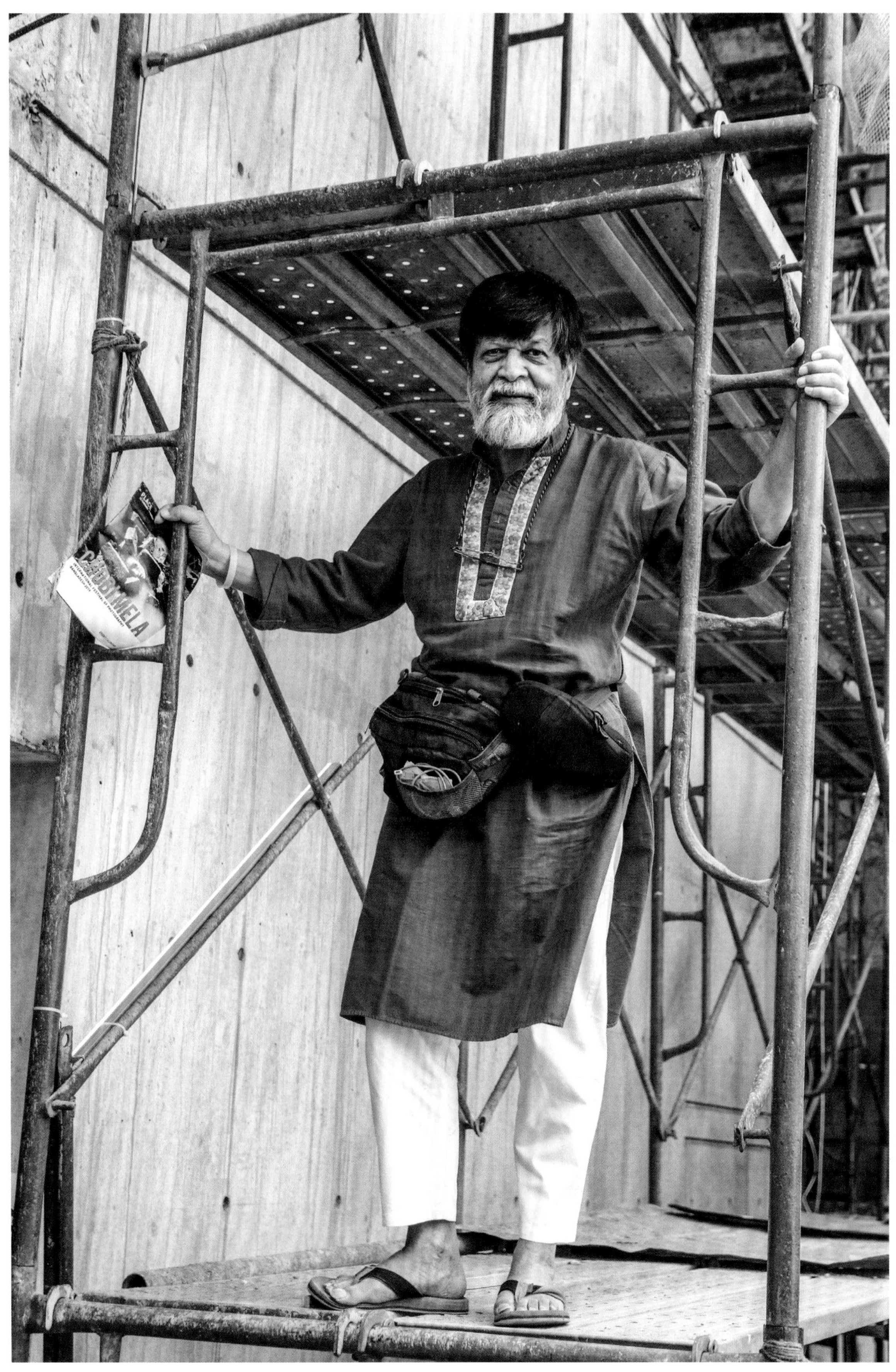

Shahidul Alam stands beside the partly built DrikPath Bhobon in Dhaka, built on the site of the original Pathshala in January 2019. Drik and Pathshala between them occupy most of the 10-storey building.

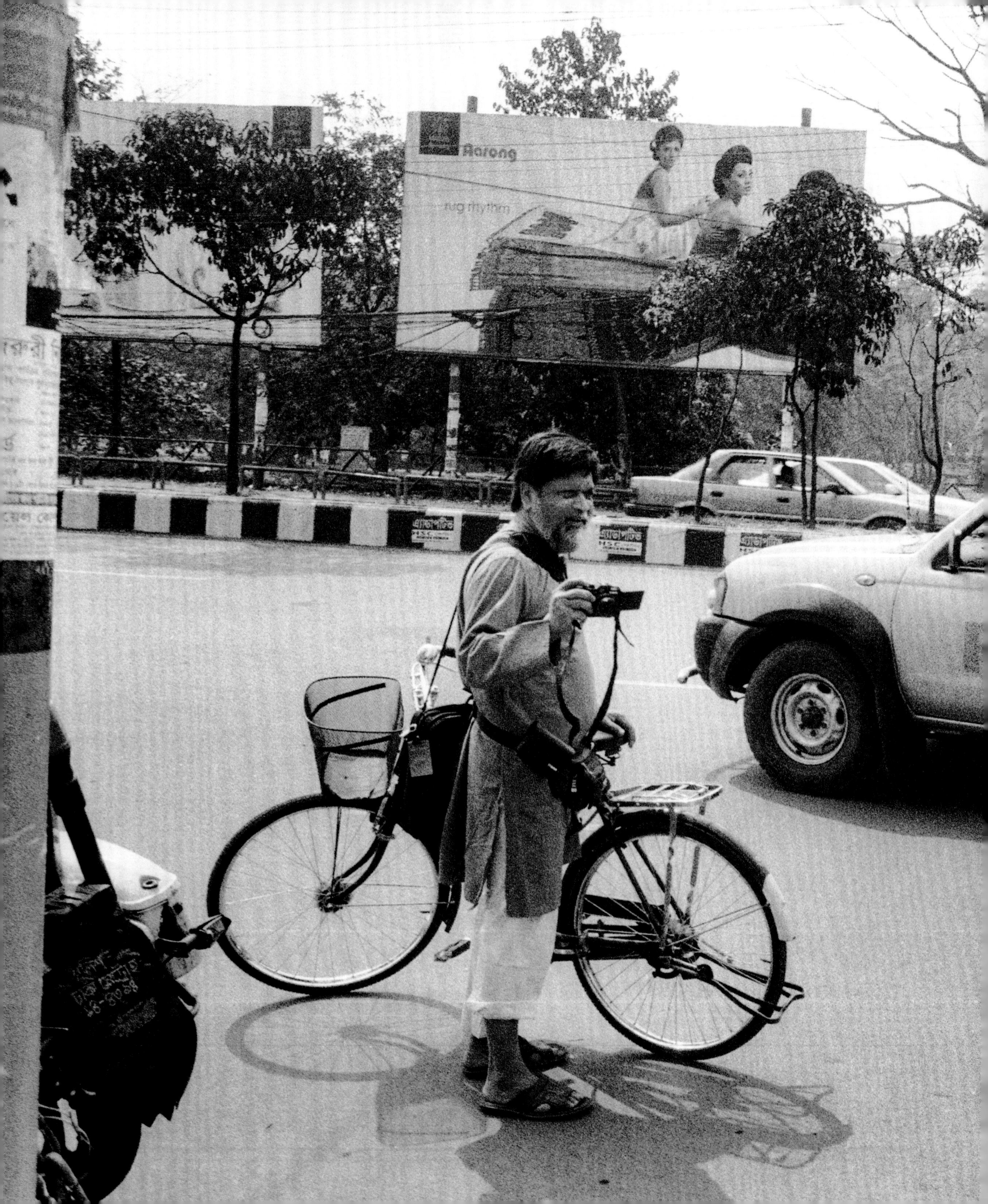
Aarong
rug rhythm

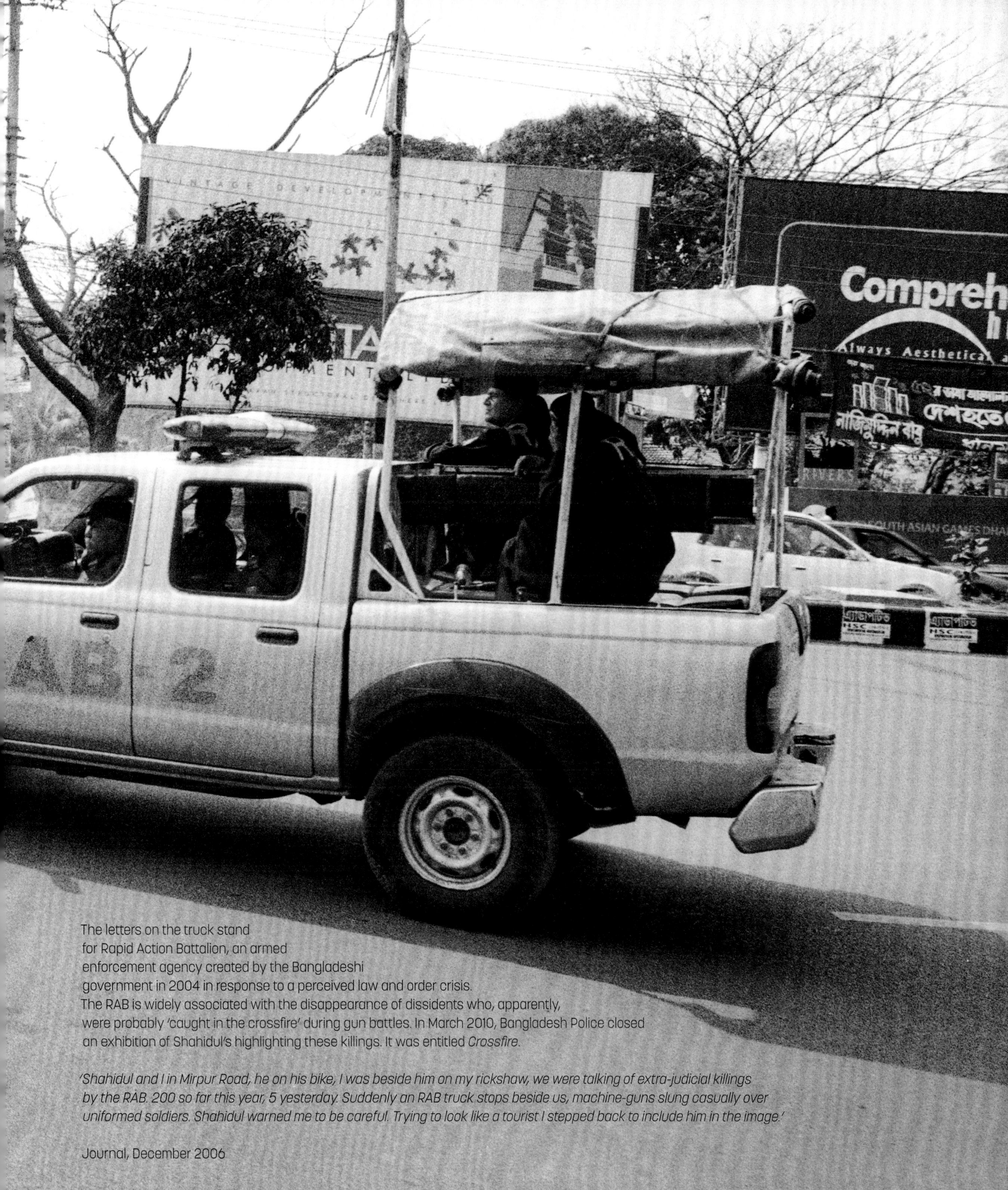

The letters on the truck stand for Rapid Action Battalion, an armed enforcement agency created by the Bangladeshi government in 2004 in response to a perceived law and order crisis. The RAB is widely associated with the disappearance of dissidents who, apparently, were probably 'caught in the crossfire' during gun battles. In March 2010, Bangladesh Police closed an exhibition of Shahidul's highlighting these killings. It was entitled *Crossfire*.

'Shahidul and I in Mirpur Road, he on his bike, I was beside him on my rickshaw, we were talking of extra-judicial killings by the RAB. 200 so far this year, 5 yesterday. Suddenly an RAB truck stops beside us, machine-guns slung casually over uniformed soldiers. Shahidul warned me to be careful. Trying to look like a tourist I stepped back to include him in the image.'

Journal, December 2006

The Rock Mine at Jaflong

There are no rocks in Bangladesh. This problem is providentially resolved by involuntary donations from India: every year the monsoon rains sweep a massive quantity of rocks down the steep-sloped Meghalayan Hills of Assam to the alluvial plains of Bangladesh, as they have done for millennia. Extraction and crushing of the rocks for use on construction began on a small scale in the 1940s. Over the last twenty years it has developed into a stone rush comparable to the gold rushes of the west: lawless frontiers in which a few got rich, most remained poor and a good many died.

In 2011, when these photographs were taken, the stone rush was completely unregulated. There was no framework for protecting the environment, labour laws were non-existent and health and safety was not part of the lexicon. The result is significant environmental and human damage. The riverbed is pockmarked with giant pits and its banks have become highways for trucks bearing rocks from the craters to the rock crushers. The rock mine at Jaflong on the Dawki River, where these images were taken, is one of several in the area north of Sylhet.

During the dry season some 10,000 men, women and children collect the rocks in baskets from the craters. They arrive at first light to begin a day of hard labour, unearthing the rocks from the riverbed with shovels, crowbars and bare hands. Bearing the baskets on their heads, they climb out of the pits in lines like ants up a tree. The baskets weigh 40 kg or more. For each journey the bearer receives a token from the foreman at the top, later to be redeemed in cash. The larger rocks are slung between poles borne on the shoulders of two or four men. The pay in 2011, when these photographs were taken, was said to be roughly US$6/day.

The pits, being in the riverbed, fill with water. Giant pumps, propelled by machines with unguarded high-speed belts, hurl water out of the pits through a spider's web of pipes. The roar of the engines pervades a landscape blighted by fumes.

On the riverbanks, lost in clouds of dust, men with boulder-breaking hammers smite boulders into fragments. The dust from their labours, and from some 250 stone-crushing machines, lingers over the plains and is absorbed into their lungs. The noise and the fumes from their engines add to the pollution. The landscape and the rivers which flow through it are now a scene of devastation and hard labour. The majority of workers are agricultural labourers in need of seasonal work. Most of them, I was told when I was there, are women and children. The attempts to control or mitigate the environmental damage initiated in 2011[19] have failed.

I spent two days there with a Bangladeshi friend, talking, listening, watching, photographing. The resilience of these workers, and the manner in which they helped and supported each other, was profoundly impressive.

Some raised a smile at our passing. Most did not. ■

19 Following High Court rulings in 2011, the government declared Jaflong an Ecologically Critical Area and prohibited all forms of stone collection. In 2016, the Supreme Court permitted the manual collection of stone. The human and environmental damage continues.

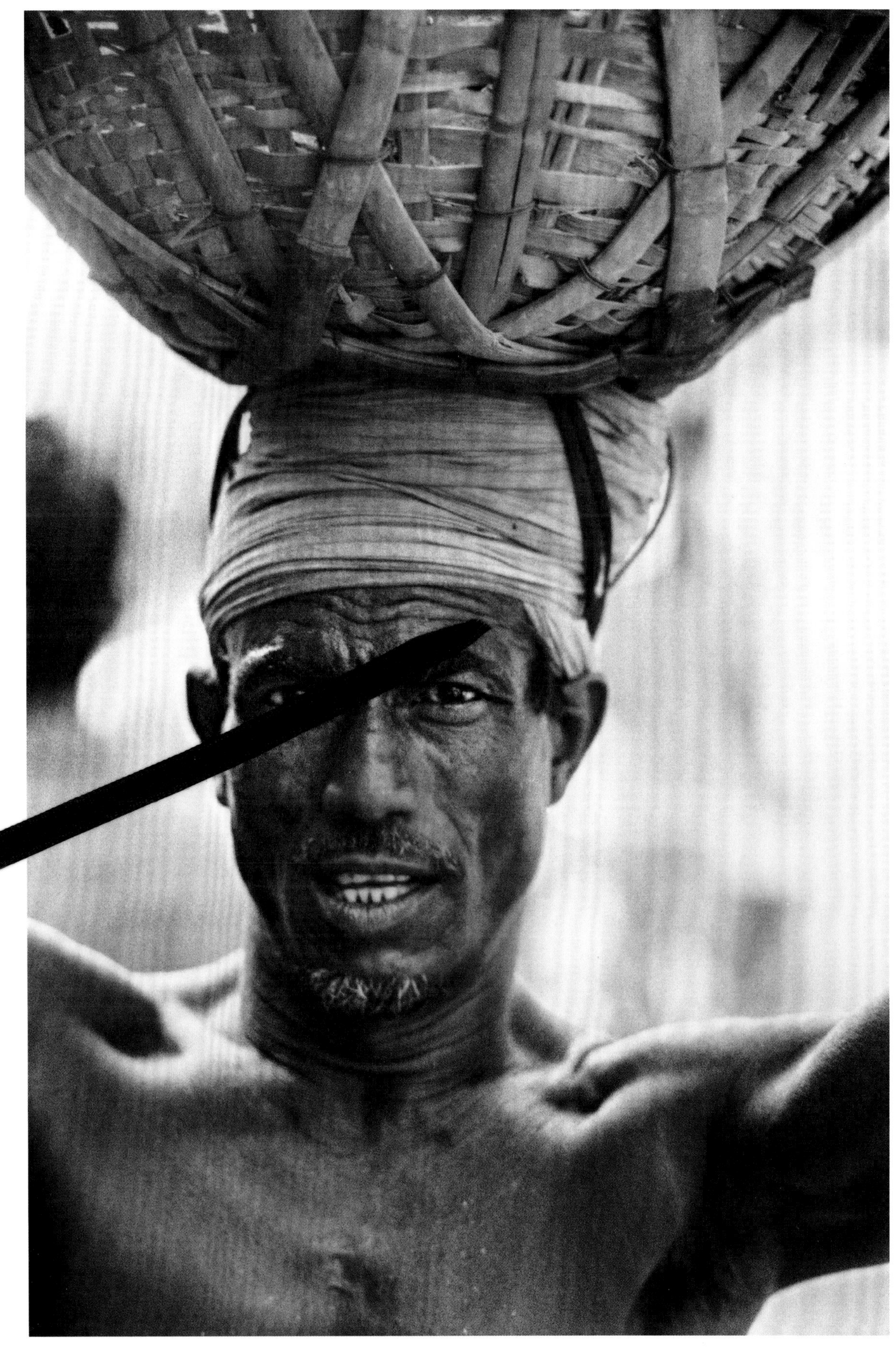

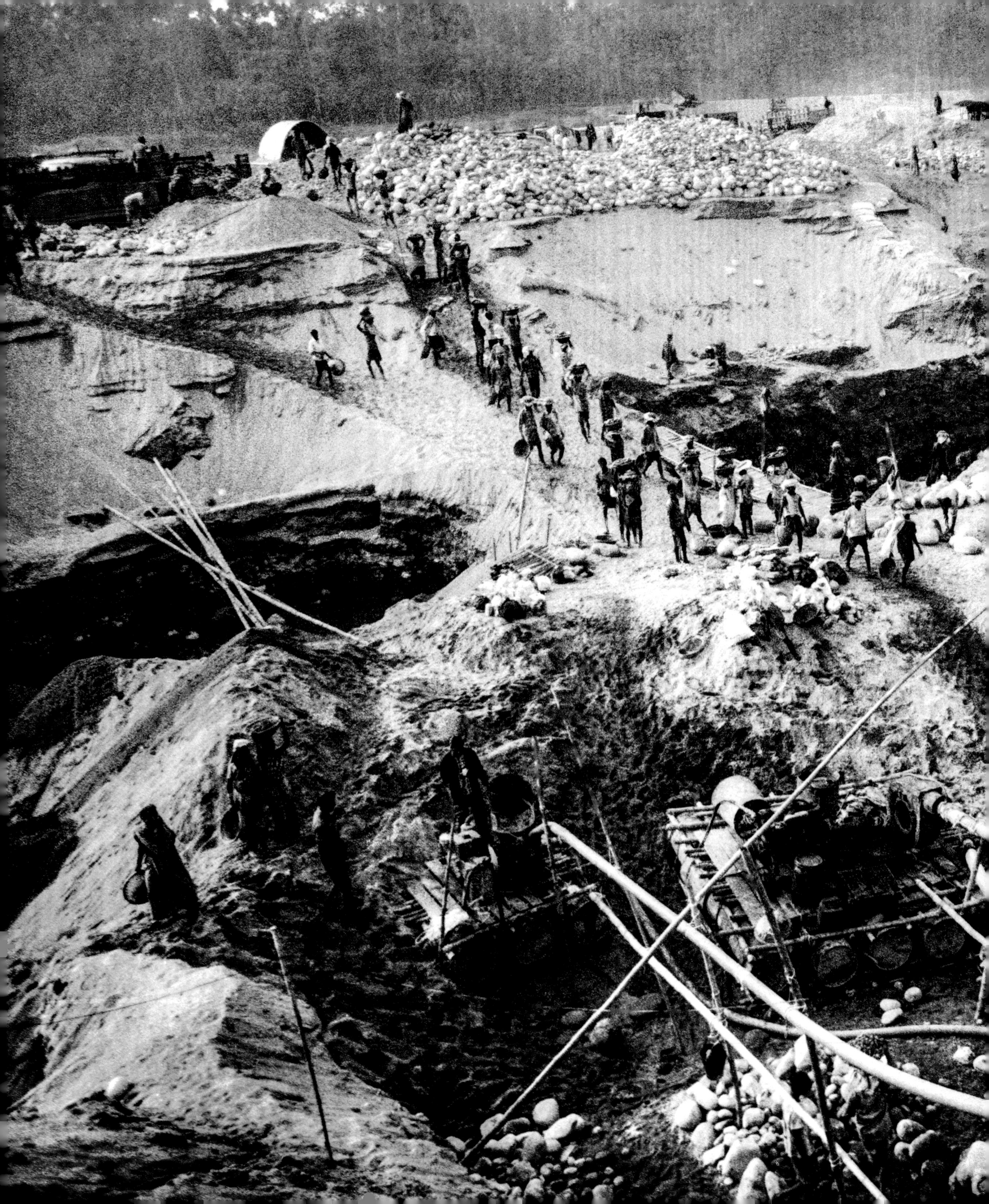

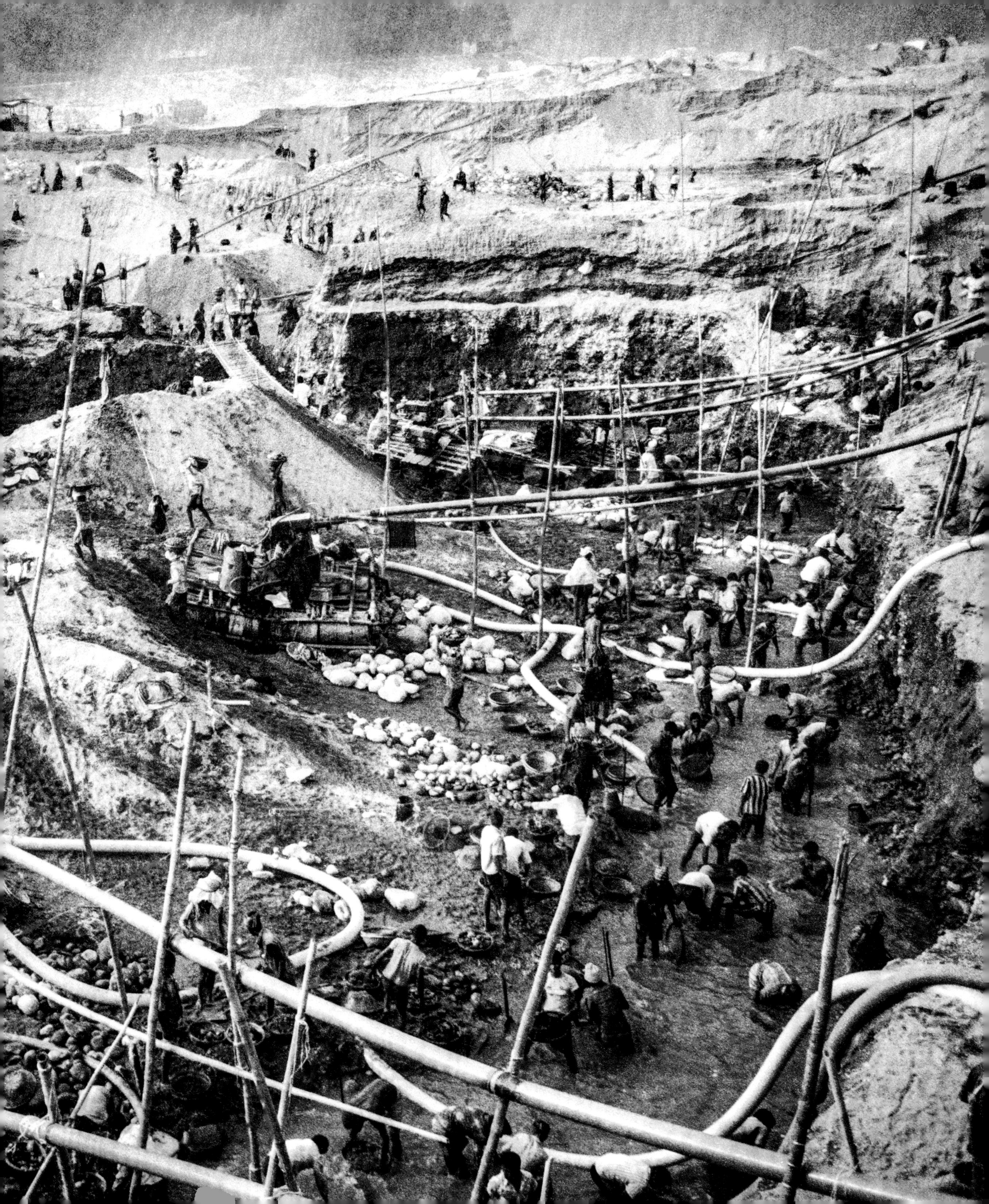

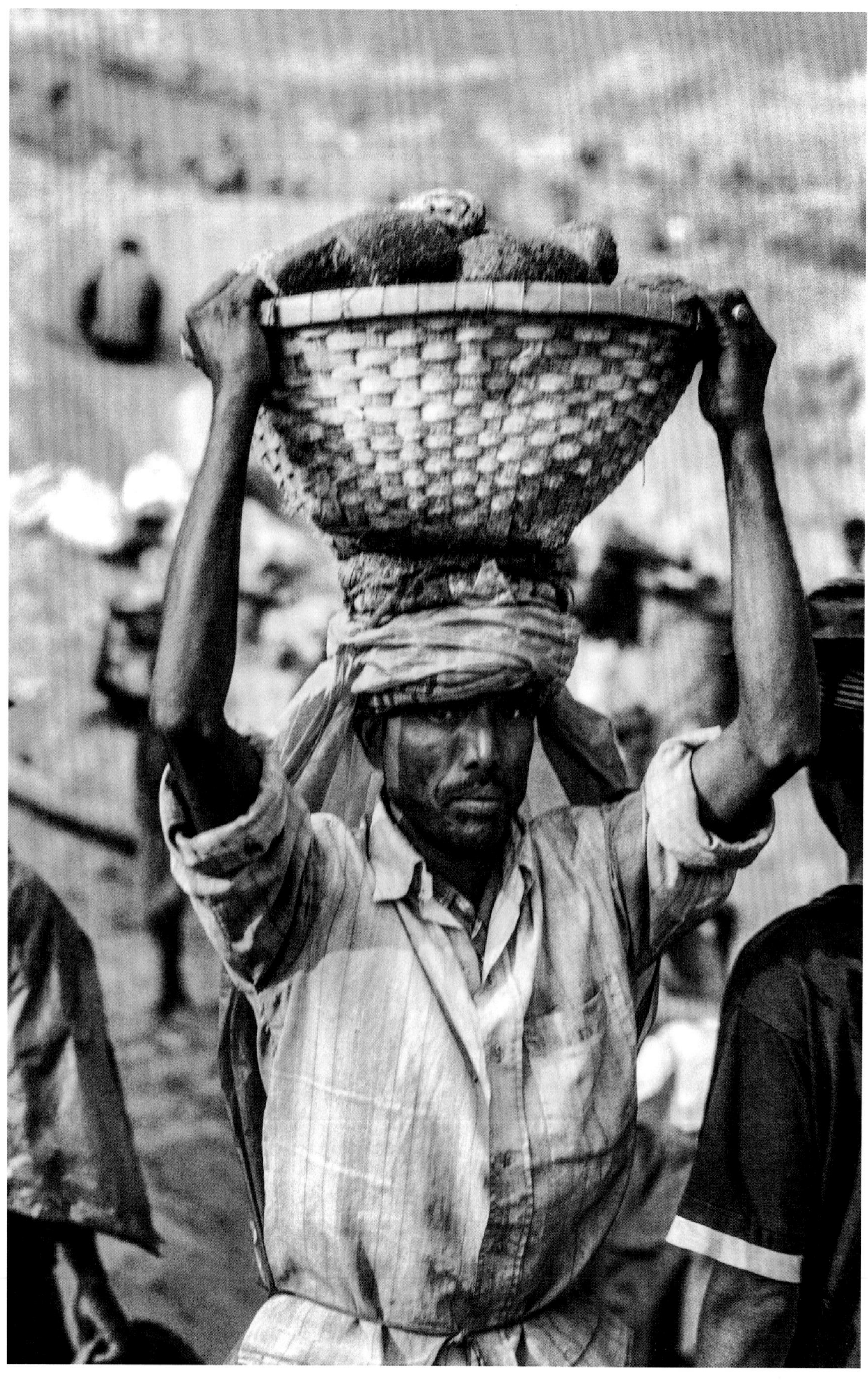

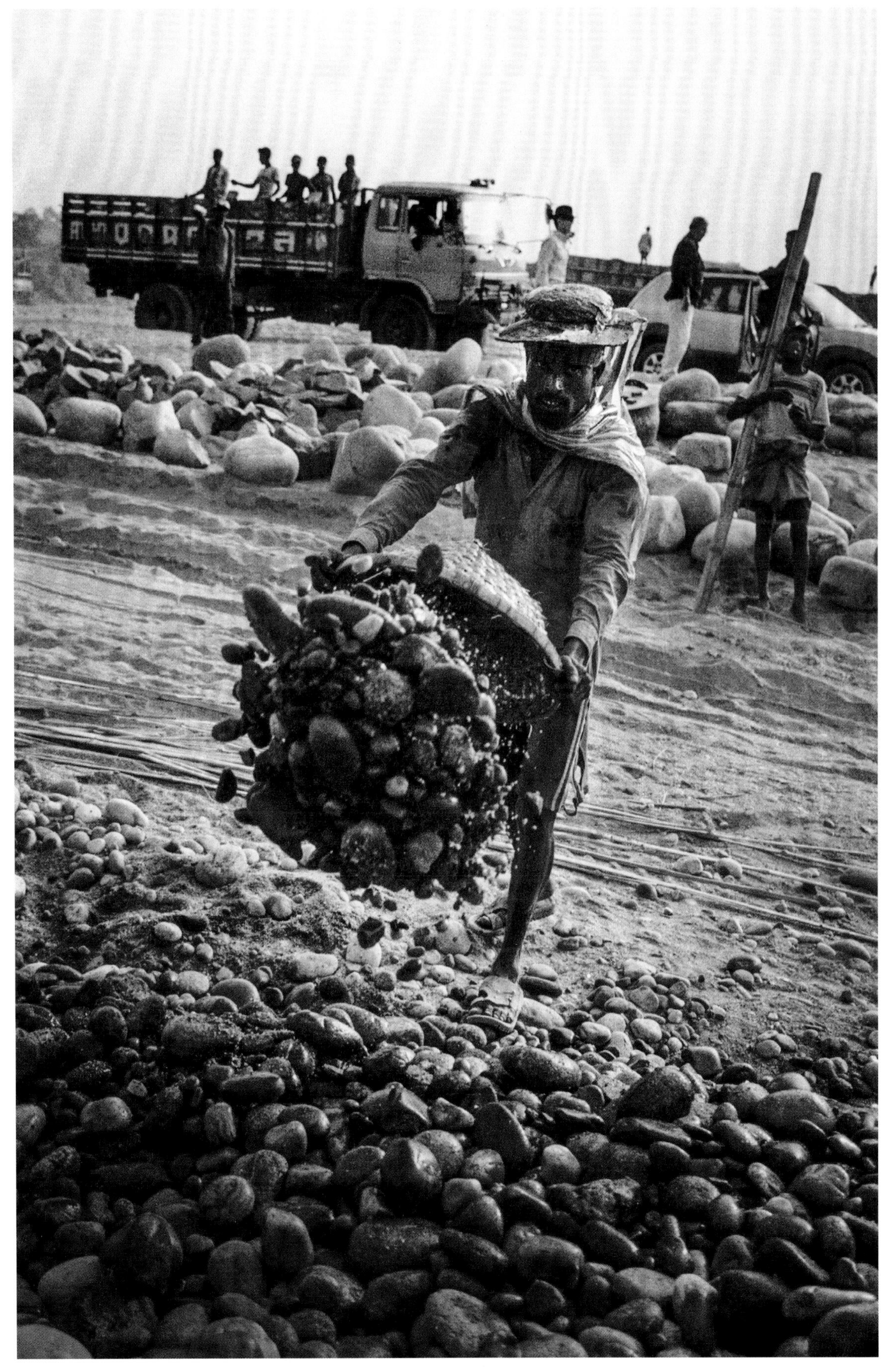

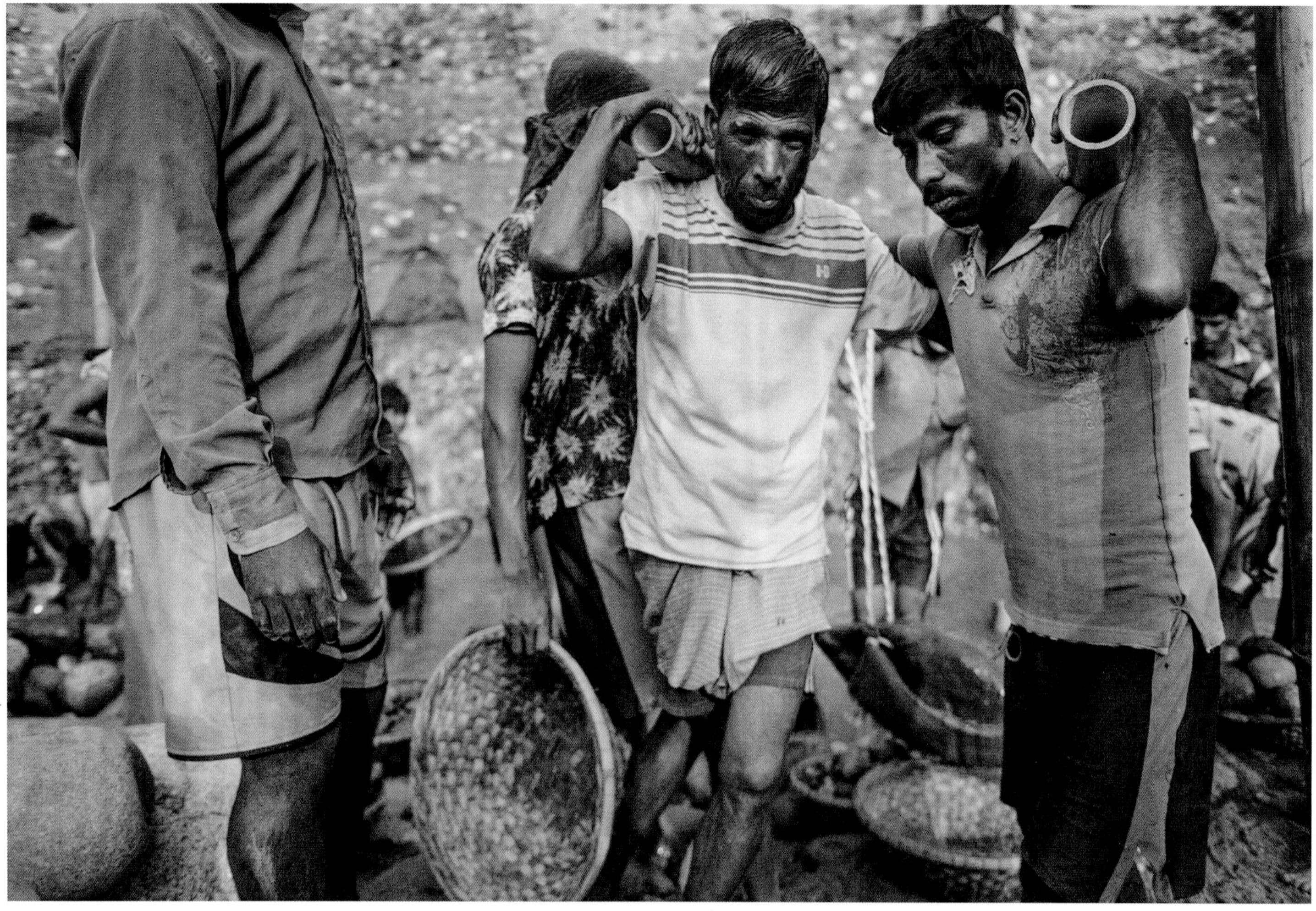

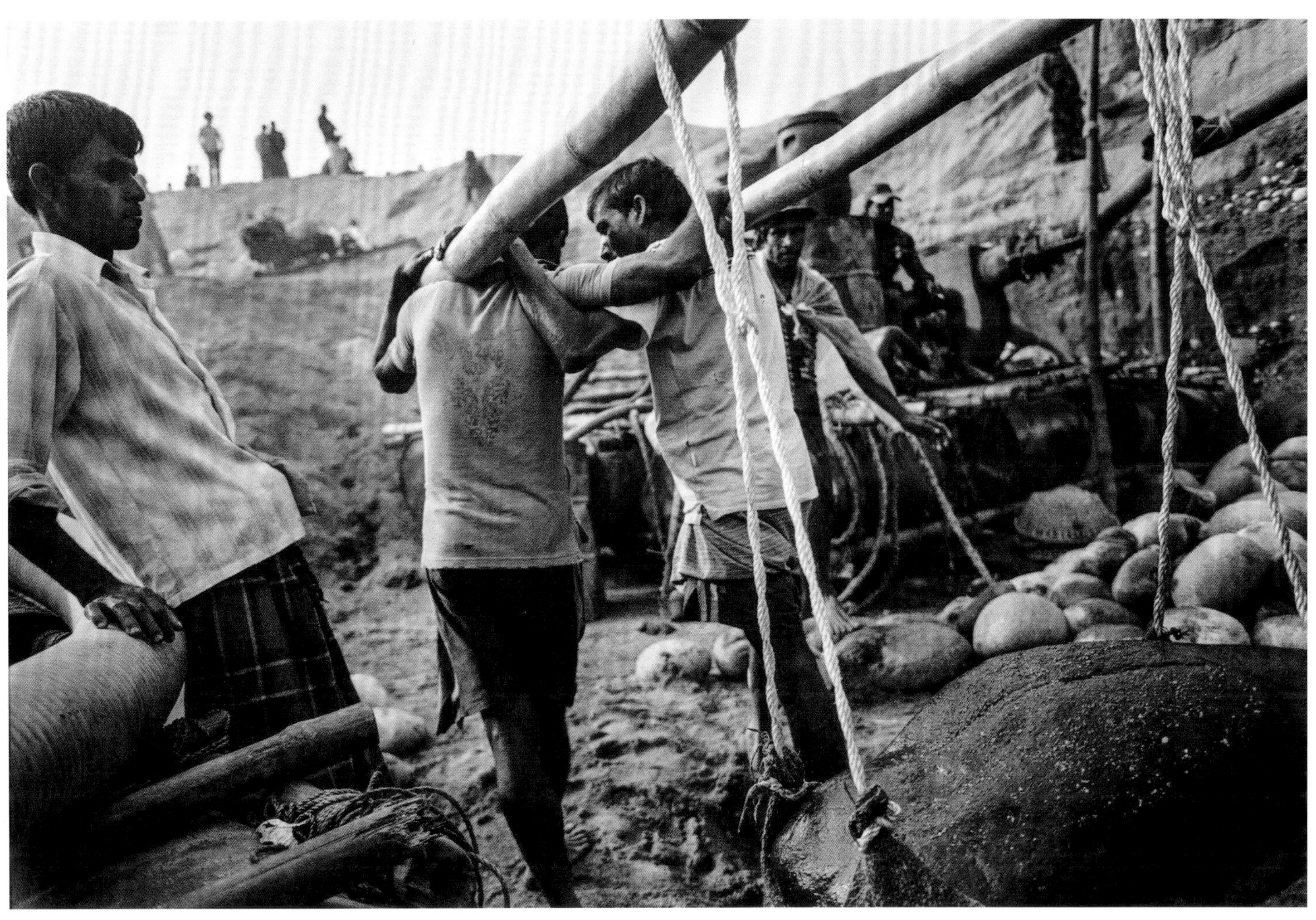

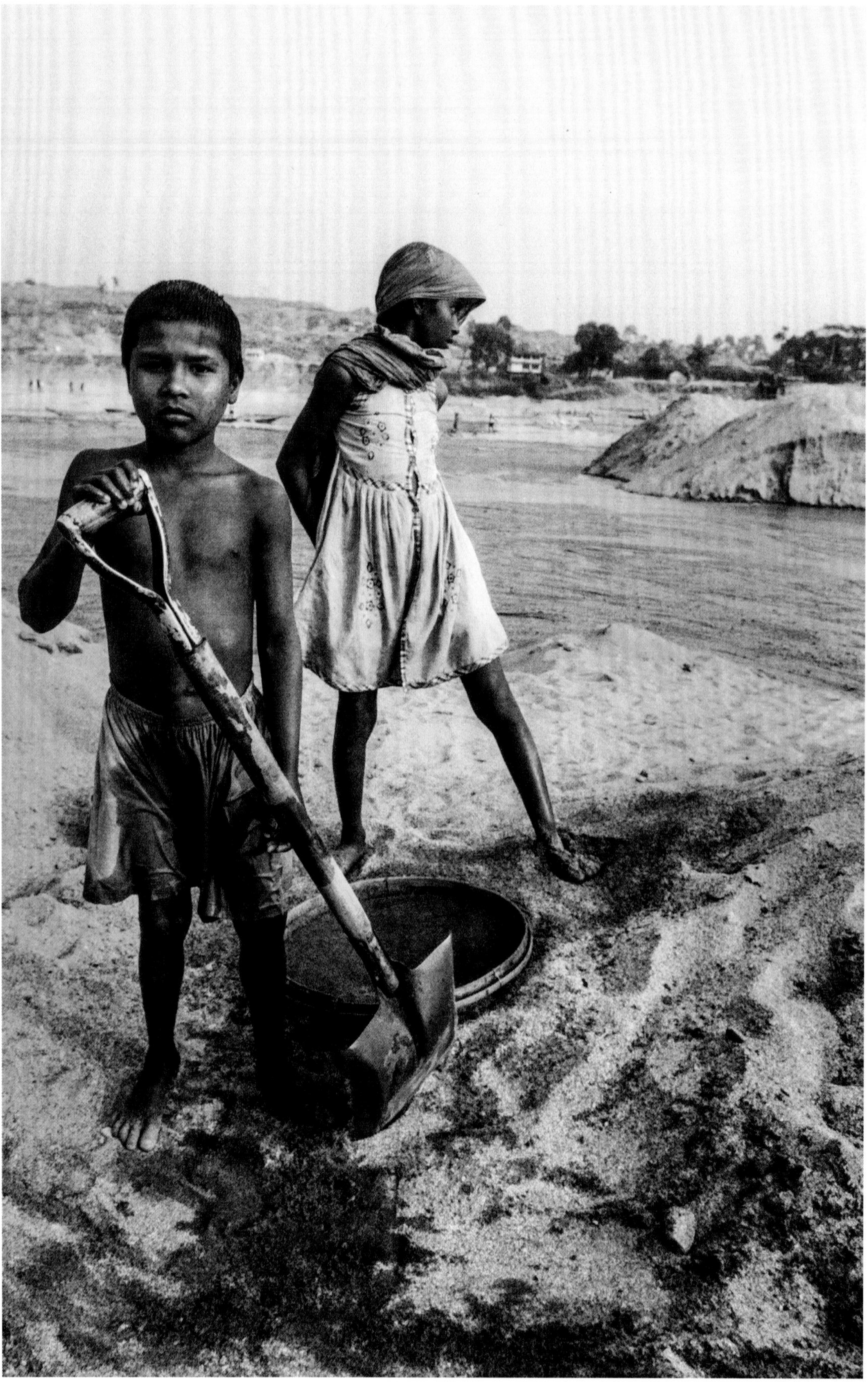

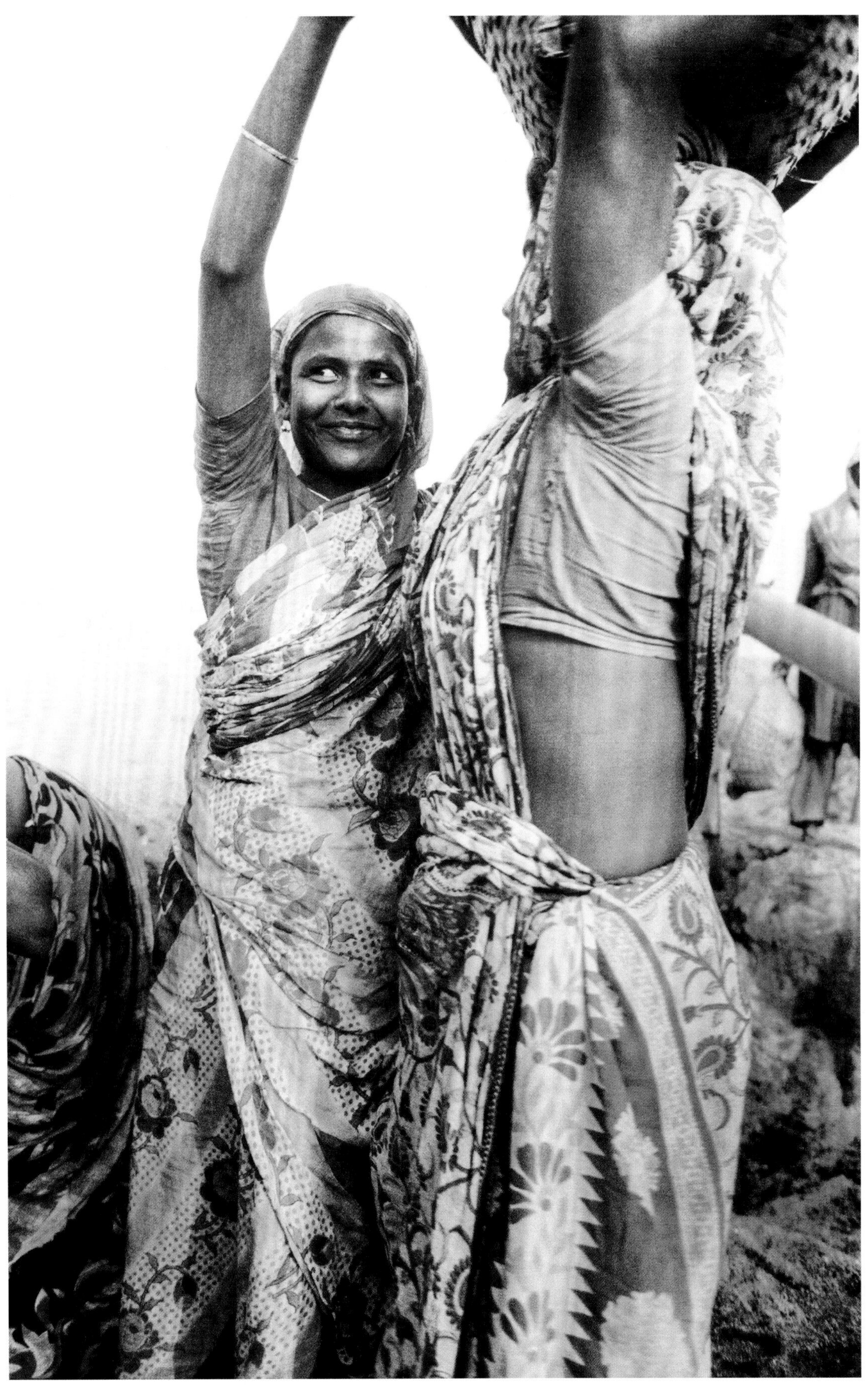

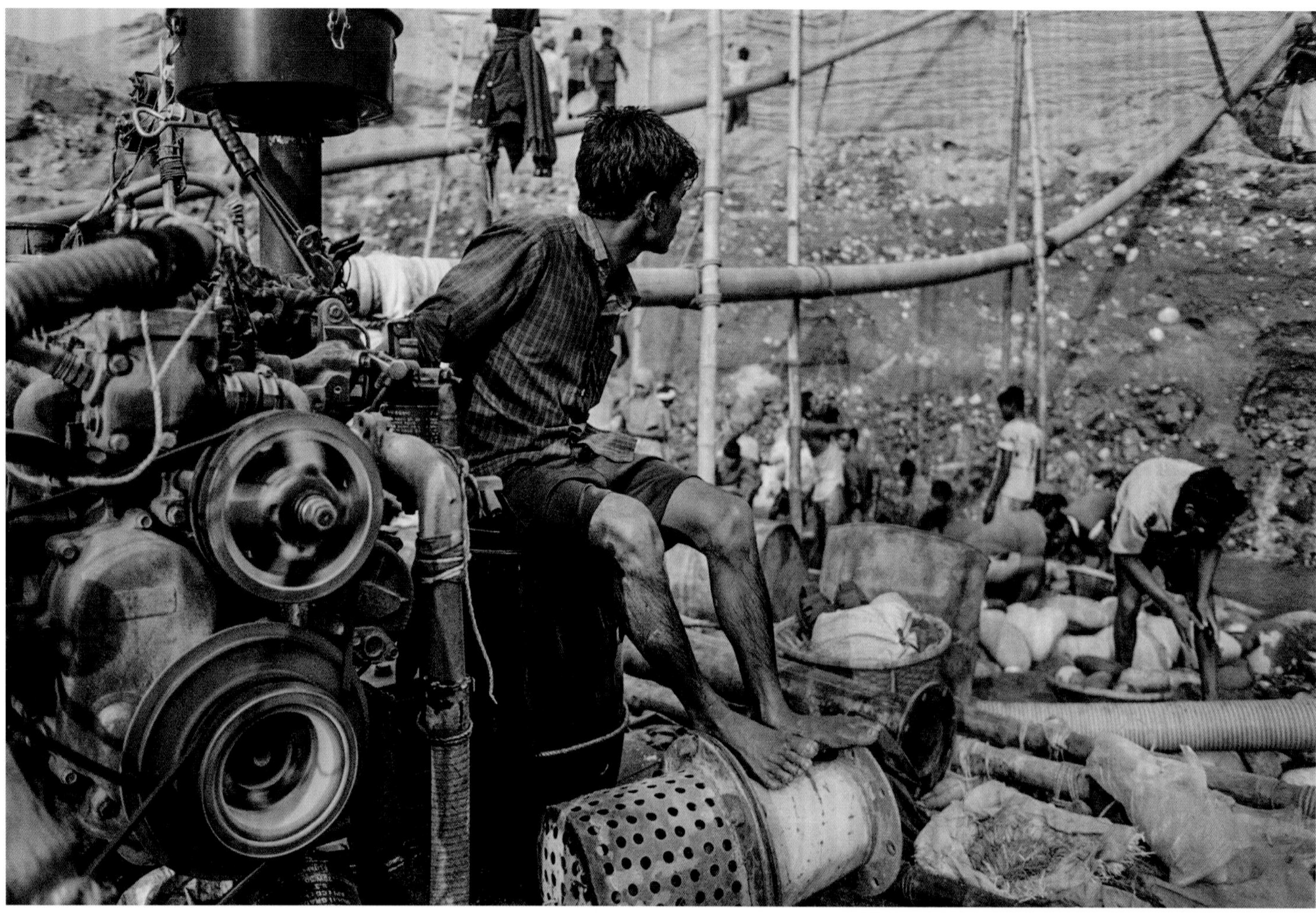

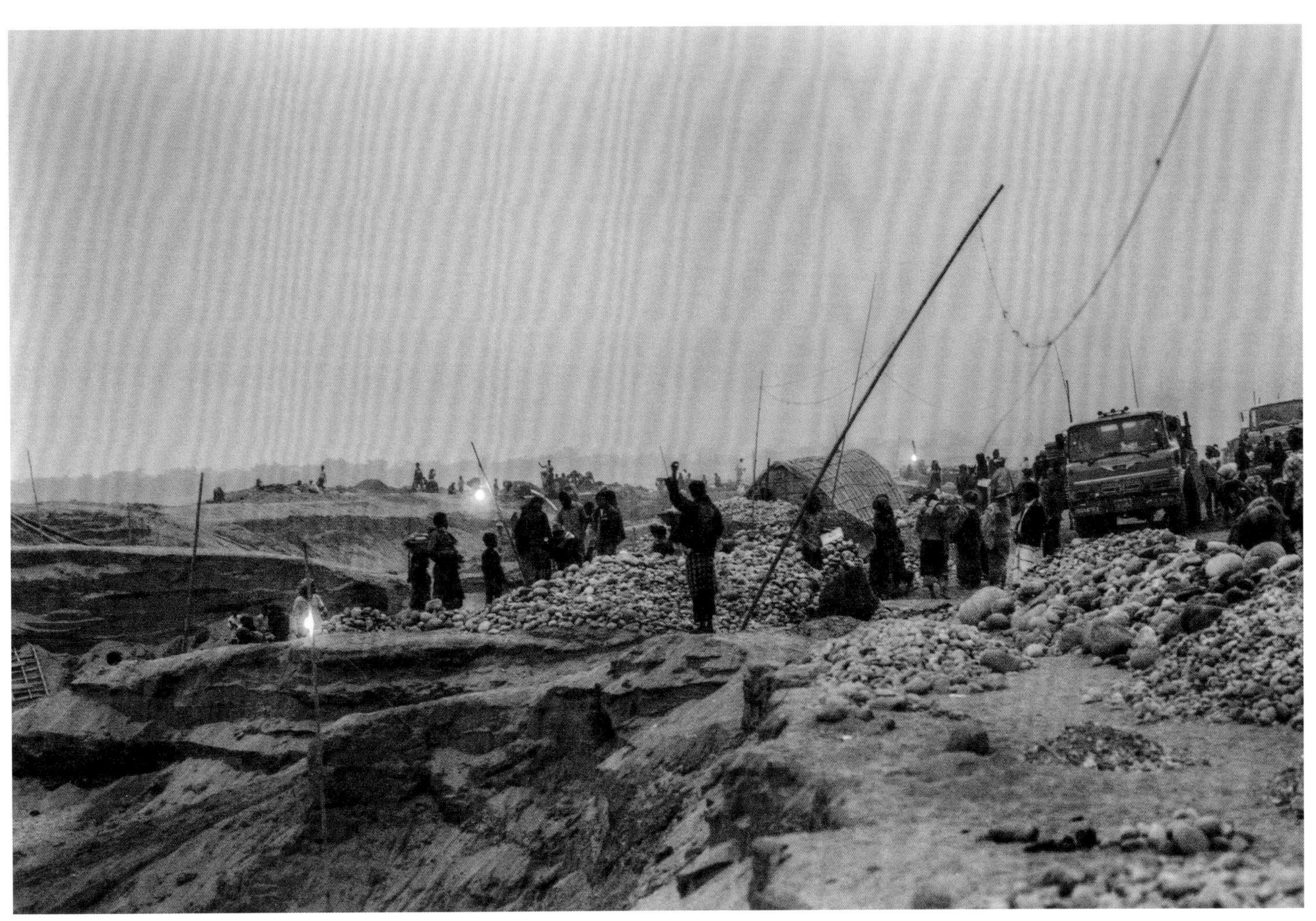

'I photographed all afternoon. As I was leaving, the scene was suddenly illuminated by light bulbs hanging from bamboos. They shed an eerie light on the basket carriers. Still the labour went on. Kamran Choudhury, [MP for the region] said that the visitors never stopped here or commented on it as they passed on their way to the Karsi villages on the far side of the river.'

Journal, January 2011

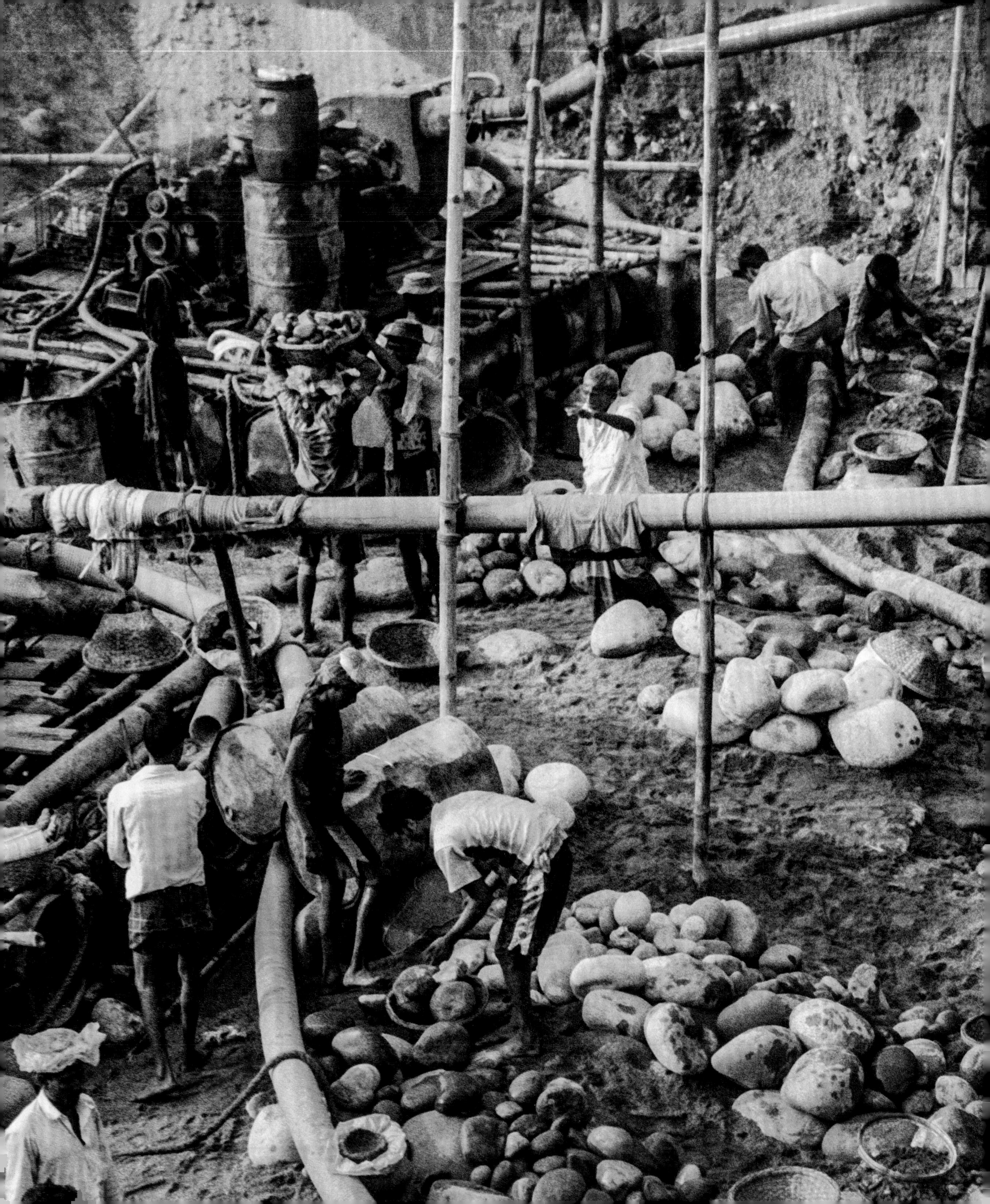

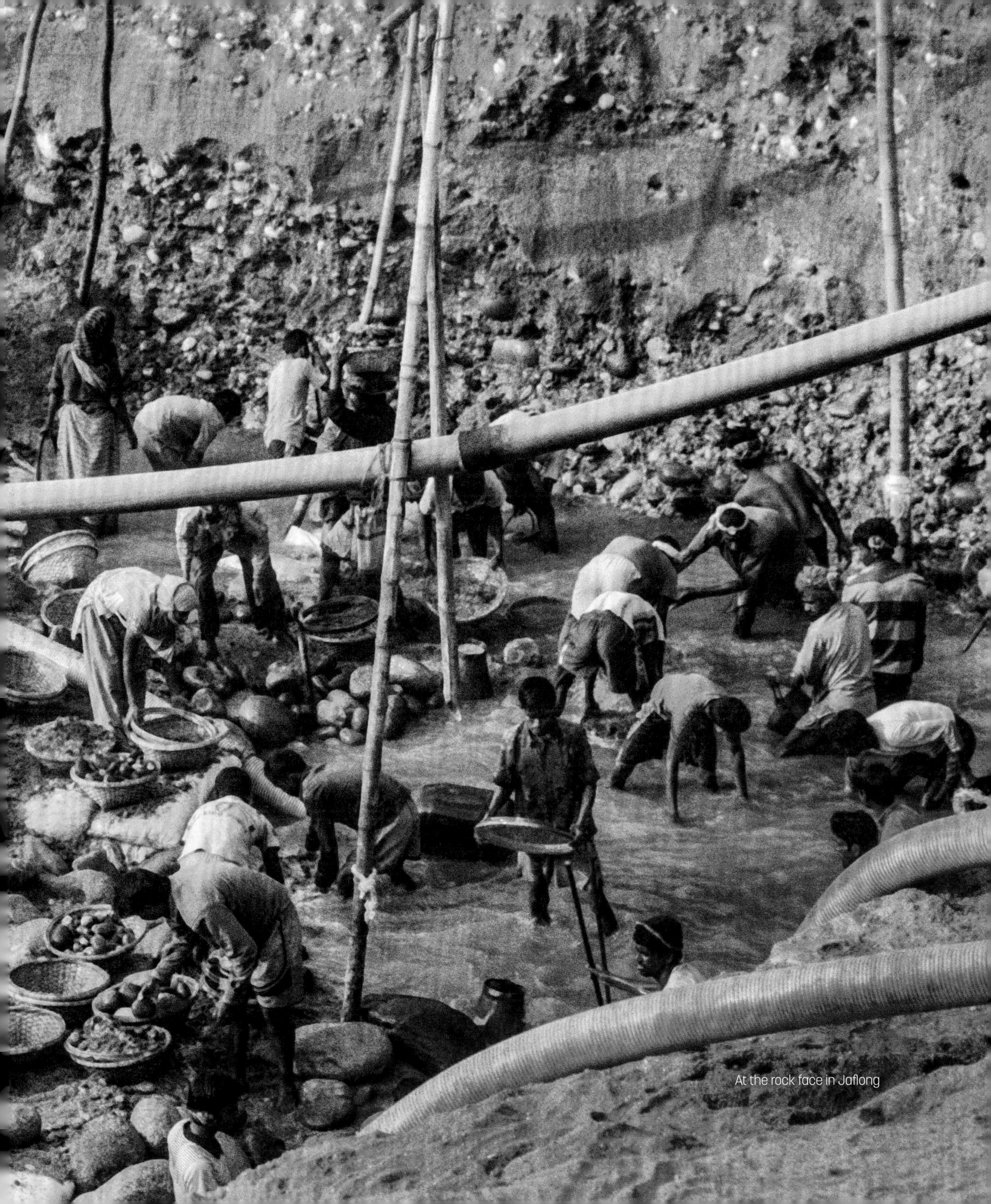
At the rock face in Jaflong

The Brickfields of Dhaka

I saw the Dhaka brickyards for the first time from the decks of a river ferry at dawn. I had slept overnight in a small cabin as the ferry motored up the Buriganga River through the warm night. It was a frugal accommodation, and the facilities were simple, but the chug of the engine lulled me agreeably to sleep. I was up at first light, for the riverbanks come to life as the sun rises and the workers of Dhaka begin their day's labour. Mostly, on the riverbanks near Dhaka, they work in the brickfields.

It was impossible to see the banks clearly. The sun was a light metal orb in a dark metal sky, barely visible through the dust which hovered over Dhaka. There, like sentinels in the mist, stood the towering chimneys of the brickyards. From them issued the smoke of the kilns which baked the bricks. Hence the haze. In the foreground were a multitude of timber craft bearing bricks over the metal-grey waters, their gunwales barely above the waterline amidships. The workers smiled atop their cargo.

They had little to smile about. Dhaka is one of the three most polluted cities in the world. Almost all of the brickyards in or near Dhaka, of which in 2016 there were over 2,000, are fired by coal and wood. They are the chief pollution culprit. The conditions in which they work are worse than any I have seen. Caught in the existential conflict between the drive for profitable development for which the bricks are required and the consequential degradation of the environment, the brickyard workers pay the price in low pay and shortened lives.

This I knew when I visited, unannounced, my first brickyard, accompanied by Wahid Adnan, a friend and a student from Pathshala. In the tin shelter near the kiln were five men. We were greeted warmly. We talked. They were pleased to see us. Yes, they were happy for me take photographs. Their constant cheerfulness was in stark contrast to the lives they led. I received similar welcomes in other brickyards.

As at the rock mines, the lives of these men – I did not see any women, though they also work in the brickyards – were, to quote British historian Thomas Hobbes, 'poor, nasty, brutish and short'.[20] Protective gear was nowhere to be seen. Constant exposure to brick dust and toxic fumes from the kilns cause chronic respiratory problems. The labour is back-breaking. Child labour is routine. Effective regulations governing conditions of work are not yet in place.

There is, however, a growing awareness of the massive damage that the brickfields are causing to the environment; the Buriganga is in places clinically dead, and environmental groups are applying pressure. Some in government are listening.

These images were taken between 2006 and 2013. ■

---

20 From *Leviathan*, Hobbes' best-known work. He is a key architect of modern political philosophy.

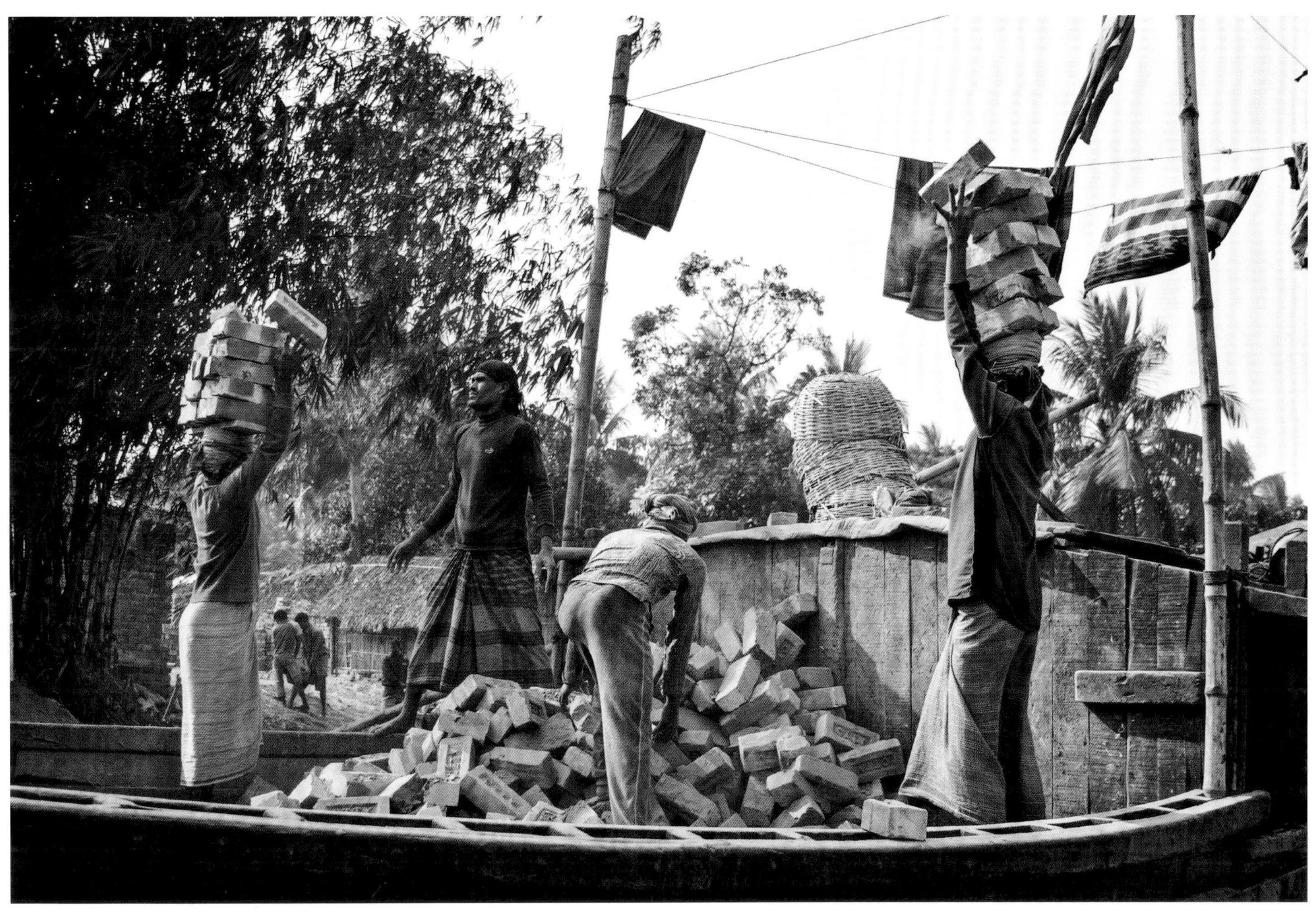

Near Khulna, in the Sundarbans, in 2013. The man on the left is throwing up the eleventh and twelfth bricks; on the right the thirteenth and fourteenth. The bricks have been fired and weigh 3.5 kg each. 14 bricks weigh roughly 50 kg, or about one hundredweight.

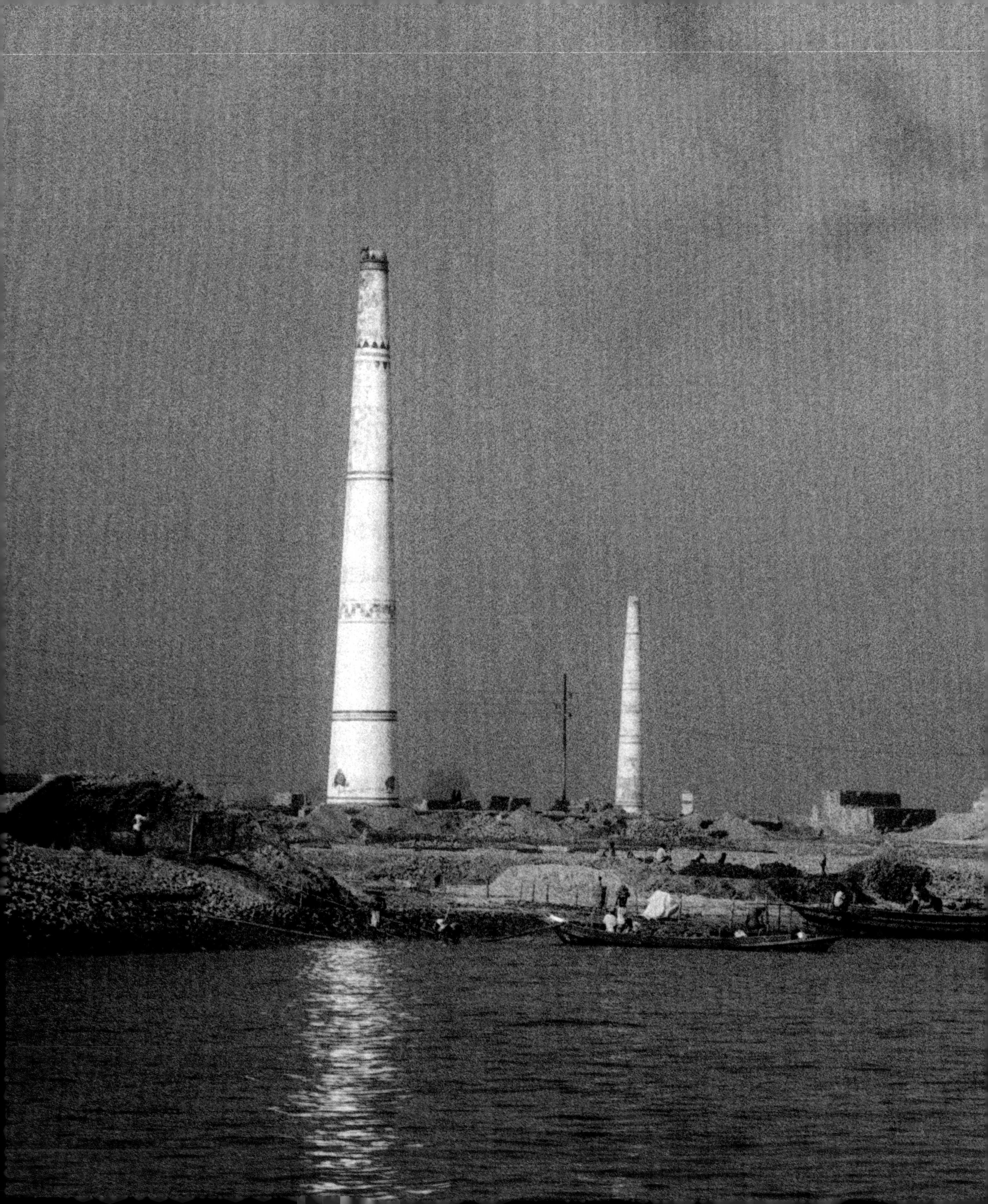

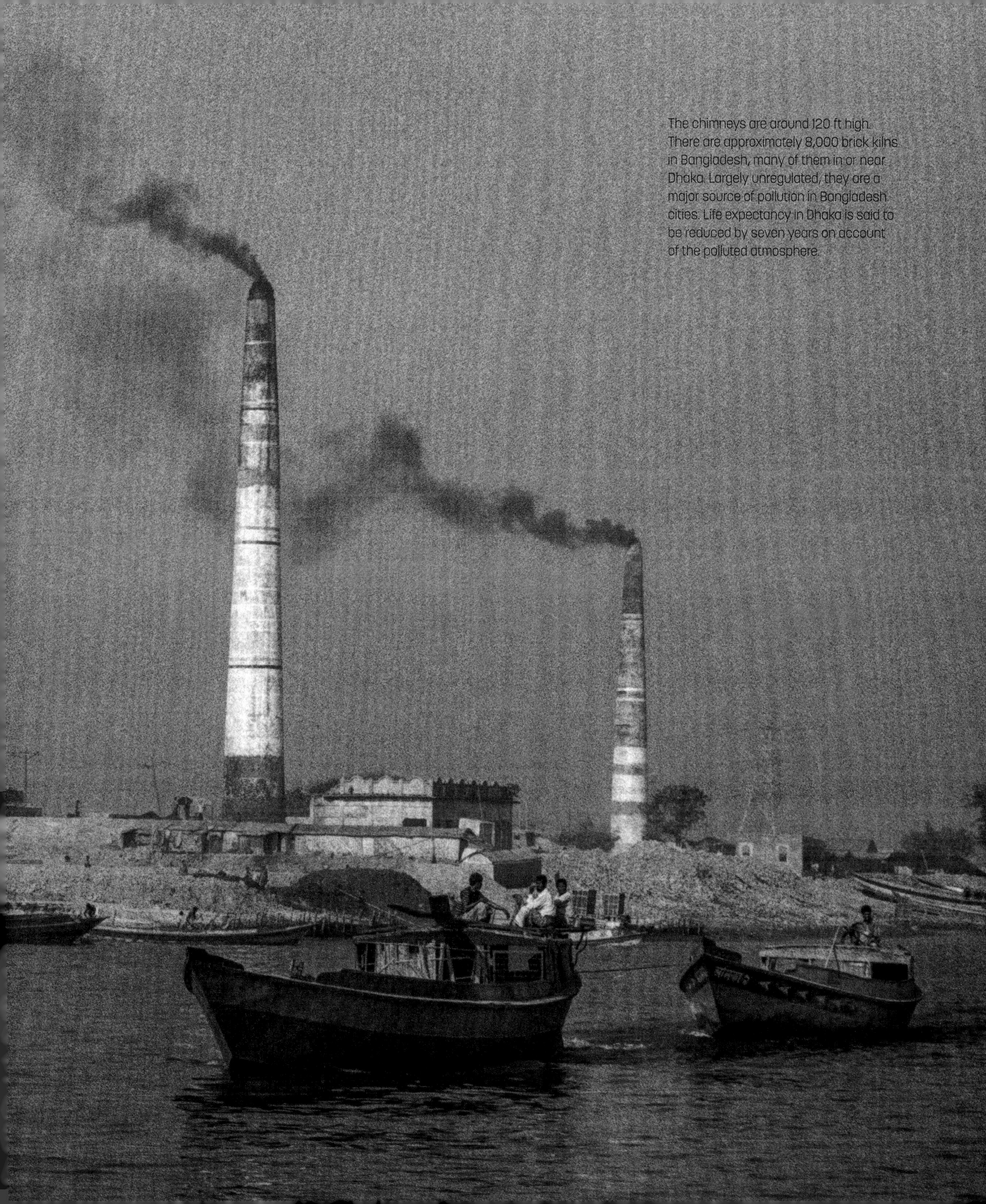

The chimneys are around 120 ft high. There are approximately 8,000 brick kilns in Bangladesh, many of them in or near Dhaka. Largely unregulated, they are a major source of pollution in Bangladesh cities. Life expectancy in Dhaka is said to be reduced by seven years on account of the polluted atmosphere.

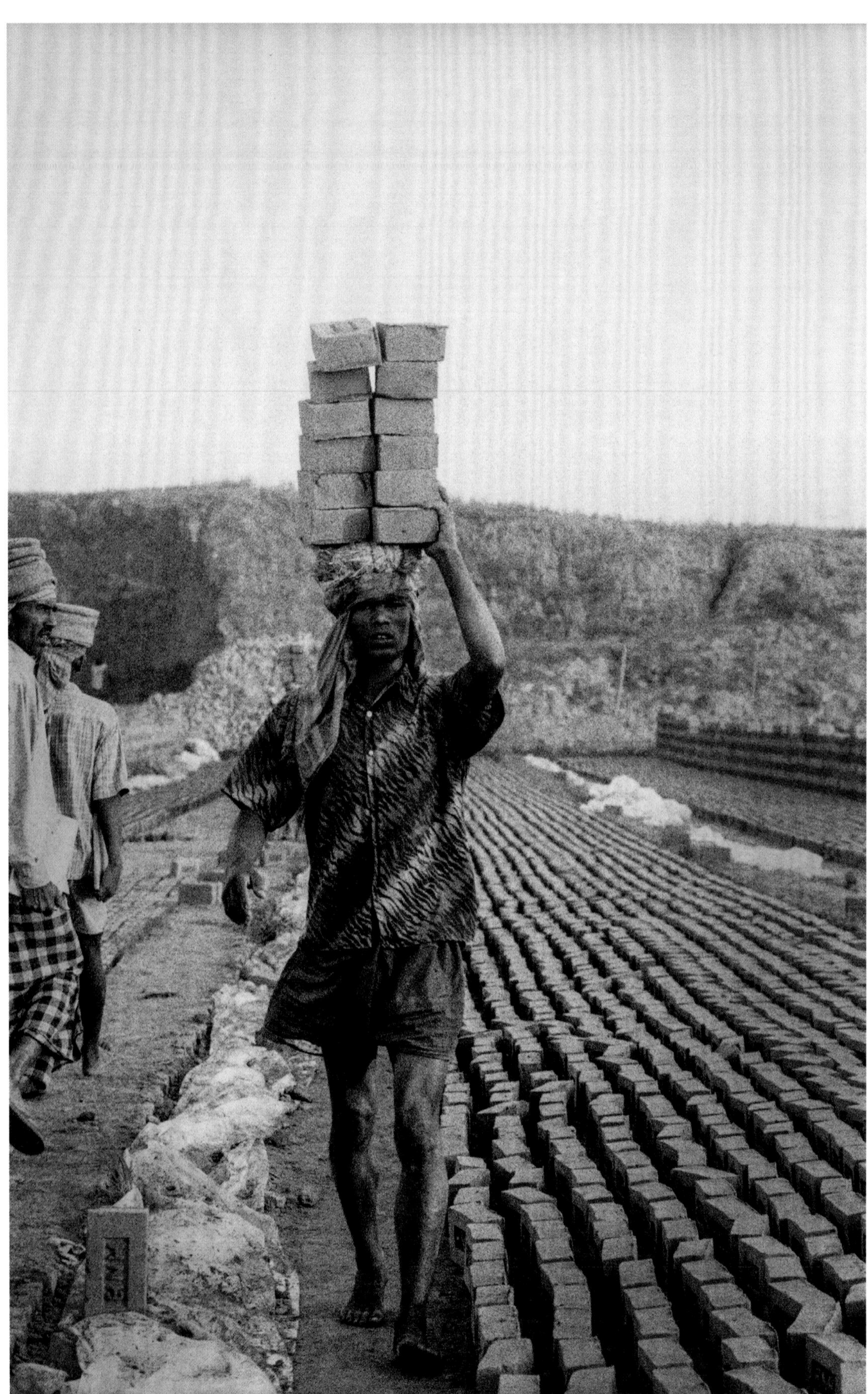

'We arrived about 6.00 am and clambered through the road gate and met the overseer, overweight and of a brutal demeanour. I shot ten rolls of film – mostly FP4 [black & white negative film] – before the sunlight lost its softness. The loads they carried on their heads were massive – ten unfired bricks at 5 kg apiece, about 50 kg or 120 lbs. Not much has changed since Imperial Rome. We left at 9.00 am, and the quiet desperation of their lives continued.'

Journal, 15 December 2006

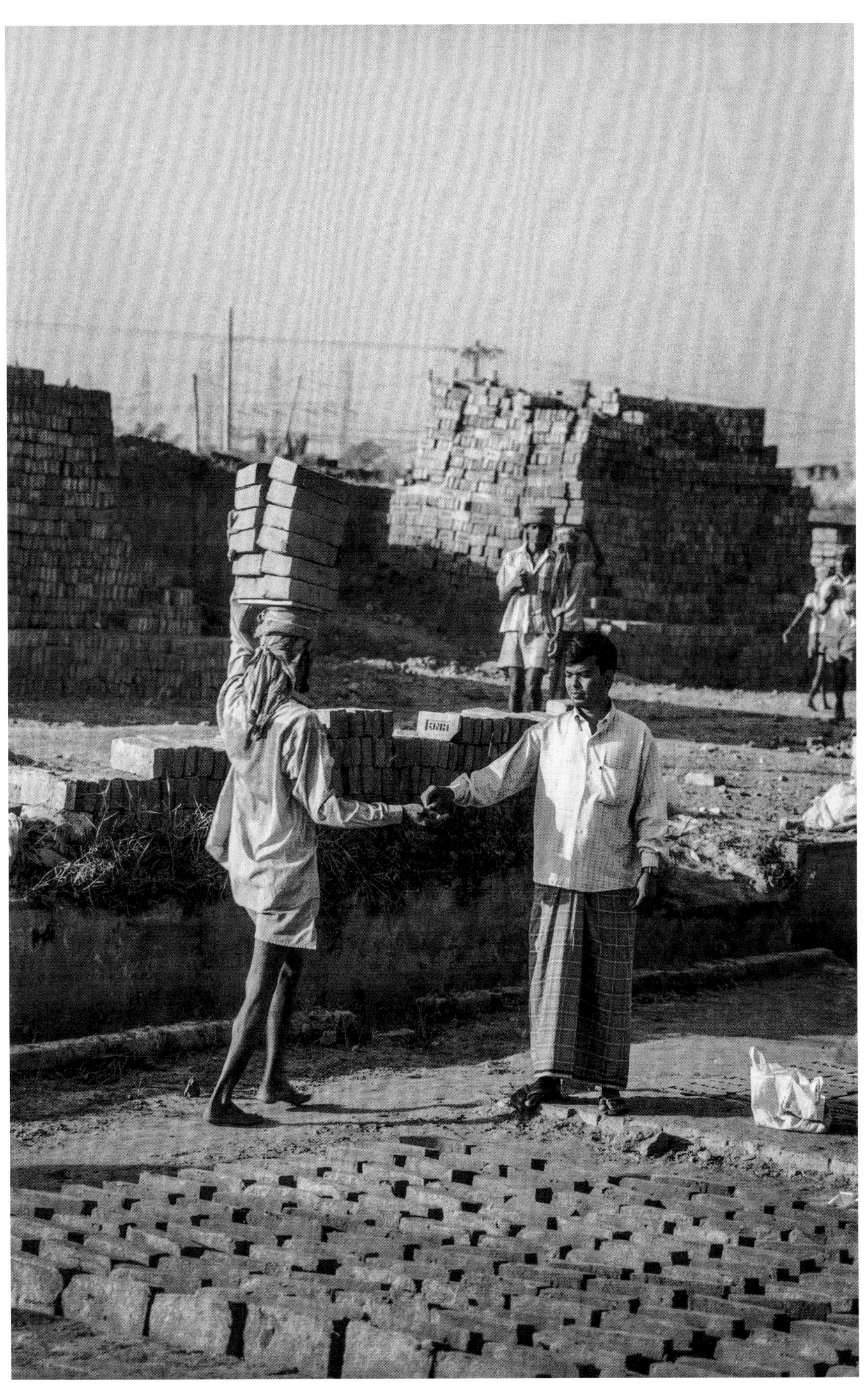

The overseer hands out tokens for each load of ten bricks, later redeemed in cash at the rate, in 2006, of 130 taka for 1,000 bricks. About £1.15 in today's money. In 2017, according to the International Growth Centre at the London School of Economics, many workers were paid less than US$100 per month.

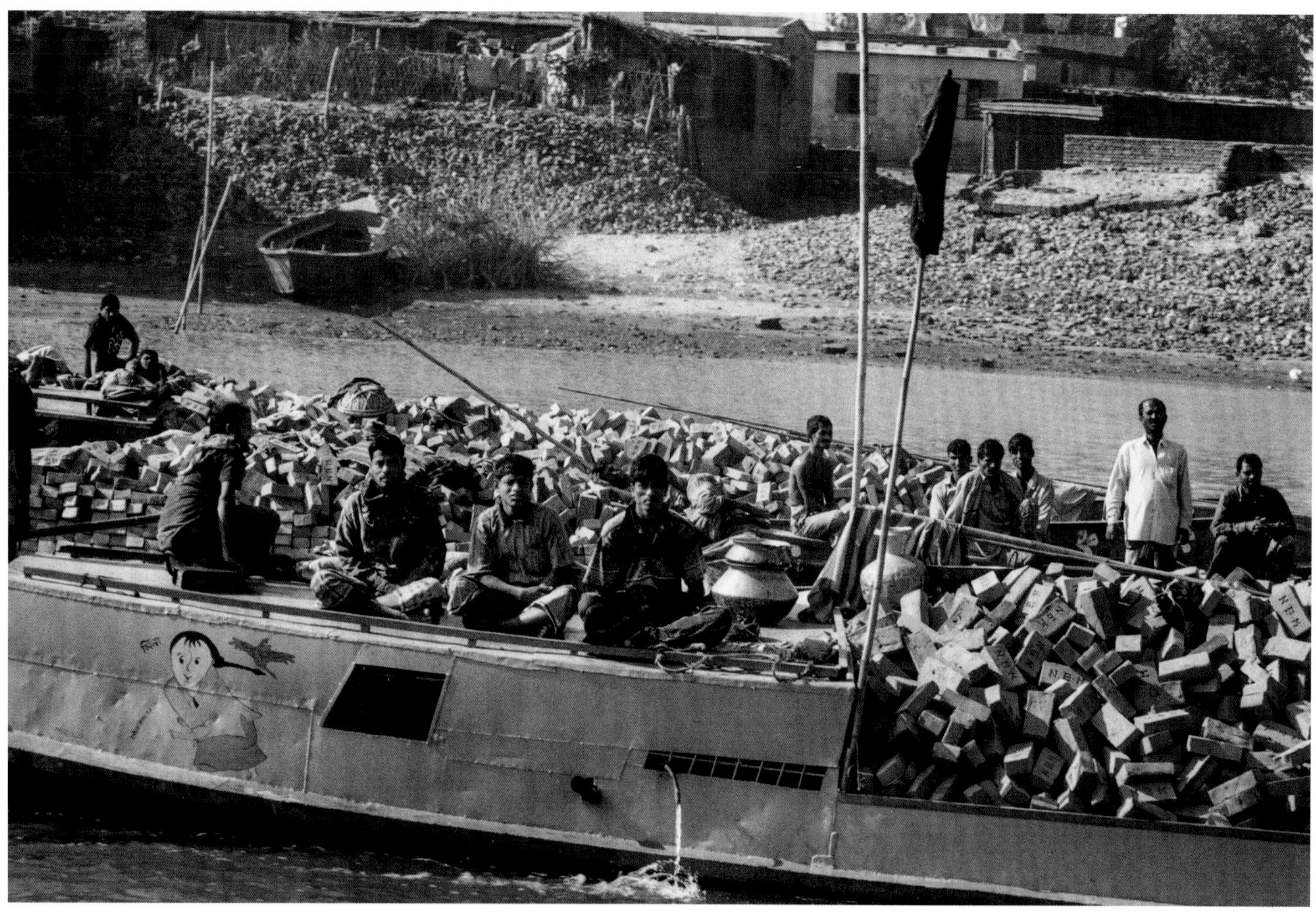

Neema, who features on the gunwales of the brickyard boat, is a spirited, nine-year-old girl who braves all the odds get to school. She is famous for her parrot, who perches as usual on her pigtail. Invented as a cartoon character by UNICEF to promote education and women's rights, she was a popular character when this photograph was taken in 2004.

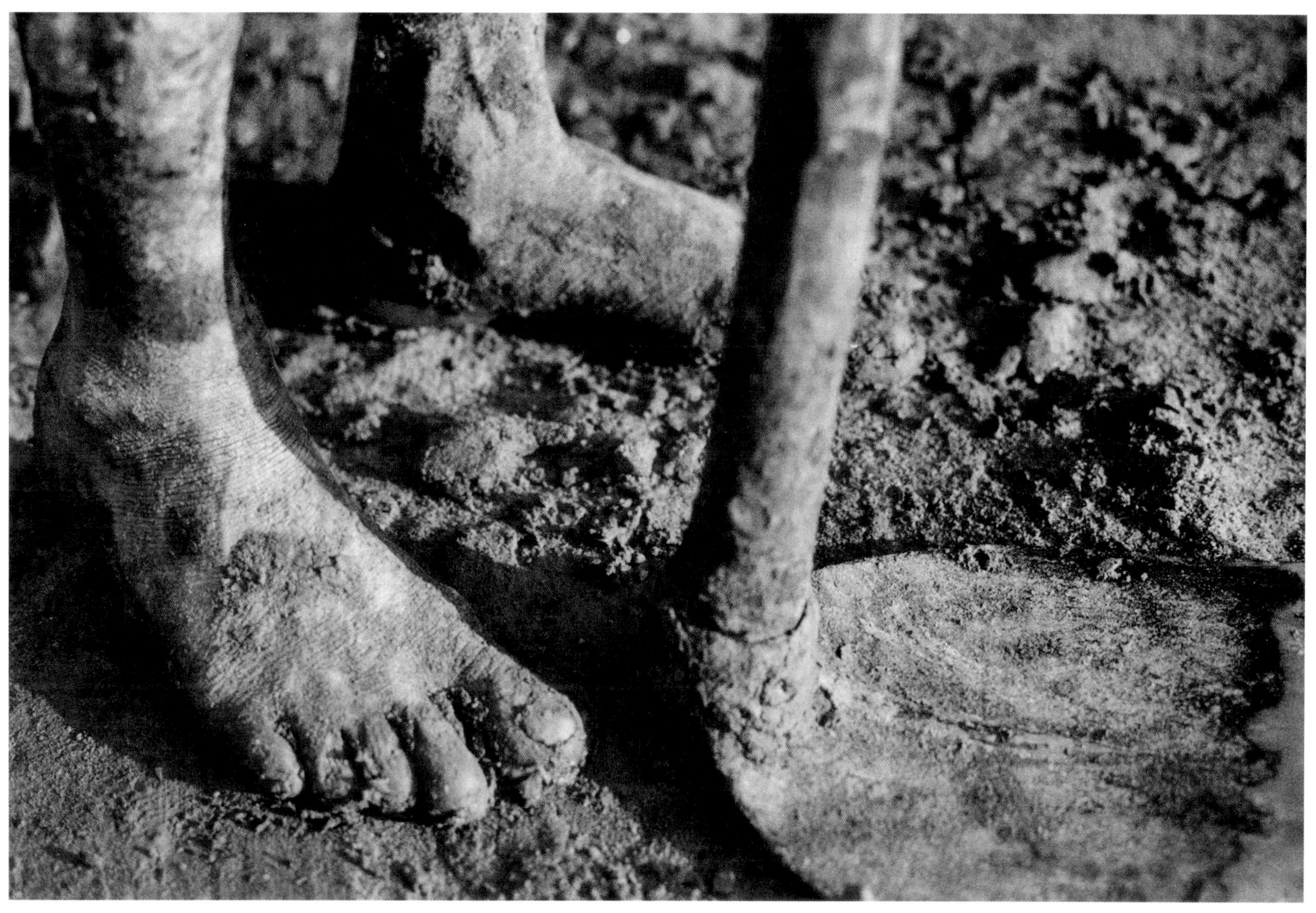

The Lutfor Brickfield in Shavar near Dhaka, in 2006. Few workers wear shoes.

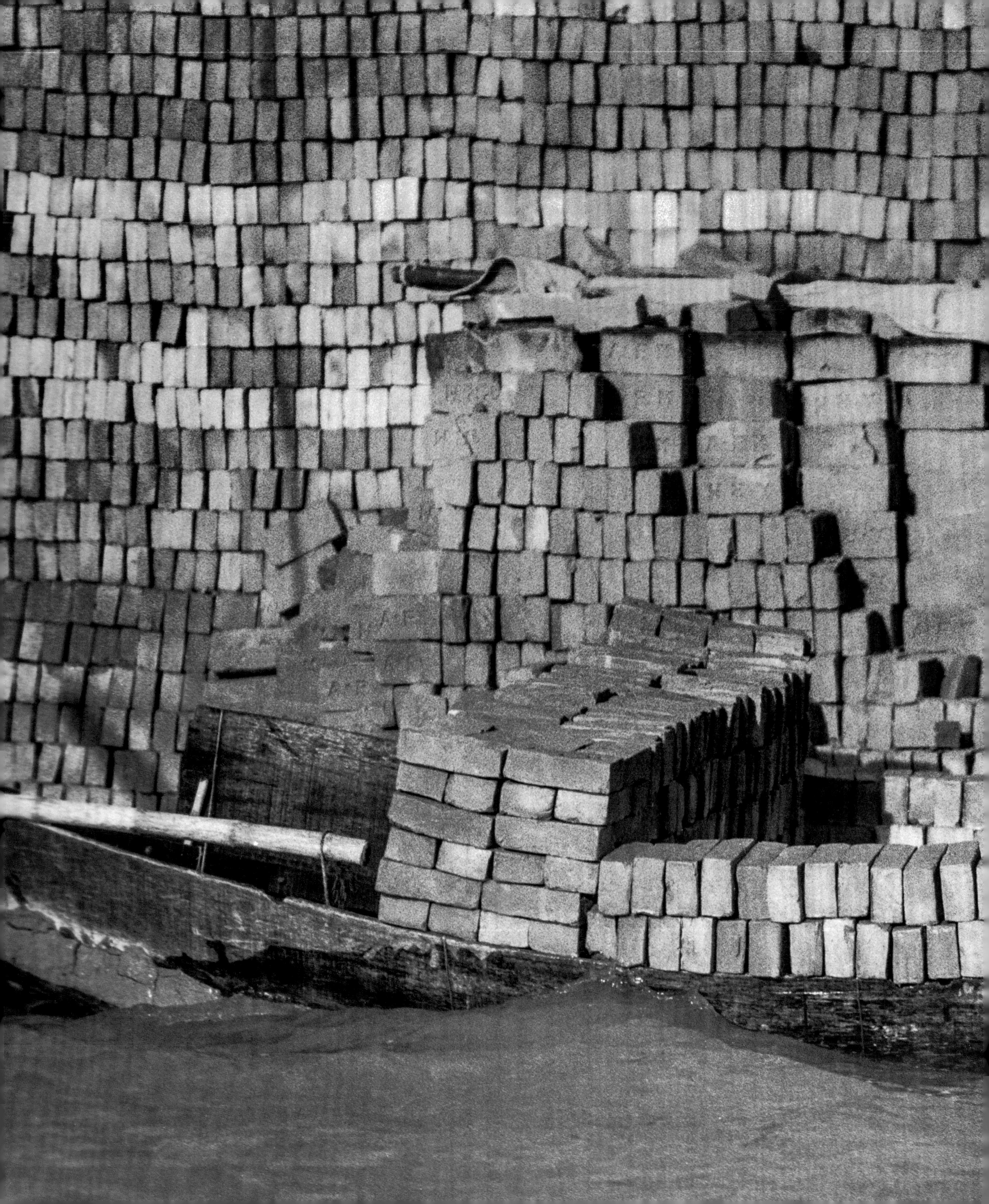

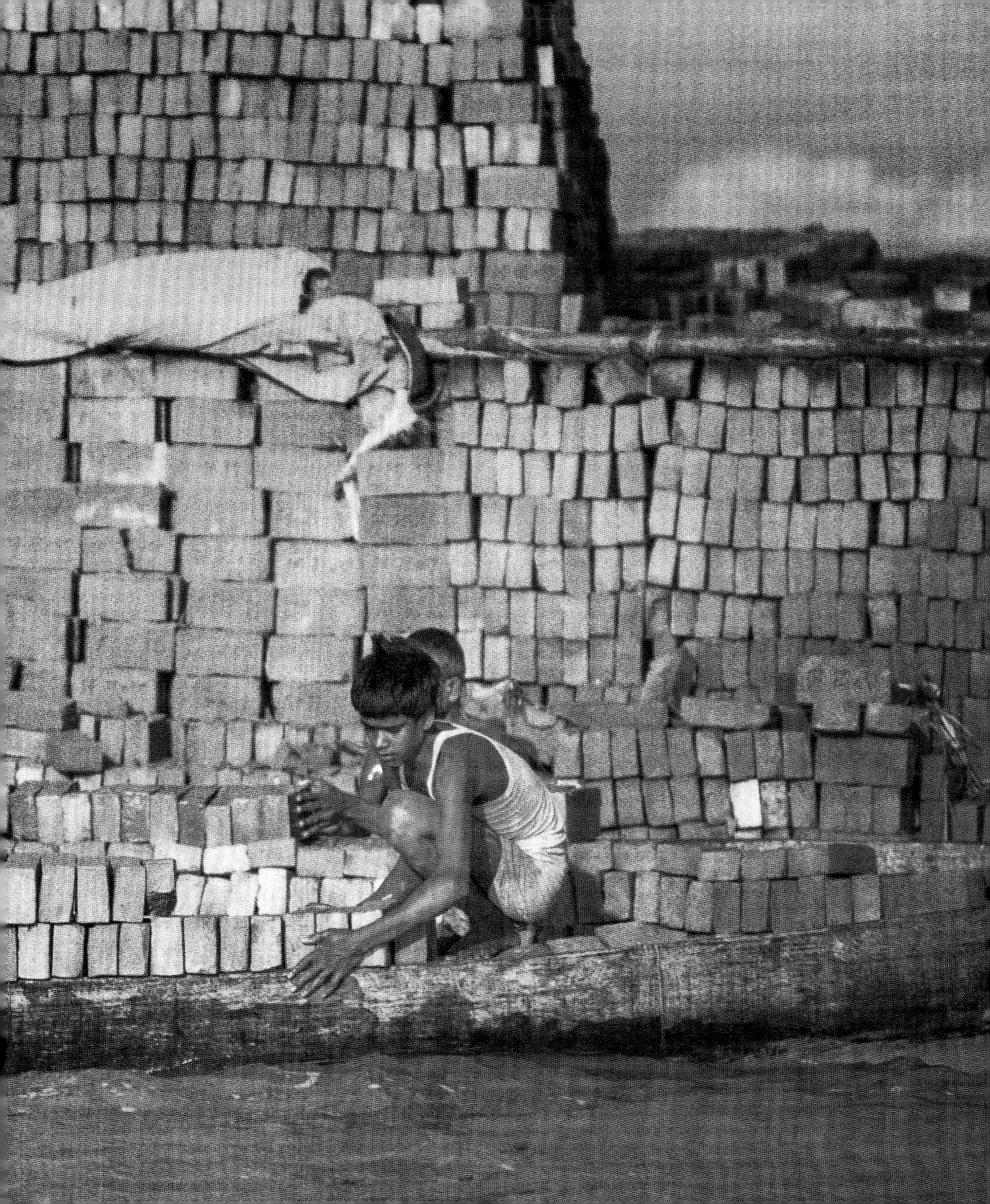

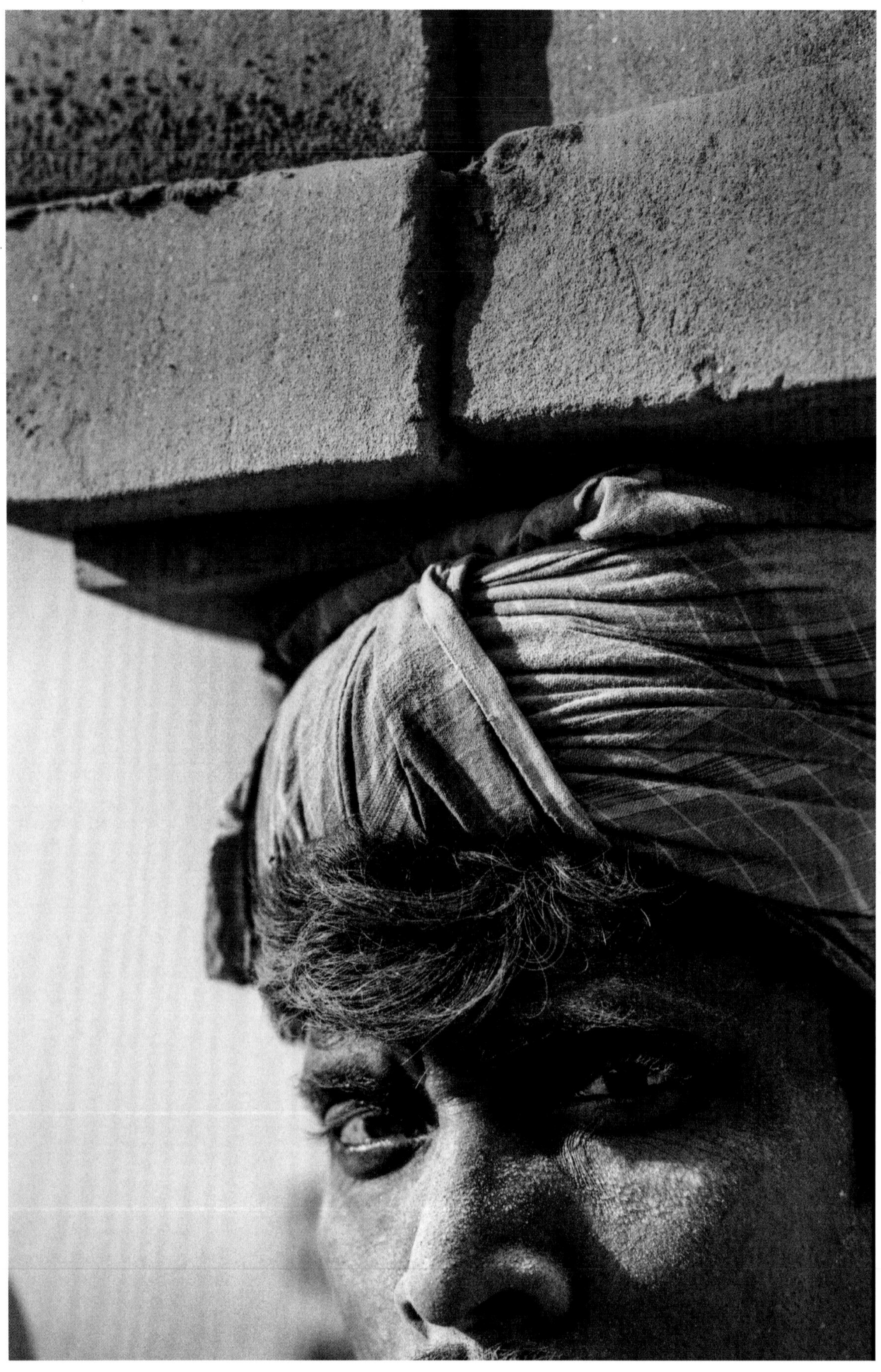

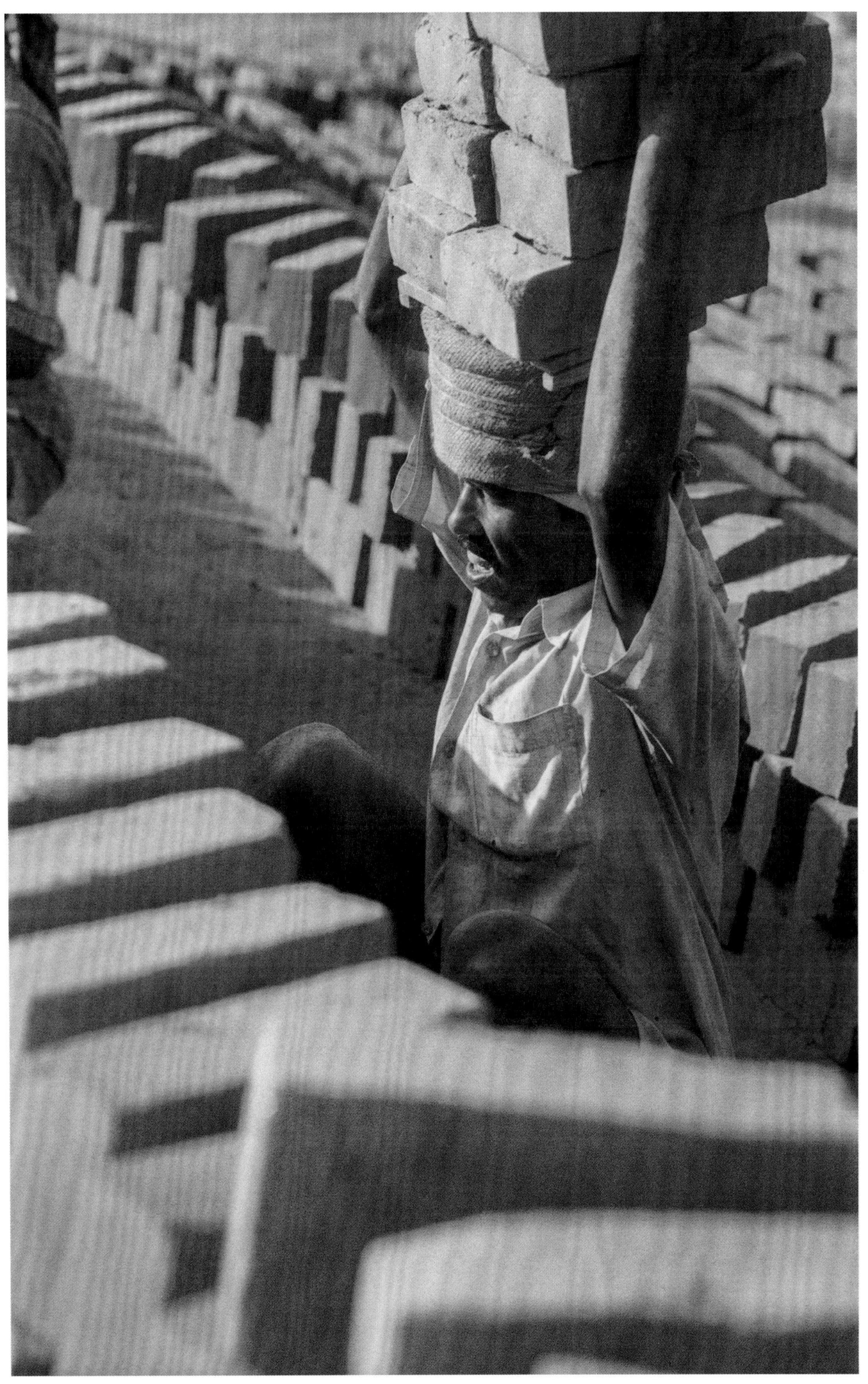

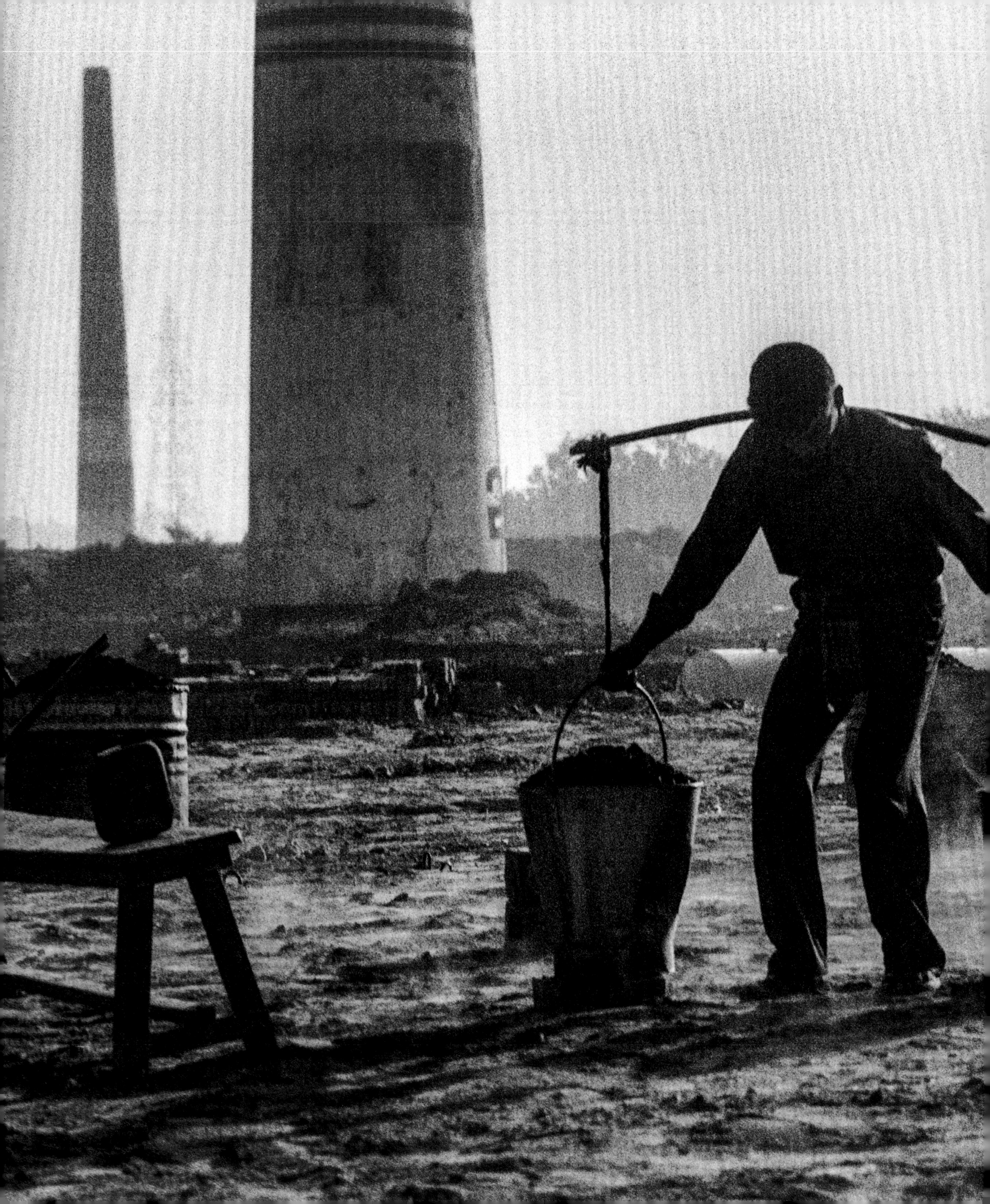

Carrying coke on the roof of the kiln in January 2006; each bucket weighs about 25 kg

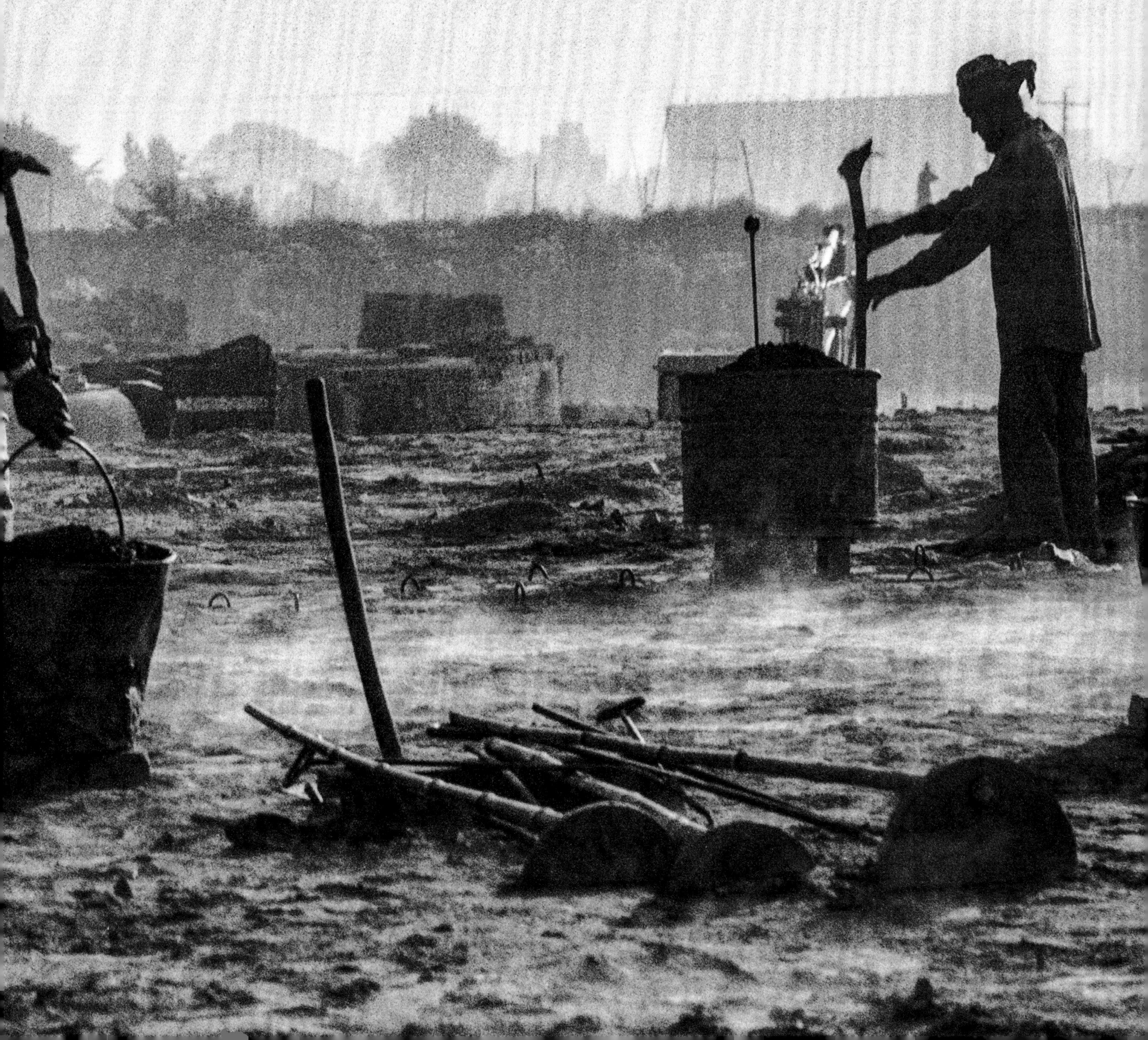

Old Dhaka and the Buriganga River

Old Dhaka stands beside the Buriganga River. Stepping off a boat at the port of Sadharghat, you enter a bewildering new reality. The wharf is dense with humanity: men with carts stacked with goods and rickshaws with passengers, women bearing vast head baskets of vegetables shouting their right of passage as they manoeuvre down alleyways to colonnaded squares where traders proclaim their wares. On the other side, as you bob and weave your way along the wharf, a myriad of boats unload passengers with goods from up-river. It is a scene to lift the heart, a moment to pause with a glass of marsala chai and relish the industry and energy that is Bangladesh.

There is a man there who irons shirts. His stall opens on to the wharf, and he is always my first port of call. His English is good and the chai stall is close at hand. From there I can observe the street life as it passes by, while asking questions about Old Dhaka.

Half a mile away, along a maze of narrow streets, is the Armenian Church, built in 1781. This is another regular port of call. Its high walls and ancient graveyard, which chronicles the lives of Armenians in Dhaka since the early eighteenth century, provide a haven of peace amidst the frenetic life of the city.

It is one of a number of listed buildings in Old Dhaka, though this by no means guarantees survival in a city consumed by chaotic expansion. I once spent a day with Taimur Islam, then their lone but passionate defender, visiting these crumbling legacies of the past. Many were occupied by sole traders engaged in small-scale manufacturing of one kind or another, surrounded by disintegrating mantelpieces and ancient pillars, their rounded bricks revealed as the lime plaster crumbles with age. One was being demolished with sledgehammers before our eyes as we came round the corner. Taimur's cry of rage rivalled the crash of hammers, the demolition crew retreated in alarm, my friends and I were abandoned and our leader vanished – to return, we heard later, with an injunction to halt the destruction, for the High Court, too, is in Old Dhaka.

Prince among these listed monuments are the palaces built by the zamindars, tax collectors for the Mughal empire and later for the British. Bengal was then the centre of power in India and the zamindars were the landed aristocracy; in due course they played a significant role in the fight for independence from the British. Their palaces are amongst the most magnificent buildings in Bangladesh. Many of them are in ruins, for other priorities than conservation prevail in Bangladesh, but they speak eloquently of another age.

One of them, now known as Beauty Boarding, is another haven of peace, in the heart of Bangla Bazaar not far from Sadharghat. The last zamindar departed shortly after partition, and its pink-walled courtyards and cool verandas became a place where writers lived and wrote, and in due course, poets conversed with politicians. Named after Beauty, the eponymous daughter of the new owner, her family still serve classic Bengali food in stainless steel bowls. Beauty Boarding is, satisfactorily and brilliantly, the exact opposite of the grand hotels on the other side of the city.

Crowding in upon these oases is one of the world's fastest-growing megacities. Streets are lined with stalls selling every kind of commodity, packed with people and bikes and flatbed rickshaws hauling goods between traders. Walking through this marvellous madness is exciting, exhausting, unpredictable, alarming, inspiring and not infrequently astonishing. Here, as Kipling remarked of the Grand Trunk Road (which passes by not far from Dhaka), is such a river of life as nowhere else exists in the world. Many of the portraits in this book are of people in Old Dhaka with whom I fell enjoyably into company over the years.

Others were taken on or by the Buriganga. On this mighty river, on account of which Dhaka became Bengal's capital five centuries ago, all manner of boats ply the waters, for it provides access by boat to the rest of the country. In 1992, when I arrived for the first time, most of them were powered by sail and the waters were alive with fish. Diesel engines have seen off the sails and pollution the fish.

The consequences of the pollution are devastating, but the rivermen live on. Their apparent optimism and cheerfulness is infectious. They live at the coalface of an environmental catastrophe, a testament to human resilience. ■

The boatyard on the far side of the Buriganga from Sadharghat

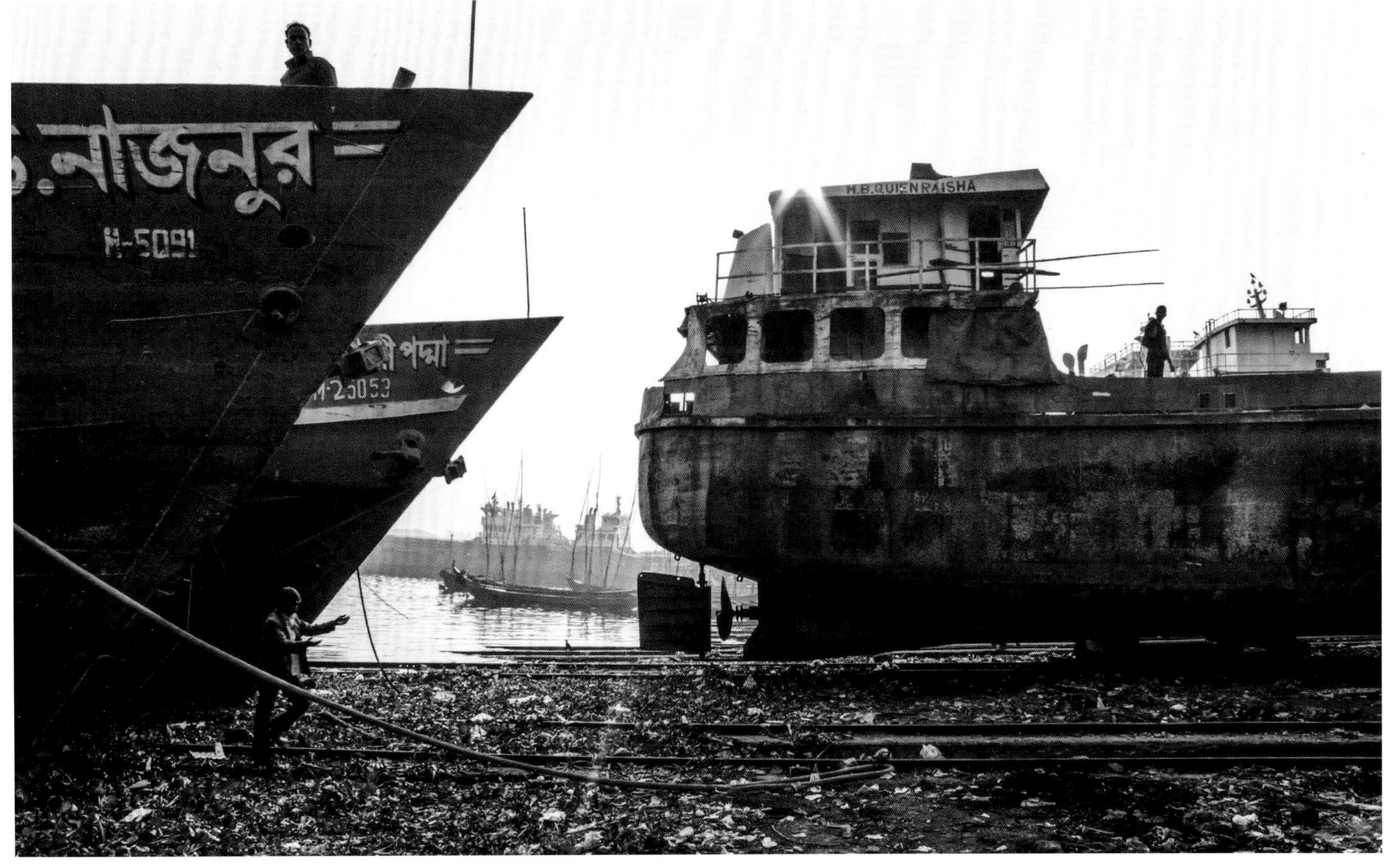

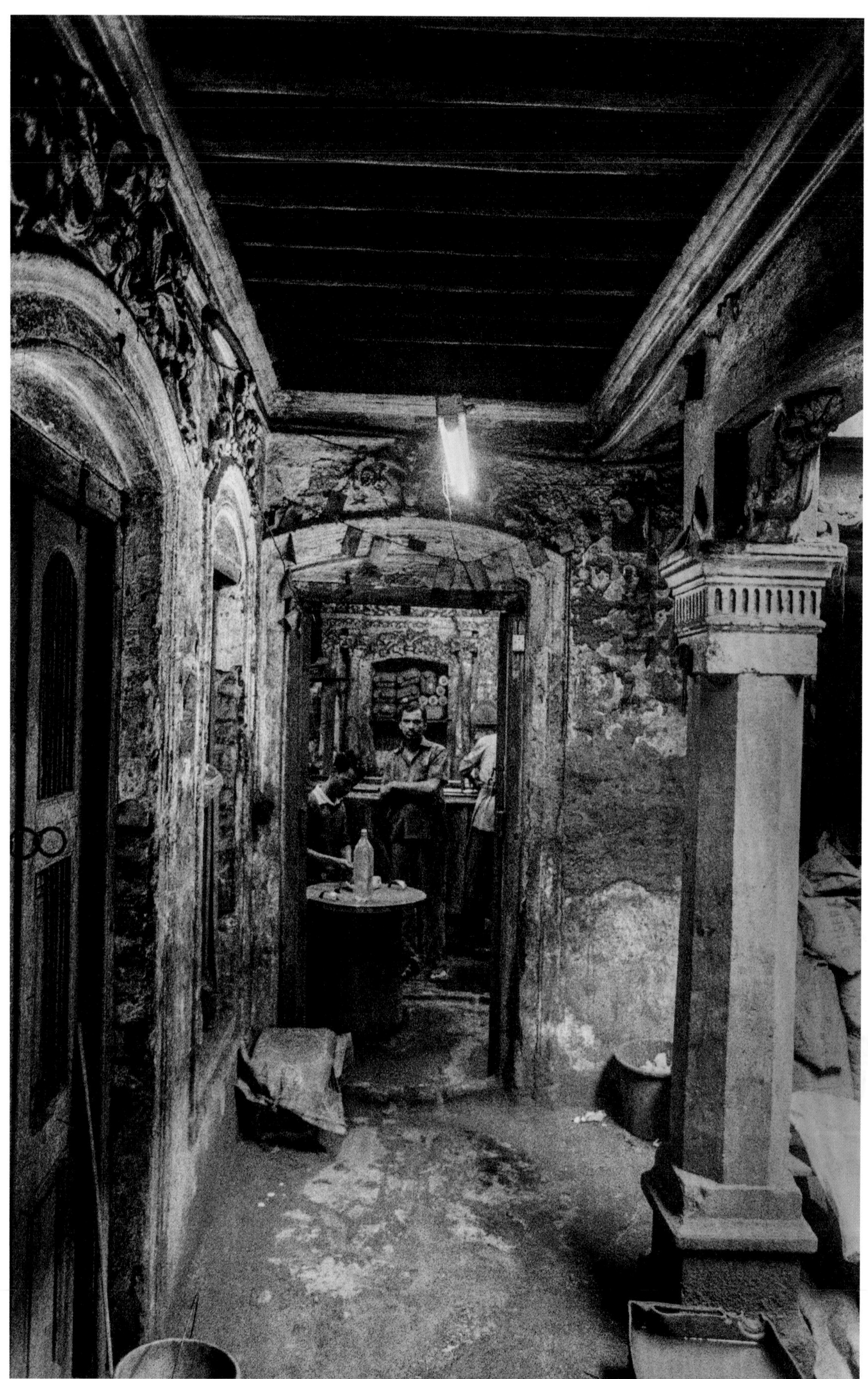

Light industry in a listed building in Old Dhaka

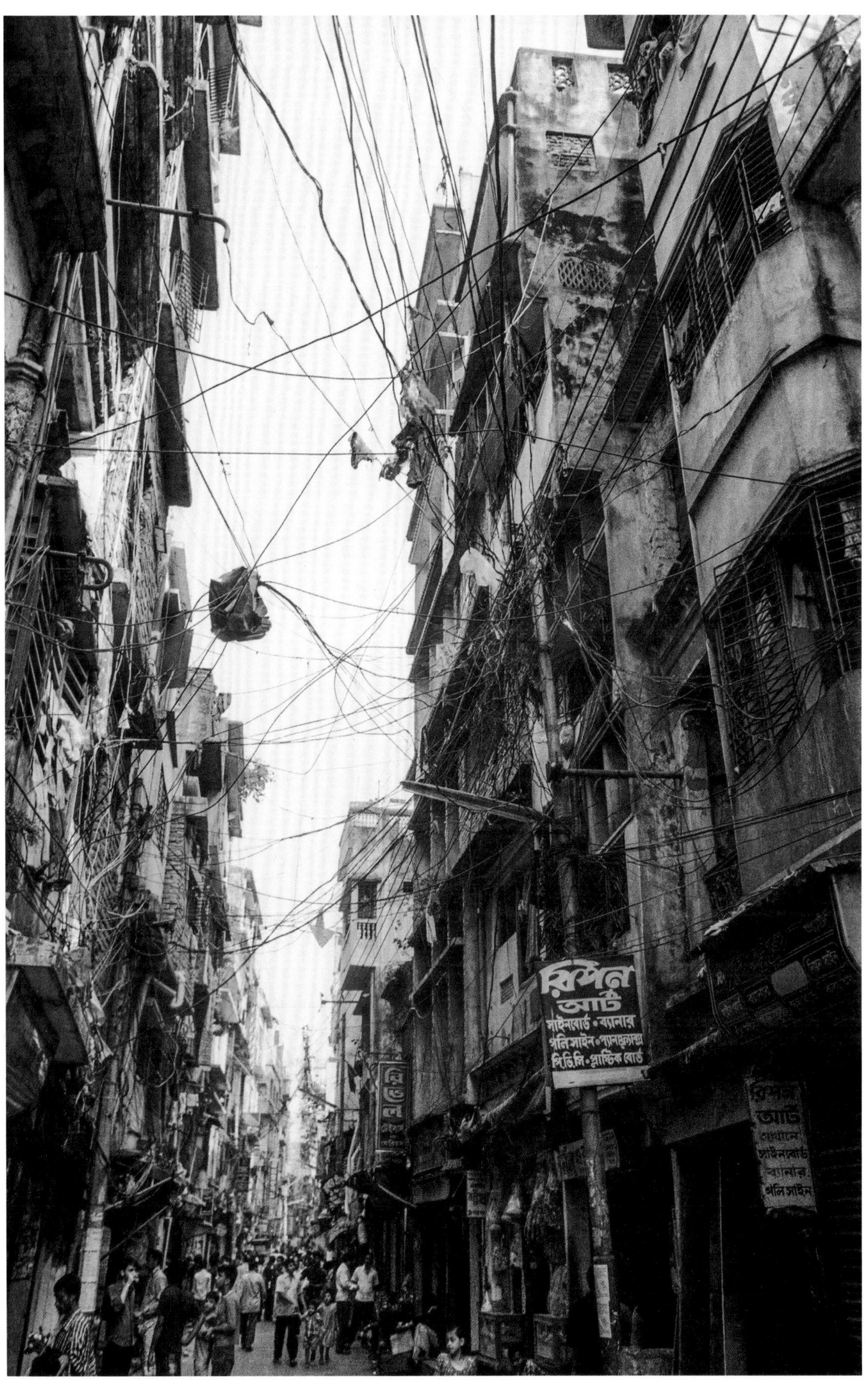

One of Dhaka's many miracles: the lights (usually) work. 2006

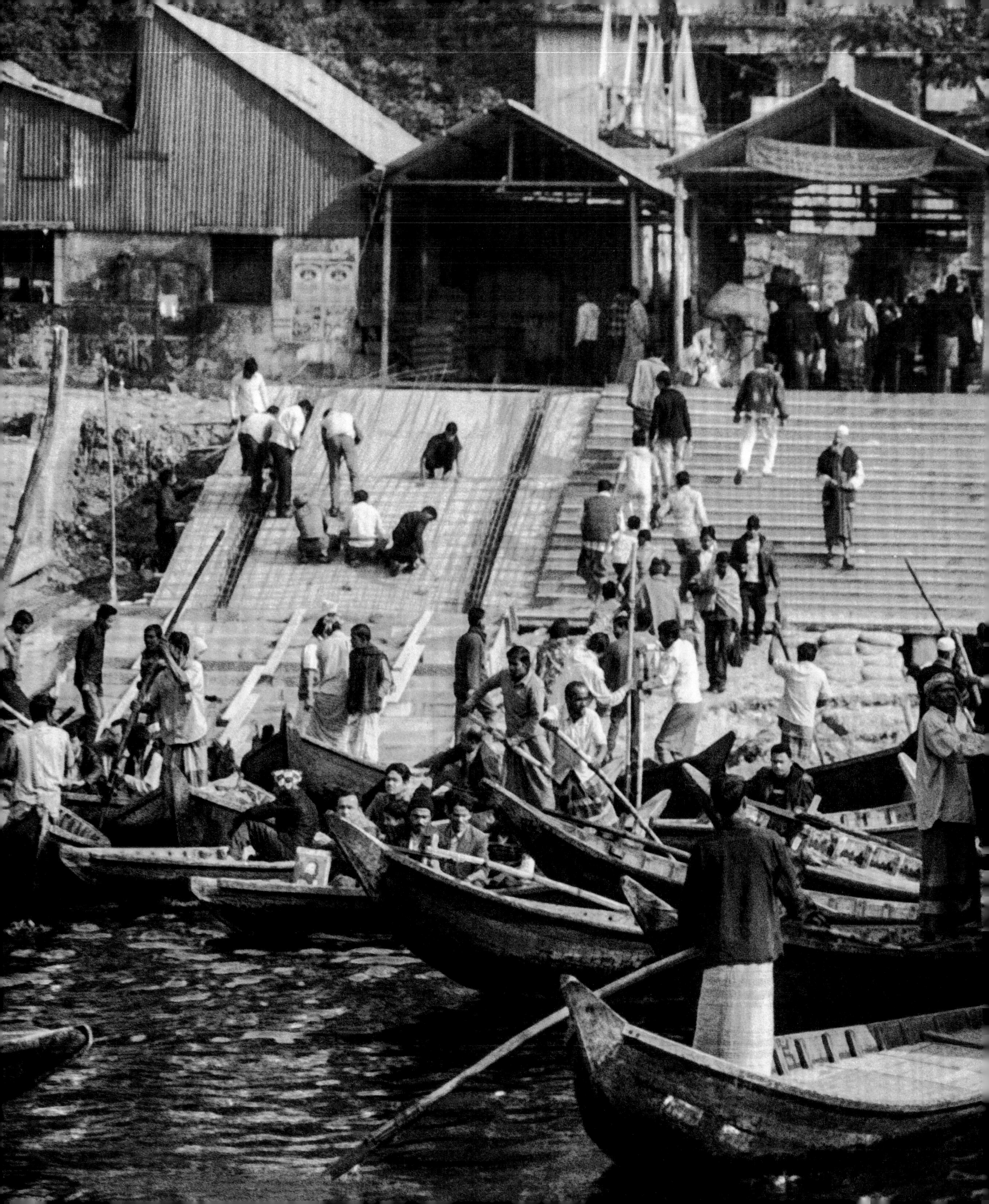

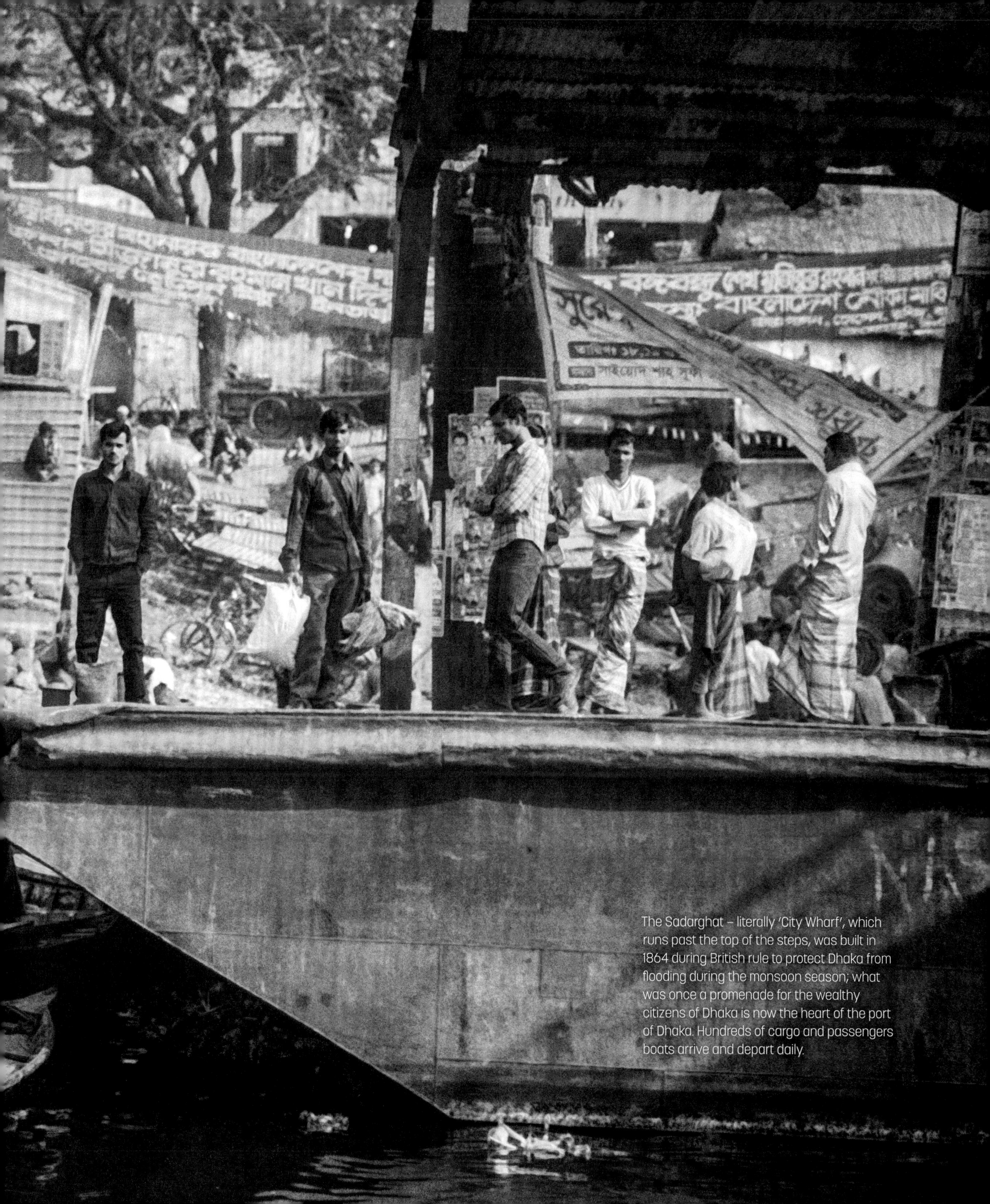

The Sadarghat – literally 'City Wharf', which runs past the top of the steps, was built in 1864 during British rule to protect Dhaka from flooding during the monsoon season; what was once a promenade for the wealthy citizens of Dhaka is now the heart of the port of Dhaka. Hundreds of cargo and passengers boats arrive and depart daily.

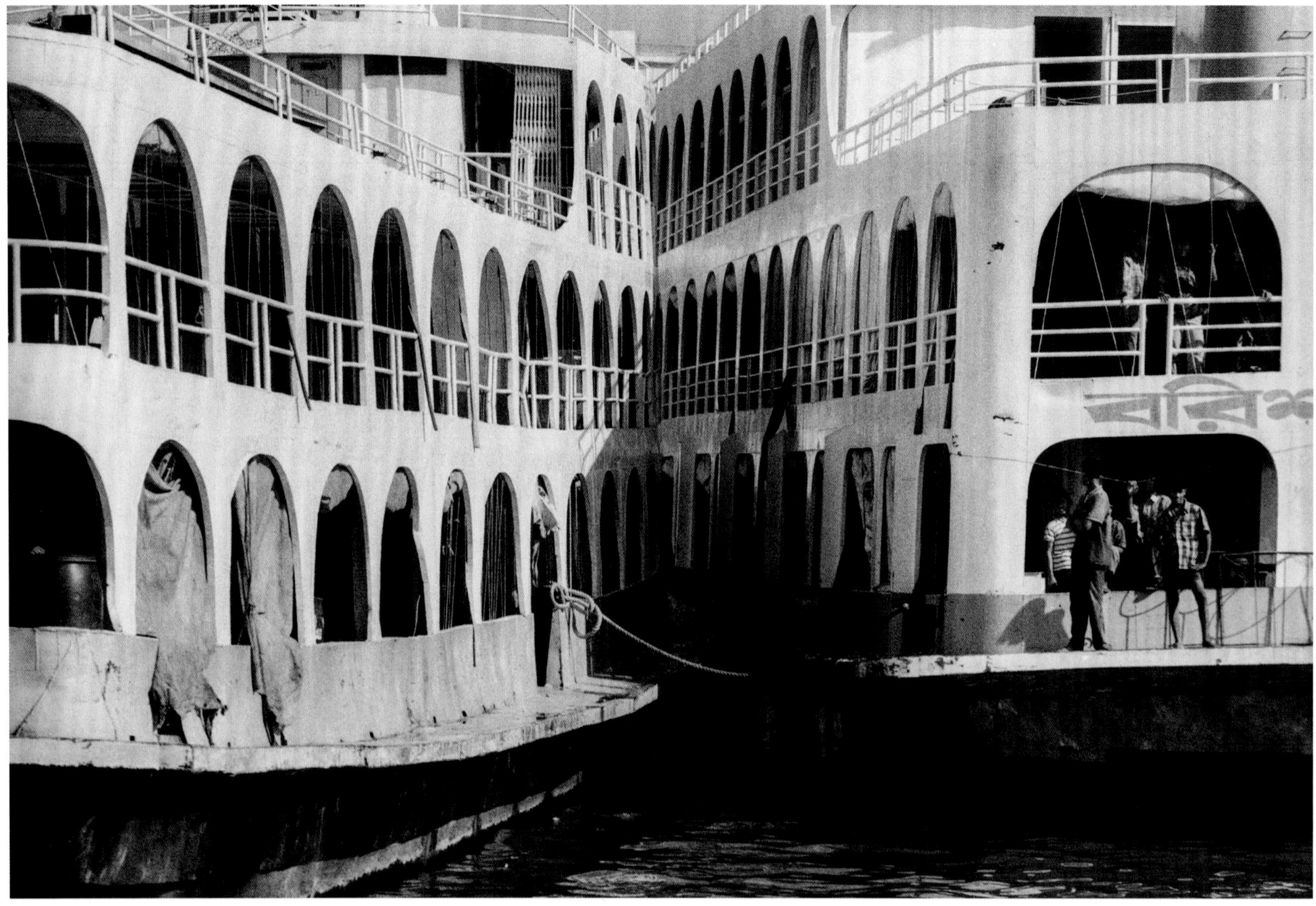

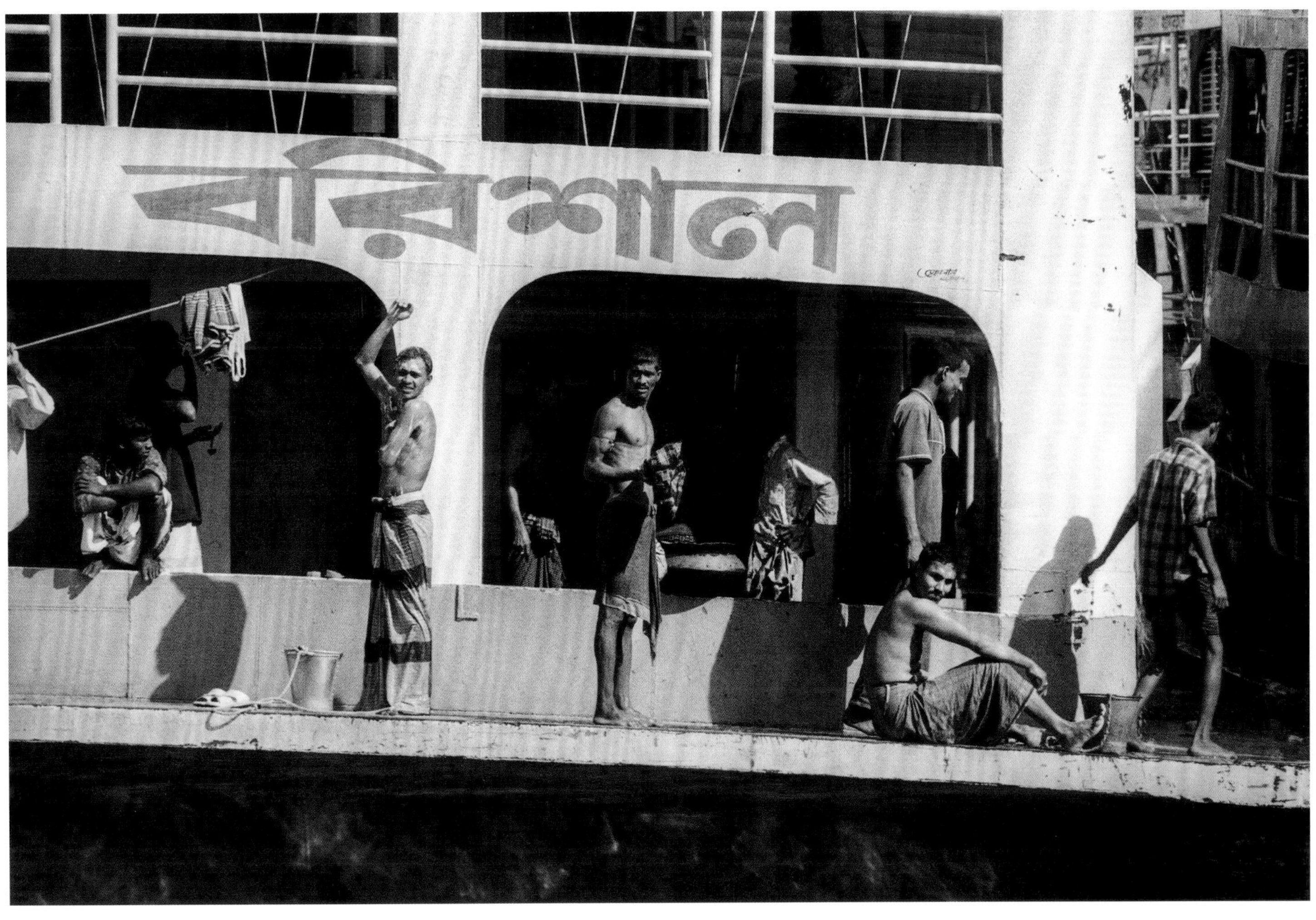

Boatmen taking baths with buckets
by the Buriganga in 2004

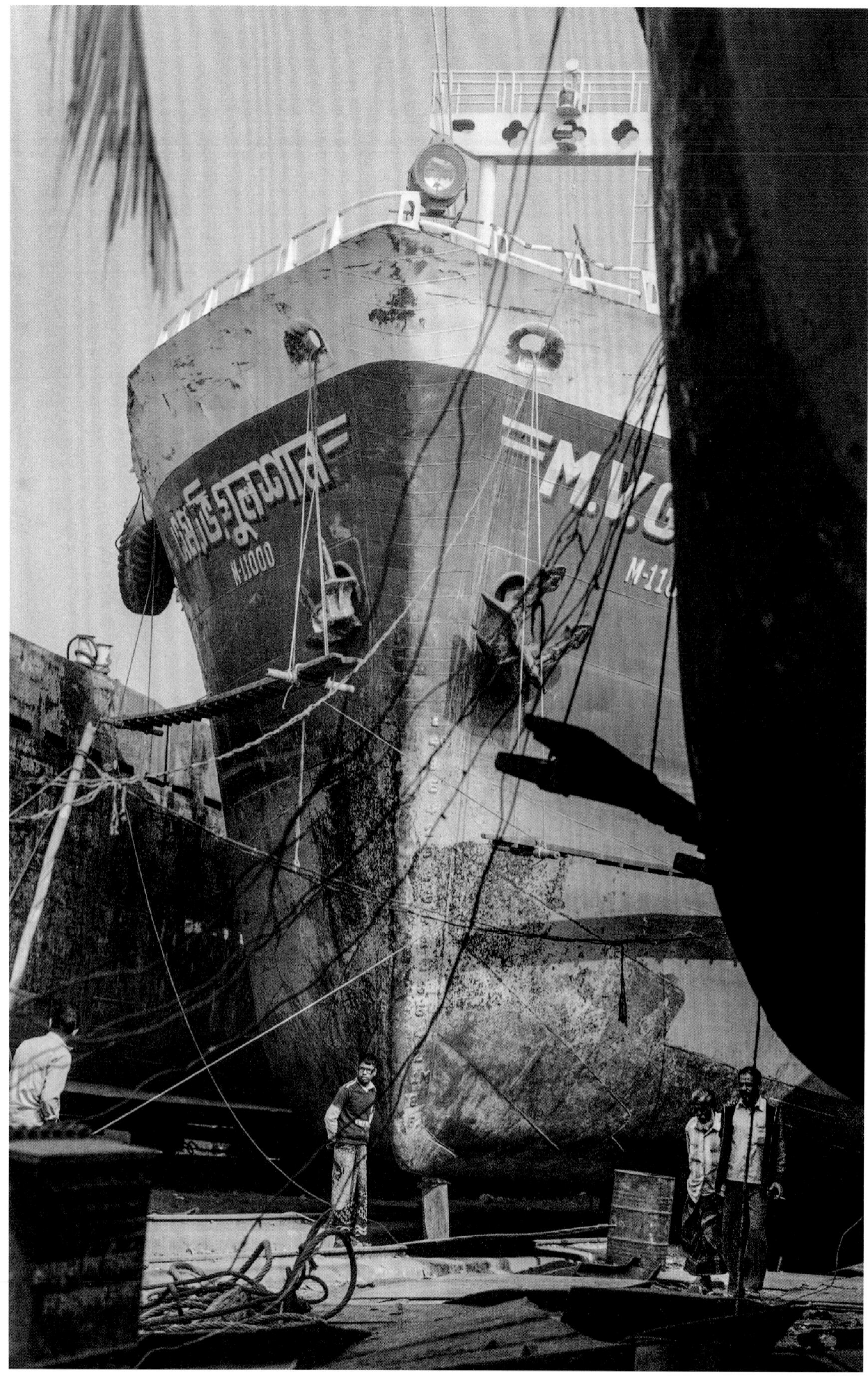
M-11000

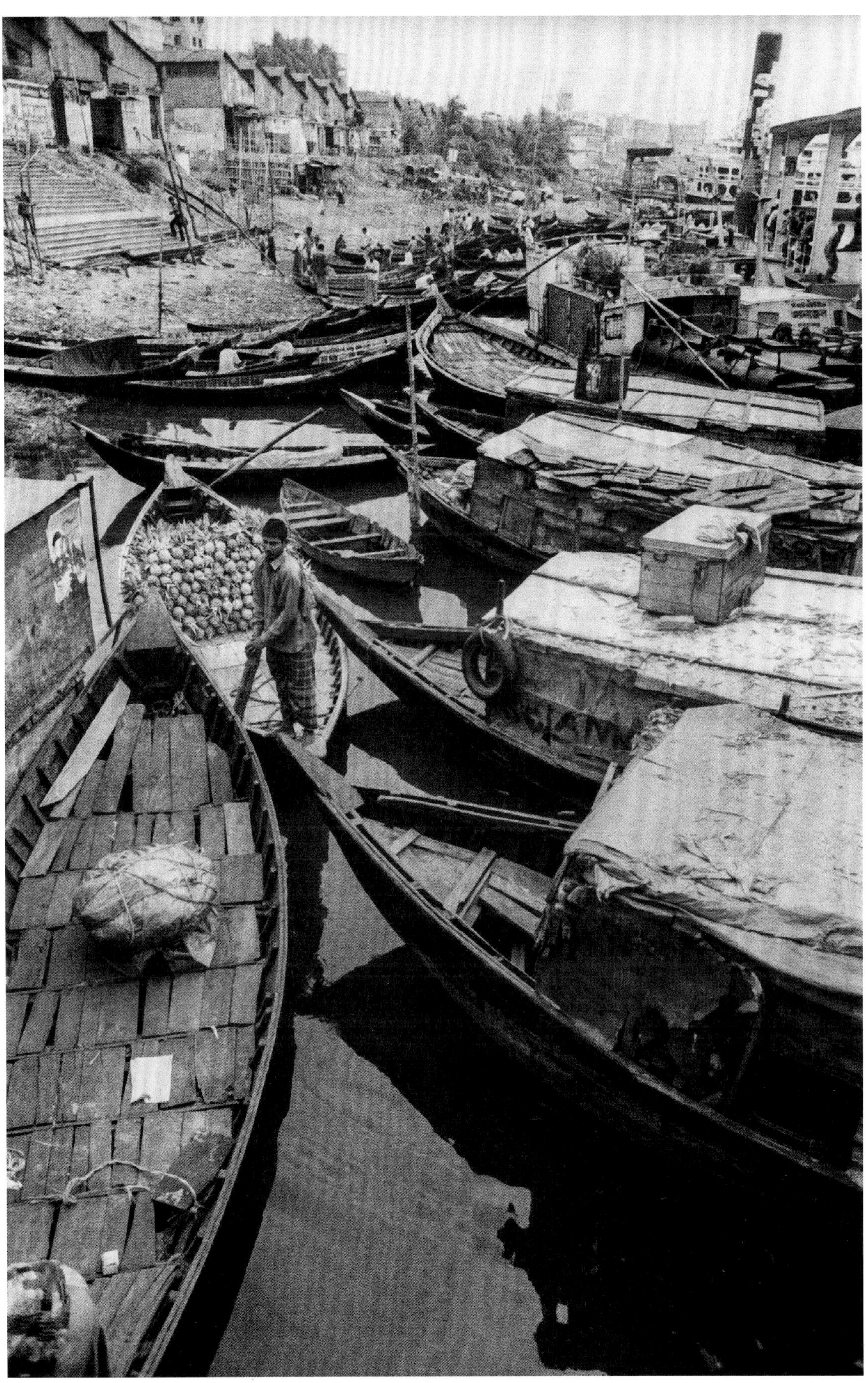

A dinghy with pineapples and other boats at the eastern end of the wharf at Sadharghat

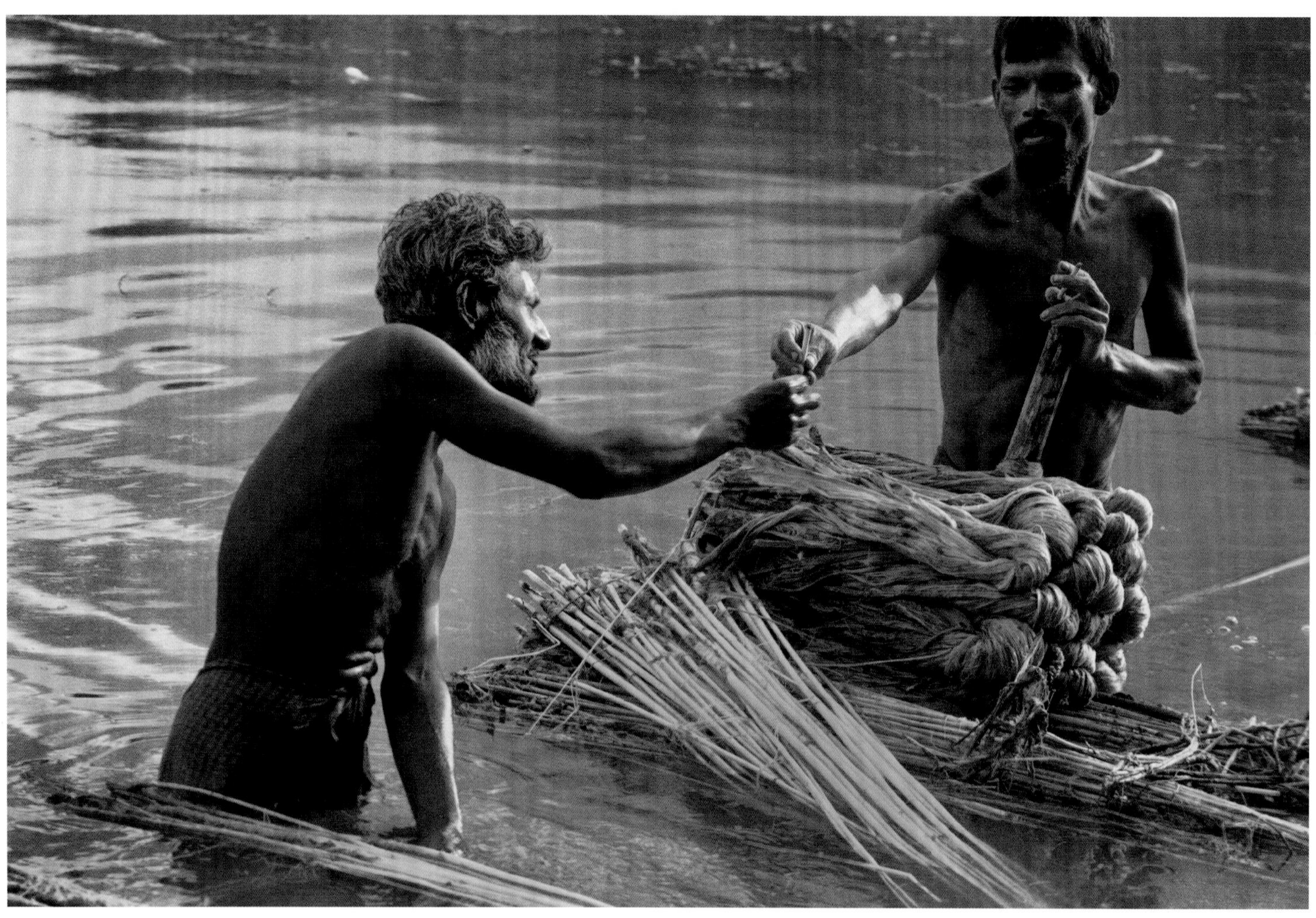

Jute-workers taking a smoke-break in the Buriganga in 1992. Bangladesh is the world's leading supplier of raw jute. The jute sticks in the foreground are used for kindling.

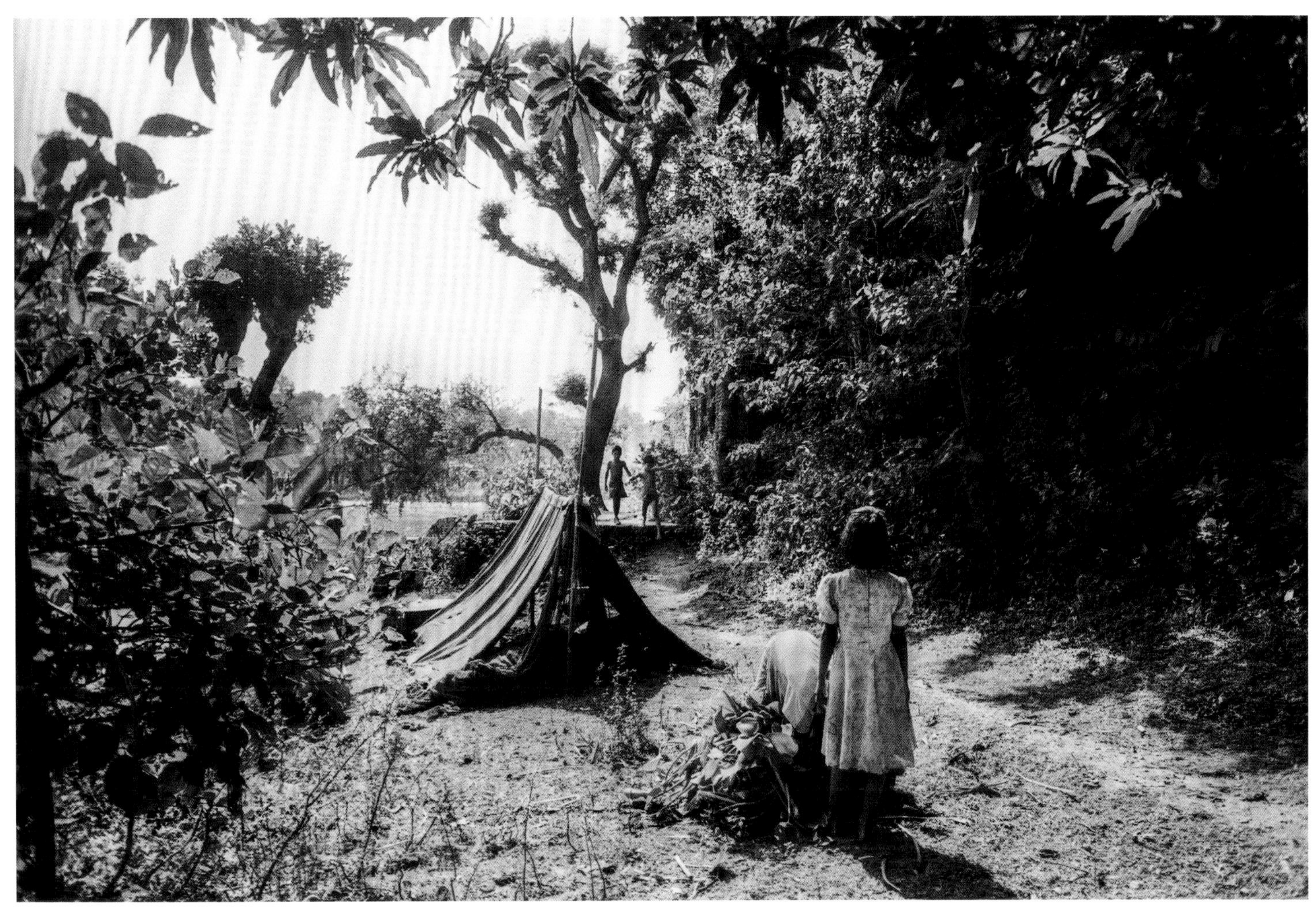

Water gypsies camped beside a tributary of the Buriganga in Old Sonargaon in 2004. River gypsies are an ethnic group in Bangladesh, known to local people as 'bedayas'. Their way of life is under threat from the drying out of rivers and urbanisation.

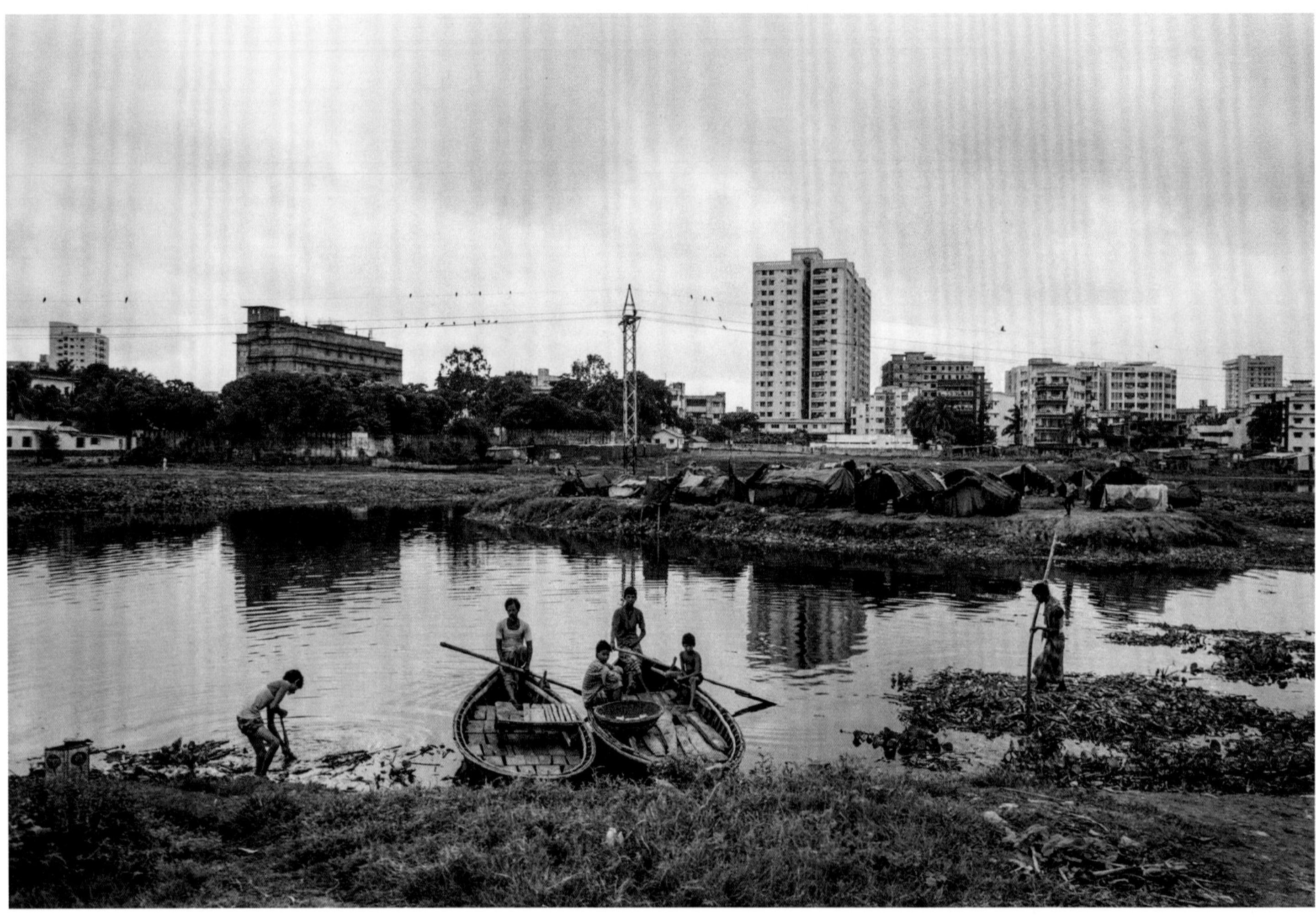

A view of Dhaka across Hatir Gheel (Elephant Lake) in 1992, highlighting the stark contrast between the new buildings in the background and the shacks where the men in the foreground live. This picture was taken from behind the Pacific Sonargoan Hotel, Dhaka's first 5-star hotel built ten years before.

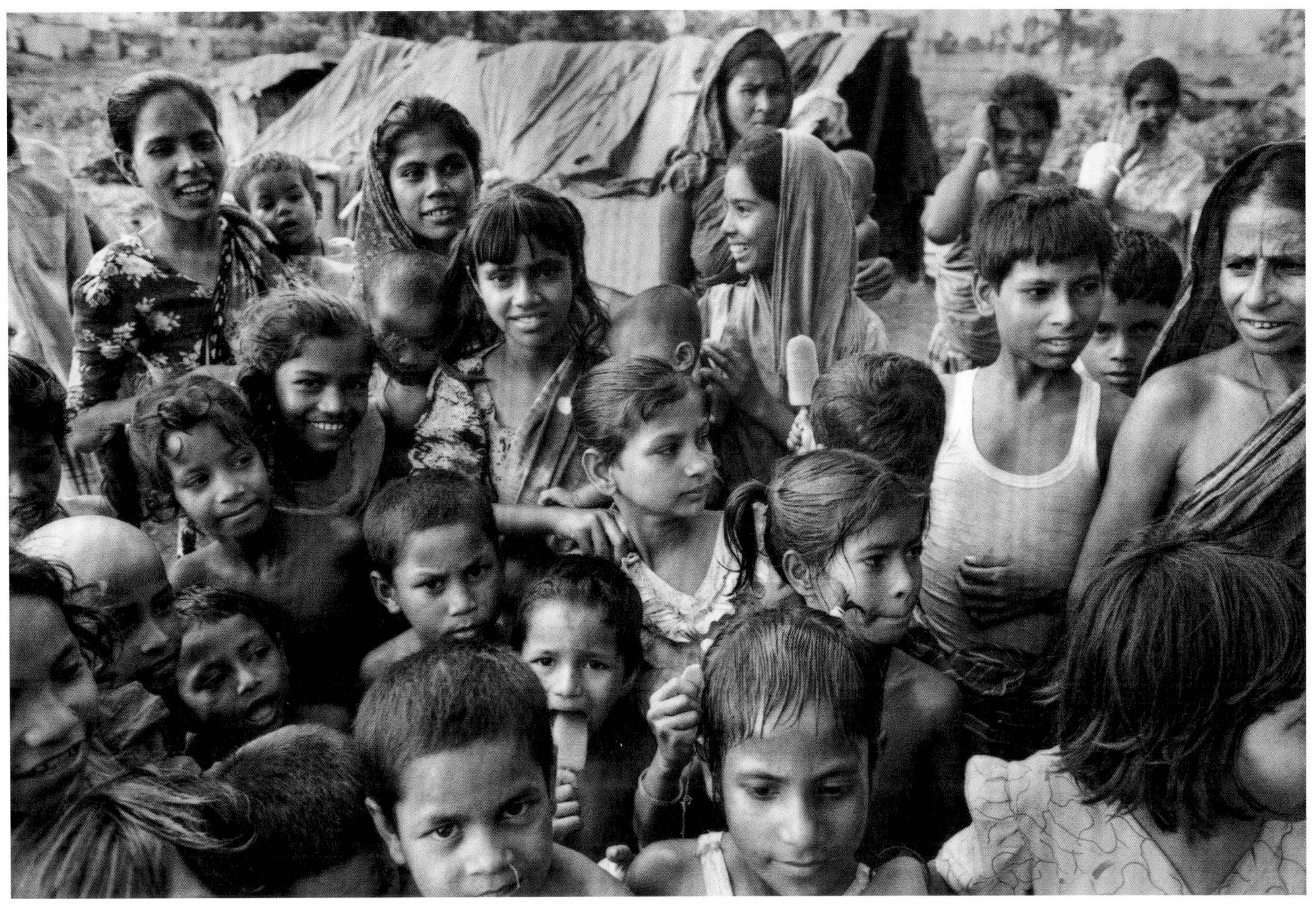

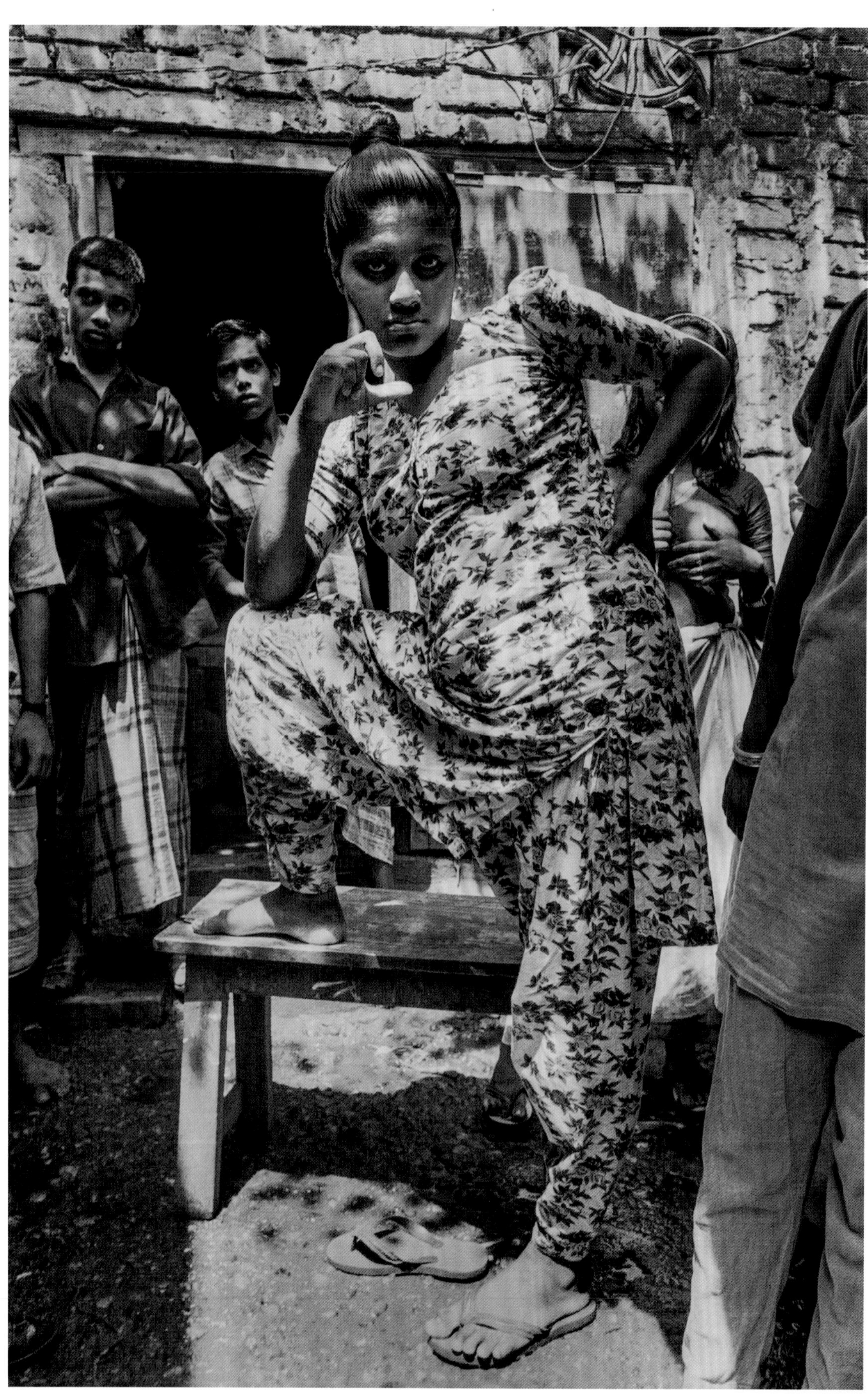

A sex-worker at a brothel in Tangail, the largest in Dhaka, in 1992; I was accompanied by Shehzad Noorani, a documentary photographer who focuses on the urban poor and marginalised. Without him I would not have been permitted to photograph there.

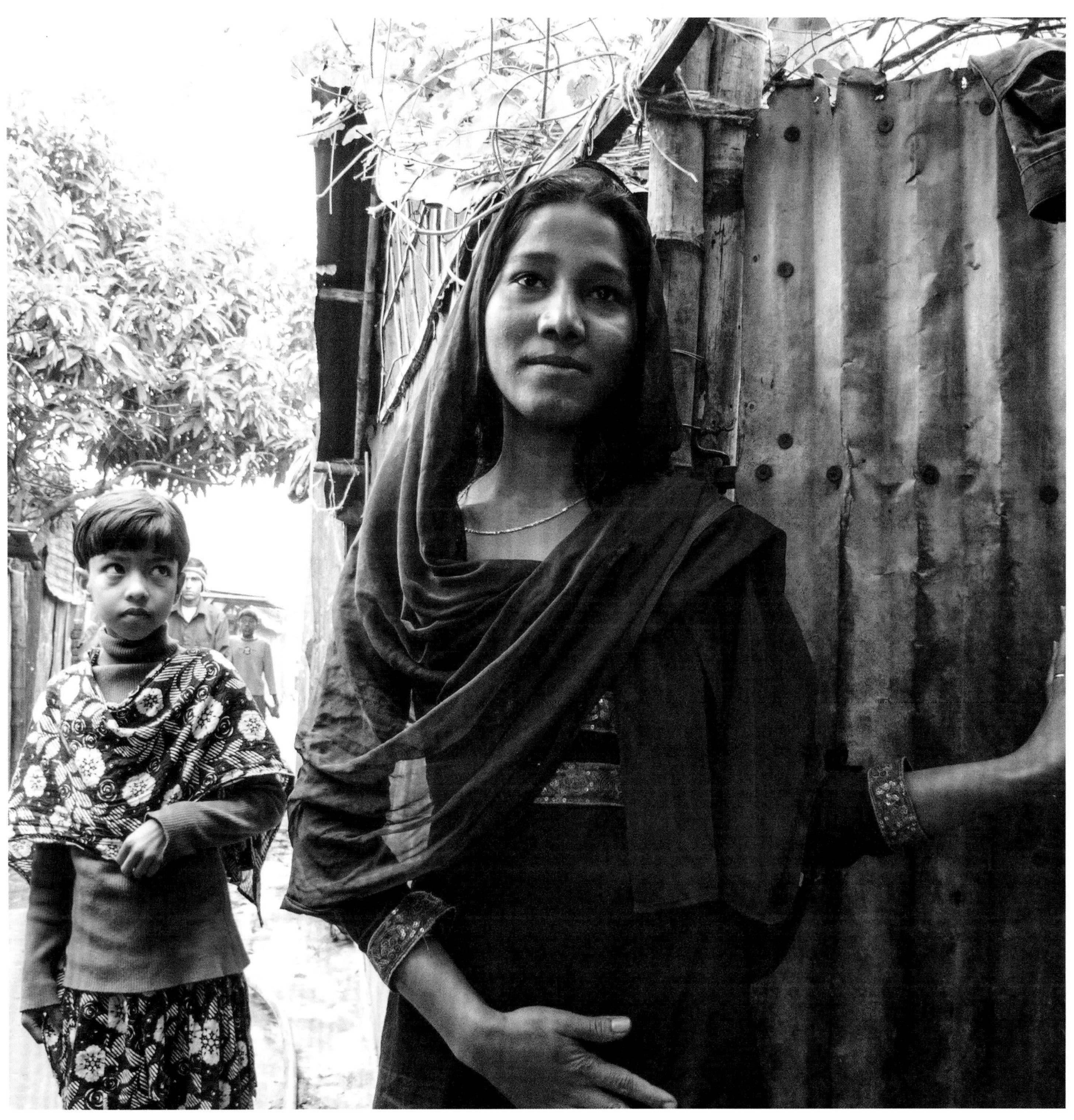

In 2011, I spent two days in Korail, one of the largest slums in Bangladesh, with David Burnett (see page 118). Our job was to photograph the water supply and sanitary fittings for Water Aid. I visited a school, where I met the girl in this photograph. It is one of the first I took with a digital camera. David taught me how to use it.

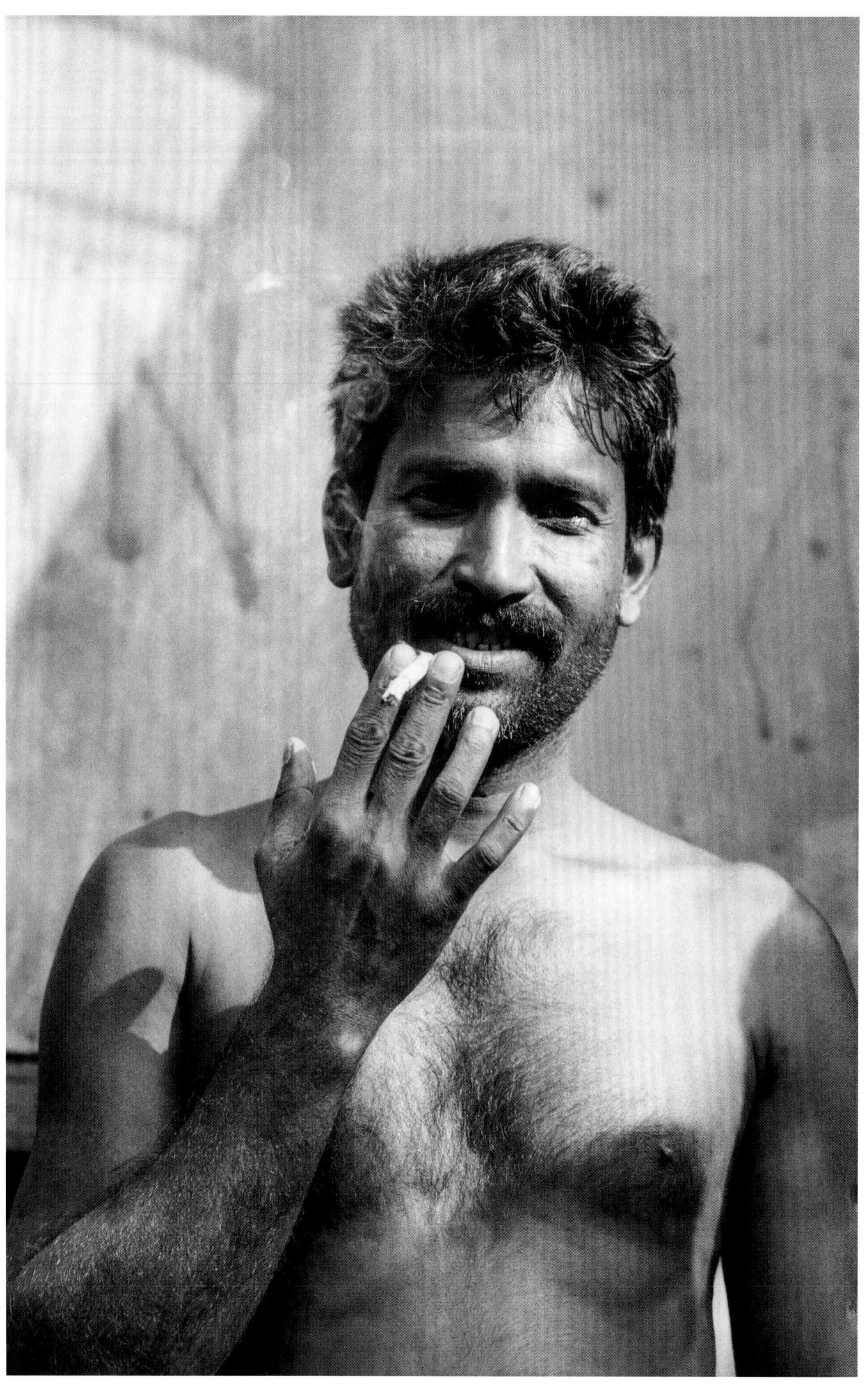

Metal worker in Old Dhaka

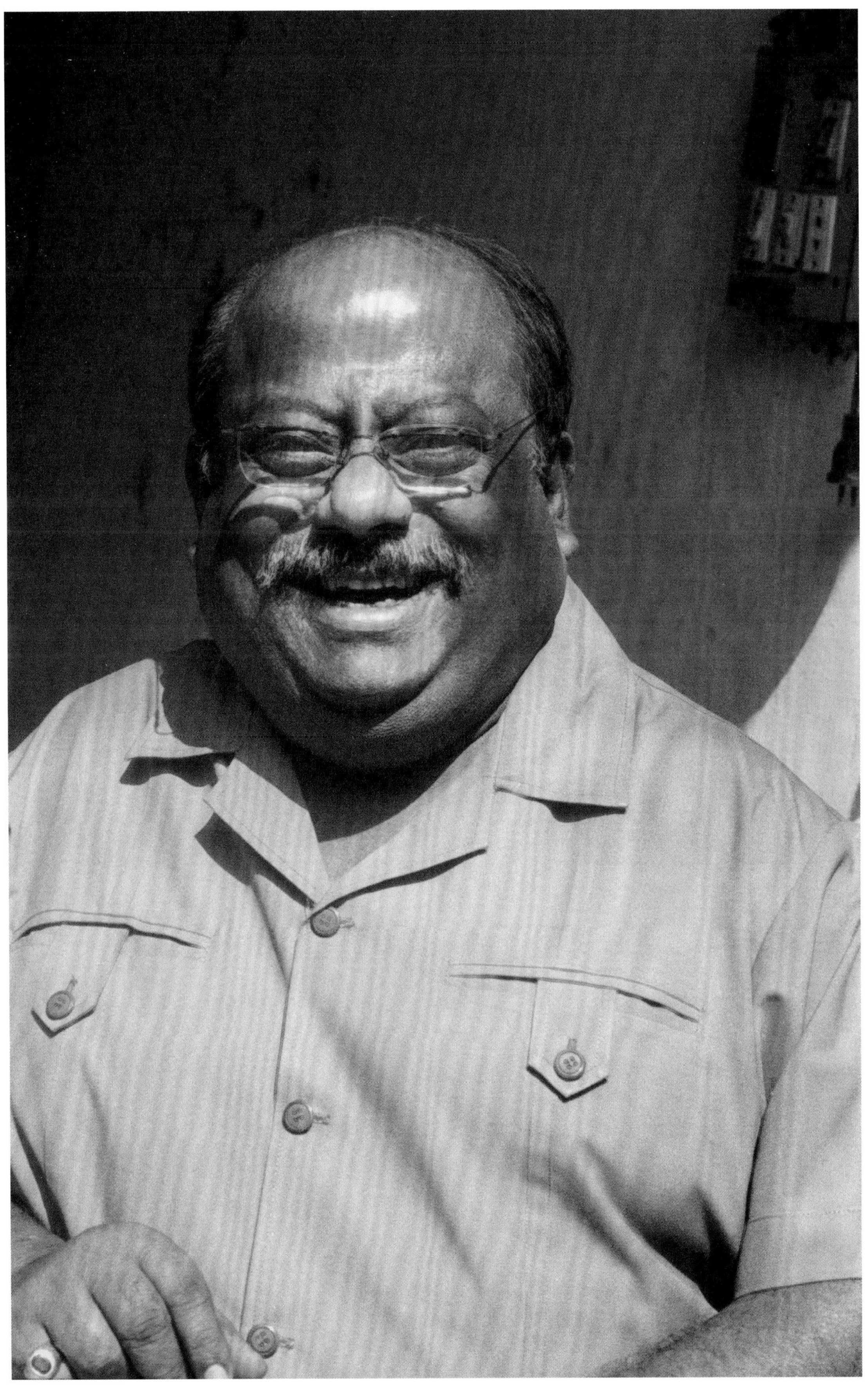

Head of Customs in Chittagong

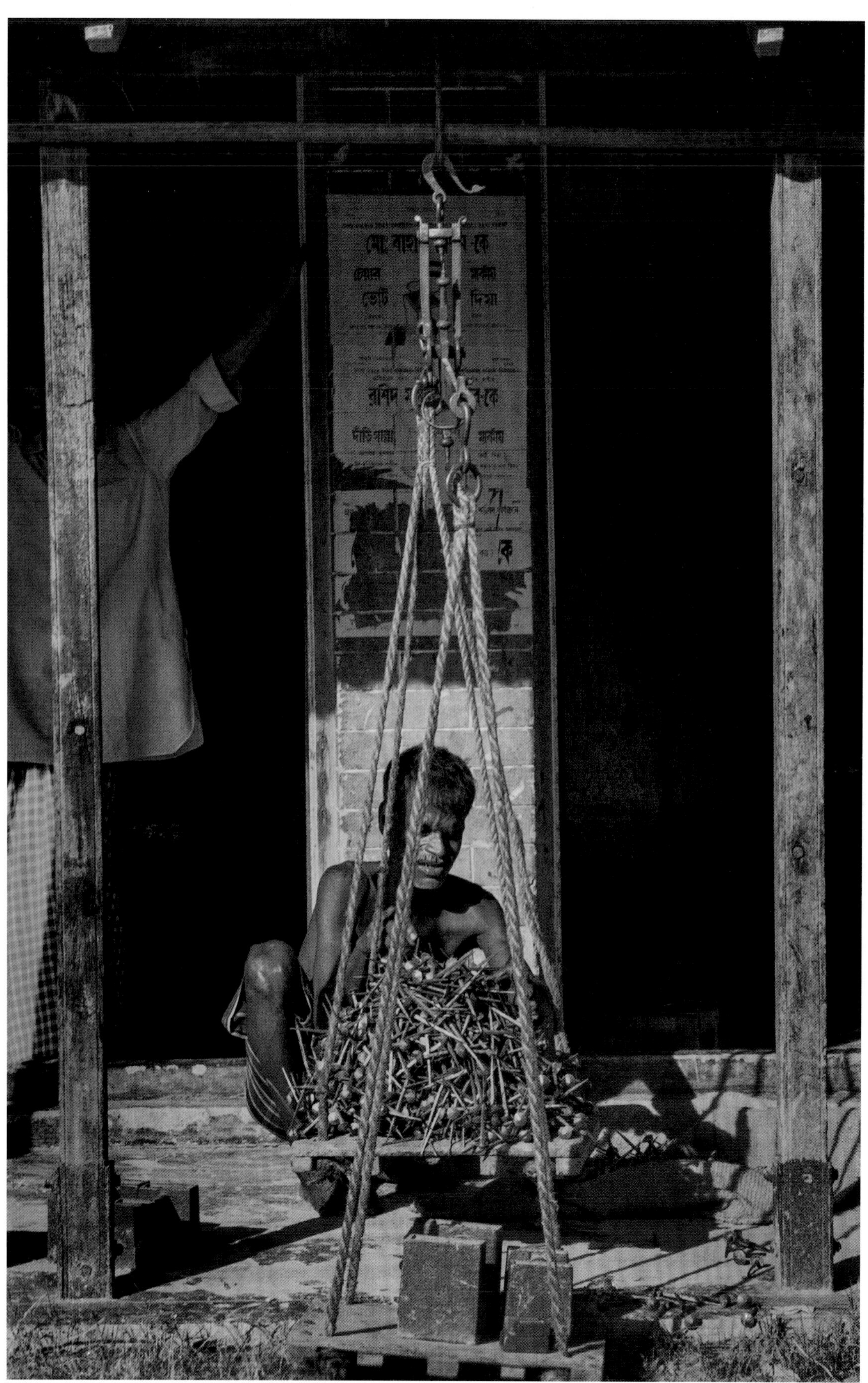

Hand-forged nails with broad heads, sold by weight. I bought 2 lbs. You could not get them in Europe at the time. 2004

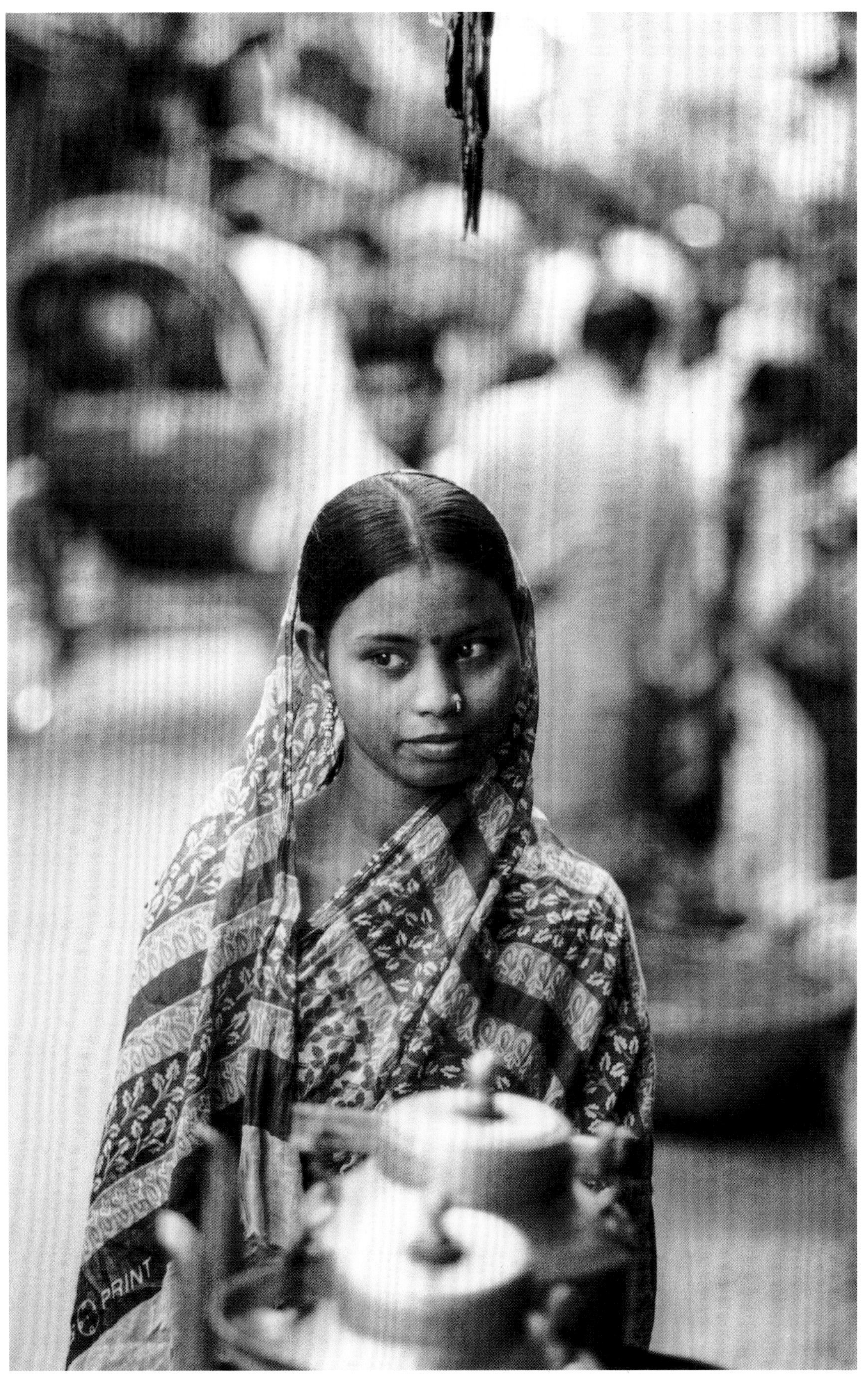

Girl with tea kettles in Old Dhaka in 2006

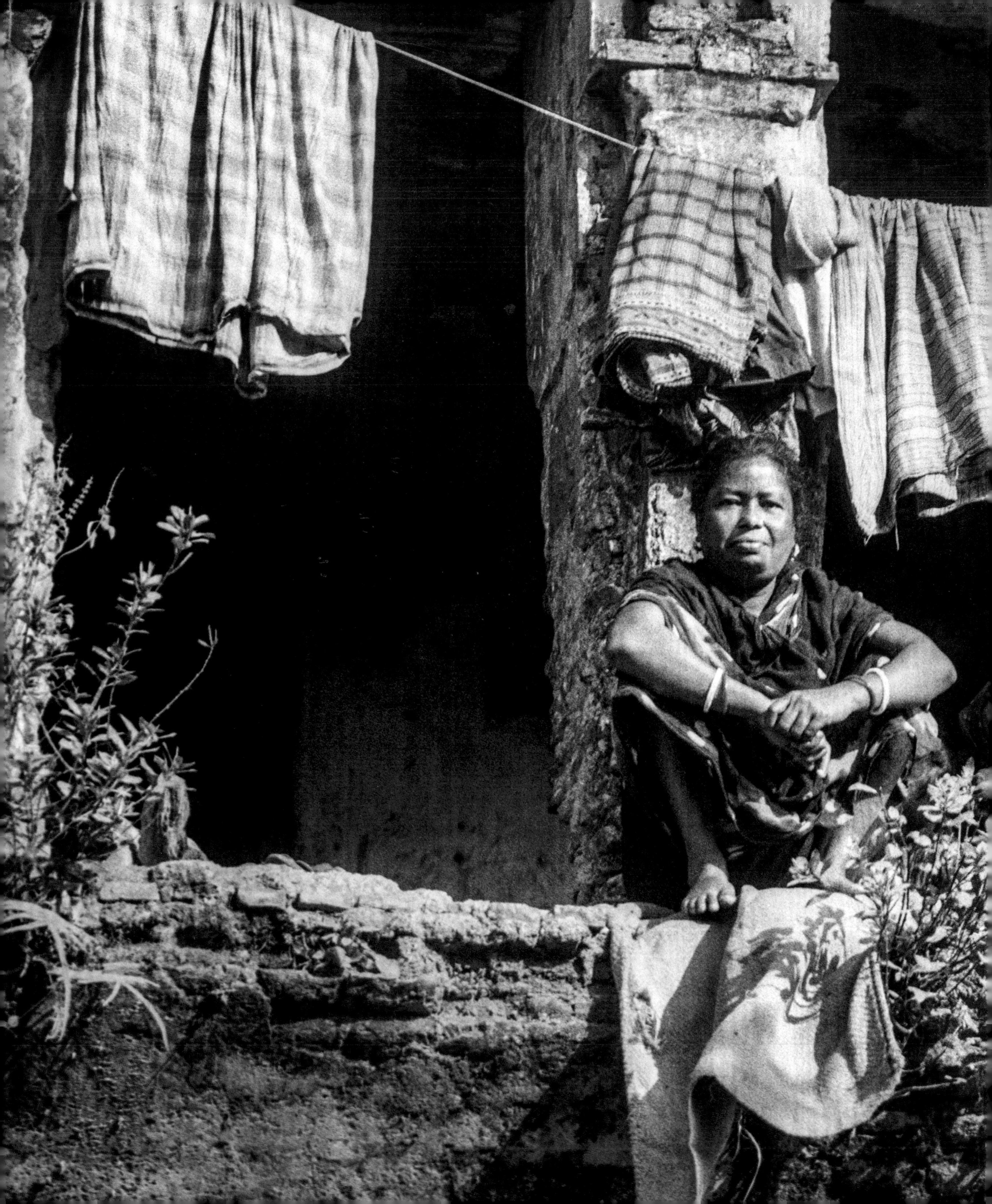

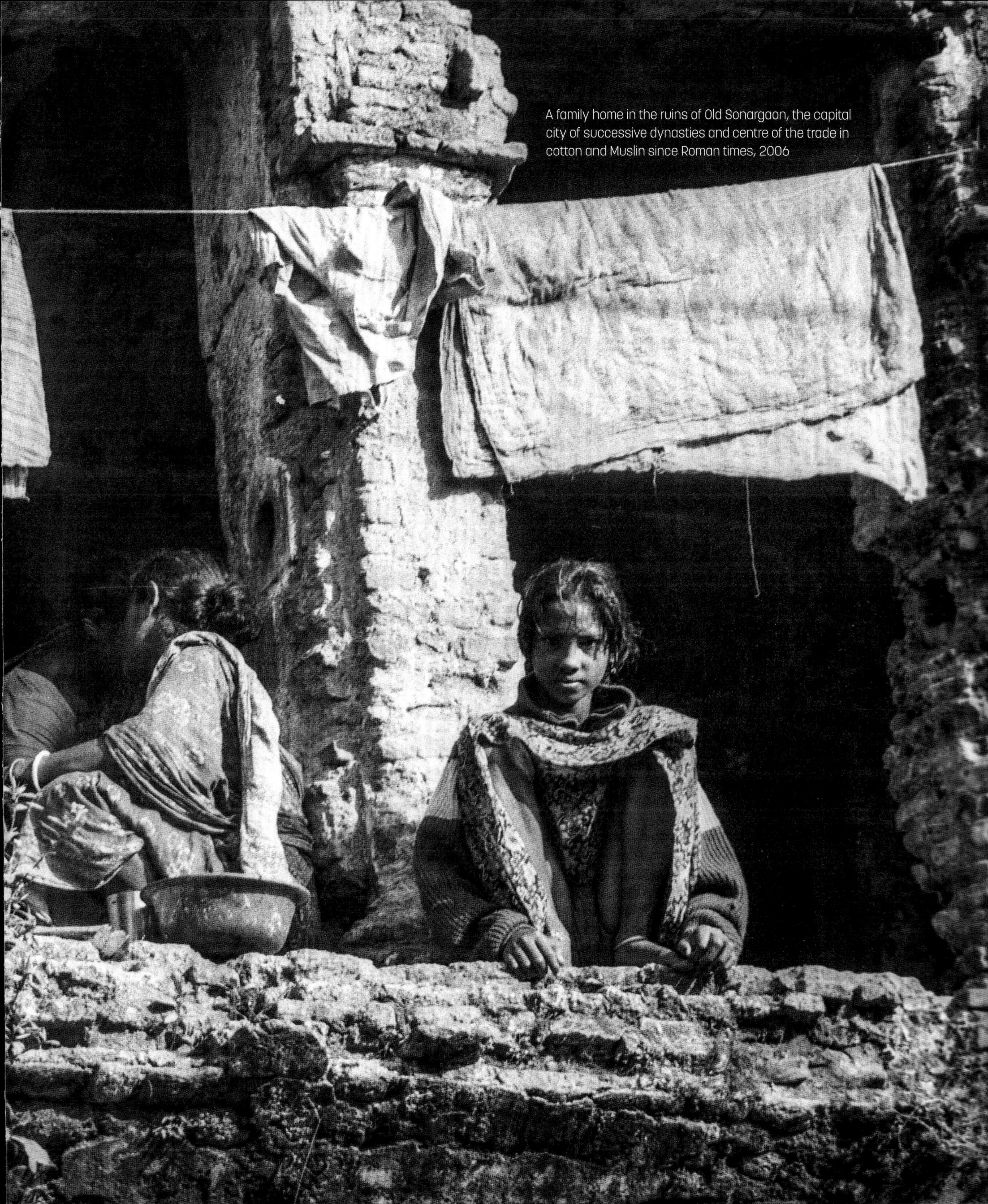

A family home in the ruins of Old Sonargaon, the capital city of successive dynasties and centre of the trade in cotton and Muslin since Roman times, 2006

'No Entry for the Rolls That Went Everywhere', 1 January 2013

In 2012, Jan and I motored across India in a battered seventy-year-old Rolls-Royce. The plan was to drive north from Bombay, across the plains of Gujarat towards the high Himalayas, and thence to the green valleys of Assam by China. Shahidul, hearing of our journey, invited us to be guests of honour at Chobi Mela VIII in January 2013.

It took three months to reach the border with Bangladesh. After a mildly hazardous journey up the Meghalayan Hills, dodging giant trucks as they thundered nose to tail in swirling dust on rough dirt roads, we made our way down the other side along a deserted narrow track to the border post at Tamabil.

We had debated at some length whether driving a symbol of wealth through a country known for poverty was altogether a good idea. The 'R-R' embossed on the silver chrome radiator spoke with evocative clarity of the British Raj. On the other hand, the dents in the aluminium bodywork told of a car that works for its living.[21] Imposing it may have been, but it wasn't flashy.

It also has a secret allure which grown-ups invariably miss and children invariably don't: running boards. Bangladeshi children, oblivious to symbols of an empire they never knew, couldn't resist a running board.[22] The combination of these things, it turned out, was a magnet. During our crossing of the subcontinent, mainly on rural roads, the Rolls drew people of all ages and backgrounds. As we pulled up at the border crossing, we had six small additional passengers riding on the running boards.

Mr Bhuyan, the Head of Customs, was charming but firm: our authority to bring the Rolls into Bangladesh came from the wrong department. He was very sorry, but British cars, as he put it, were 'not allowed'. As Jan correctly observed, it simply wasn't going to happen. So we wrapped the Rolls in a large canvas tent, established a warm rapport with Mr Bhuyan, appointed a masterly chowkidar[23] called Babul to watch over it and headed south to Dhaka to solve the problem. Back in London, *The Times* considered this turn of events to be newsworthy. The headline on page 5 was, 'No entry for the Rolls that went everywhere'.

Shahidul, who is probably the most well-connected activist on the planet, came to the rescue. He fixed a meeting with the ultimate authority, namely the Chair of the National Board of Revenue. I told him the story of the car and the journey, and Shahidul assured him that I had no intention of selling the car. He generously granted us permission to bring the Rolls into Bangladesh and stay for a month.

Thus it was that the Rolls, with Shahidul cross-legged on the roof-rack like a deity above the fray, led the boisterous trumpeteering Chobi Mela crowds through the streets of Dhaka on the opening day of the festival. Children jumped on and off the running boards, as did old friends and fellow photographers.

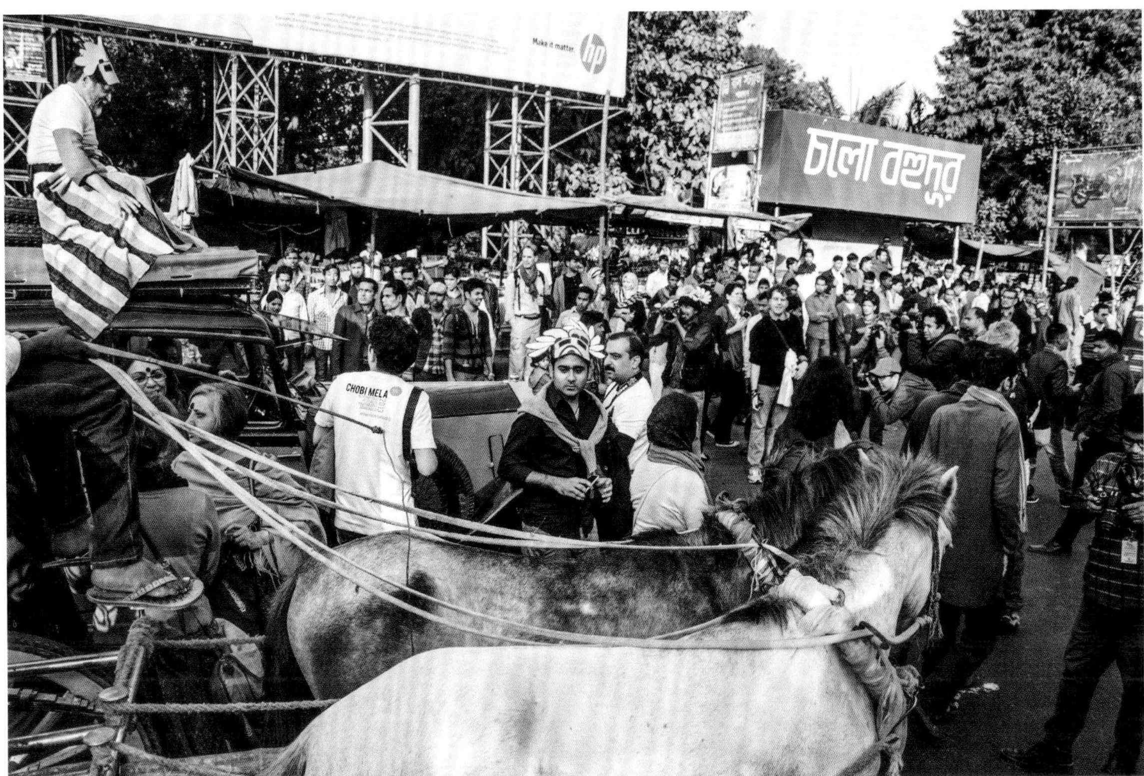

Shahidul Alam on the roof of the Rolls during the opening rally of Chobi Mela in January 2013

The Rolls, as Shahidul remarked later, had changed from being a symbol of empire to a catalyst for friendships which reached across boundaries, dismantled prejudices and celebrated cultural and historical differences. Jan made a similar remark, as she sat beside me in these extraordinary moments: 'This is no longer our journey. The Rolls has merged with the force for change that is Chobi Mela and we are being carried along with it.'

We spent a month in Bangladesh. There were exhibitions to see, photographers with whom to re-establish friendships, dinner parties to join. I gave a lecture on copyright. We spent a week on a fishing boat in the Sundarbans with two of our three daughters.

On the penultimate day of our allotted one month, we took a ferry across the Ganges and turned west towards India. That evening a hartal[24] was declared for the following day: cars seen on public roads during the hours of daylight were at risk of being destroyed.

We rose at 3.00am and raced to the border, past groups of hartal watchmen crouching by fires silhouetted against the dawn sky. This was no time to take photographs. We reached the border at first light. ■

---

21 It has done 330,000 miles.

22 We strengthened the running boards before we left home with this in mind, and added internal hooks so that when children hung on to the door handles the doors didn't fly open.

23 A watchman or gatekeeper.

24 A national shutdown of workplaces, shops and roads, it amounts to a form of civil disobedience similar to a labour strike. It is often used, as on this occasion, as a means of political protest.

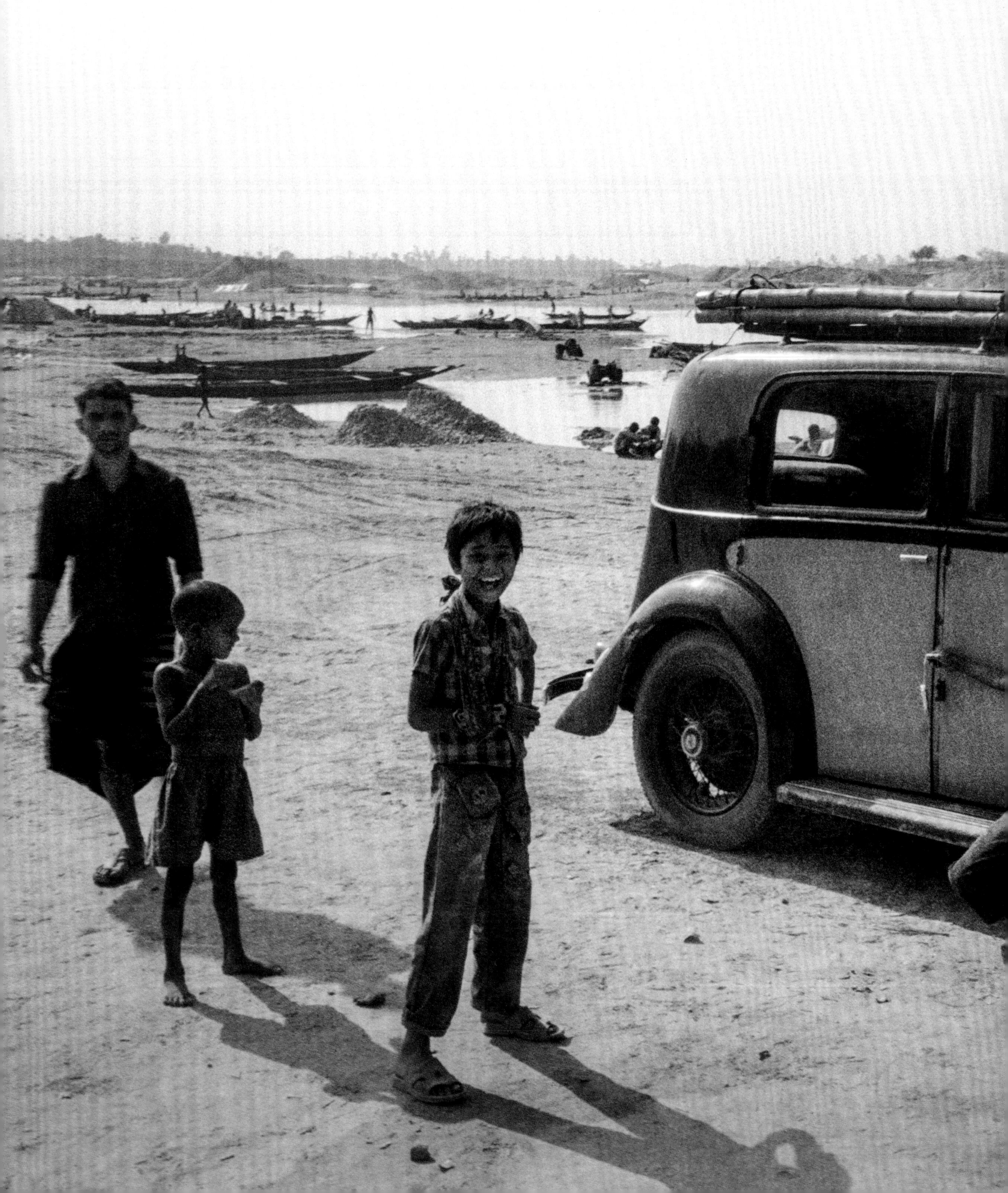

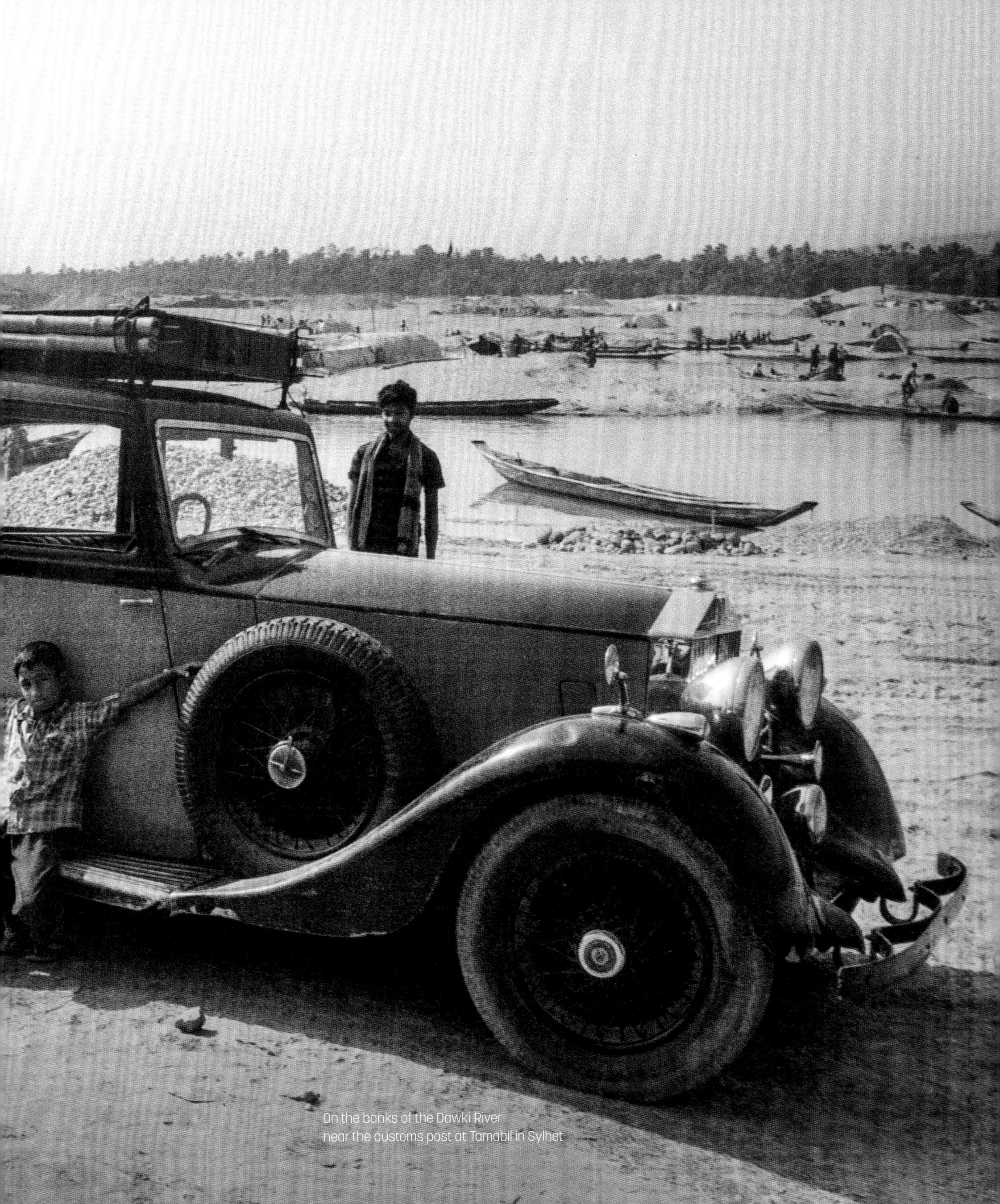

On the banks of the Dawki River
near the customs post at Tamabil in Sylhet

Victory Day, 16 December 1971

On this day over 93,000 Pakistani troops surrendered to the Bangladeshi Liberation forces. It was, and remains, the largest surrender of armed forces since the Second World War. The war was one of the most violent of the twentieth century. The cold-blooded massacres perpetrated by the Pakistani army are now widely regarded as genocide. The photographs of the war have since then been used as propaganda tools by political parties to sway public opinion and to harness nationalism in Bangladesh.

Amongst the Western photographers who covered the war was a young David Burnett, now one of the world's most respected photojournalists. Forty years later he returned to Dhaka for the fortieth anniversary. I and a few other photographers were with him.[25] The day was widely celebrated in cinema, literature, history lessons at school and across the mass media. The streets were packed, musicians played, flags flew, street-stalls sold out, goodwill was in. The day was joyous.

There was a gathering that evening at the Ambrosia, a local hotel frequented by visiting photo-journalists and Bangladeshis alike. David spoke to us of his life as a photojournalist; many Pathshala students were there. He showed us a selection of images, from times of peace and times of war. Amongst them was one which David had not shown before.

He and Nick Ut, a Vietnamese-American photographer, took shelter in a ditch as a napalm bomb exploded in a village in Vietnam on 8 June 1972. A naked nine-year old girl ran screaming down the road. Nick had one frame left in his camera. David had none. They both ran, David loading film as he went. Nick pulled ahead and took the photograph which appeared on the front cover of *Time* Magazine a few days later and won the Pulitzer Prize in 1973. David, film loaded just in time, took the picture of the man taking the picture which is widely thought to have triggered the end of the Vietnam war.[26] Downing their cameras, they took the girl, whose name is Phan Thj Kim Phuc, to hospital.

There was a long silence when David finished speaking. He had reminded us, directly and graphically, of the power of the camera and the role of the photojournalist: to inform national leaders of the consequences of their decisions and the injustices over which they preside, and to likewise inform those they represent so that, by public protest and through the ballot box, they can have a voice in what sort of world they want to live in.

Exactly what Victory Day was about, from the man who witnessed the war it commemorated. Relevant also to a time when, in many parts of the world, freedom of speech is under threat and political repression is growing. ■

---

25 We were brought together by Photographers 4 Hope, a collective formed by Anna Wang.

26 The image acquired its own title: 'The Terror of War'.

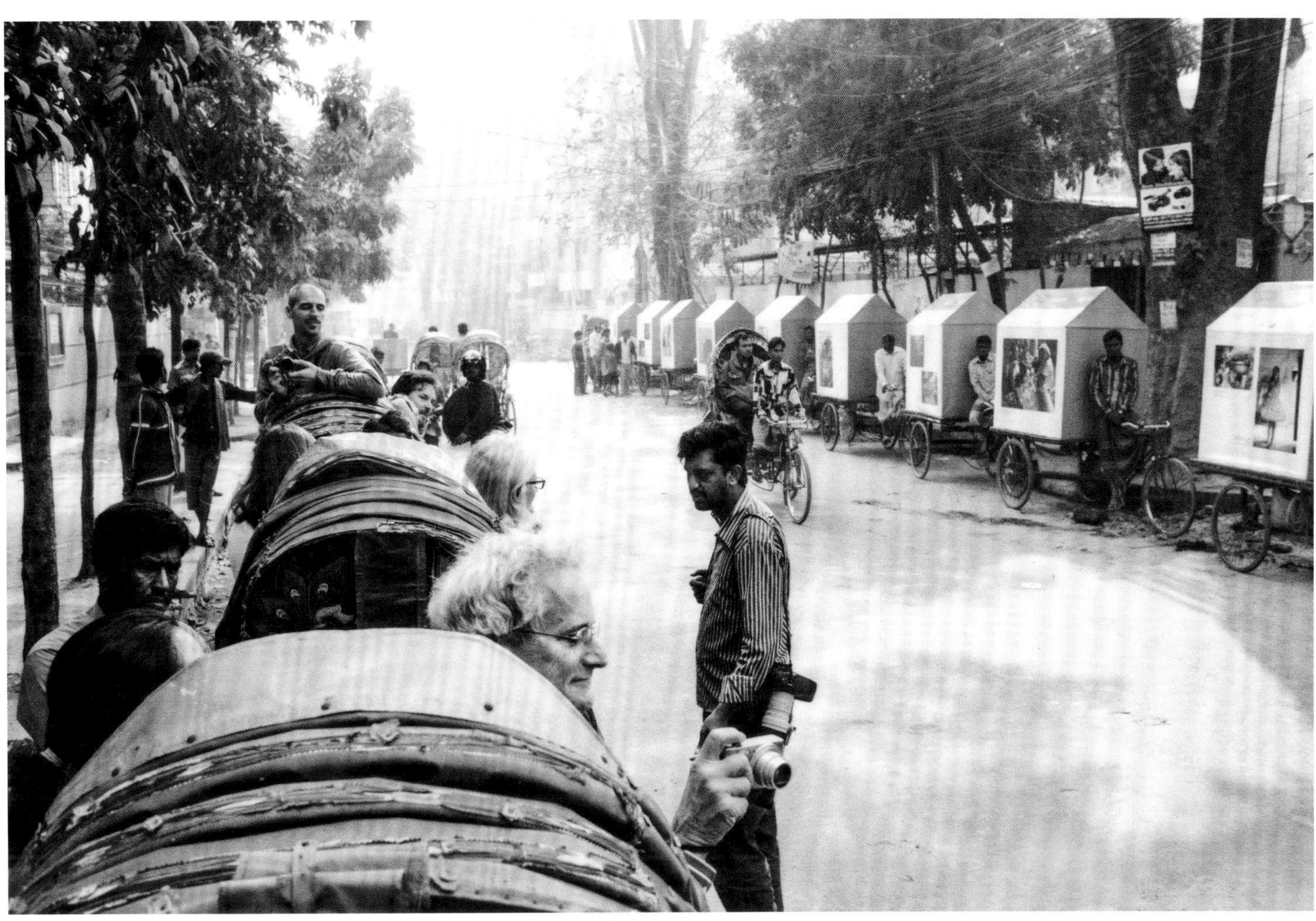

David Burnett setting out to photograph Victory Day in 2011 with Photographers 4 Hope; the flatbed rickshaws on the other side of the street are the travelling exhibition of the images taken by the group for agencies to whom we were respectively attached. I was with Water Aid.

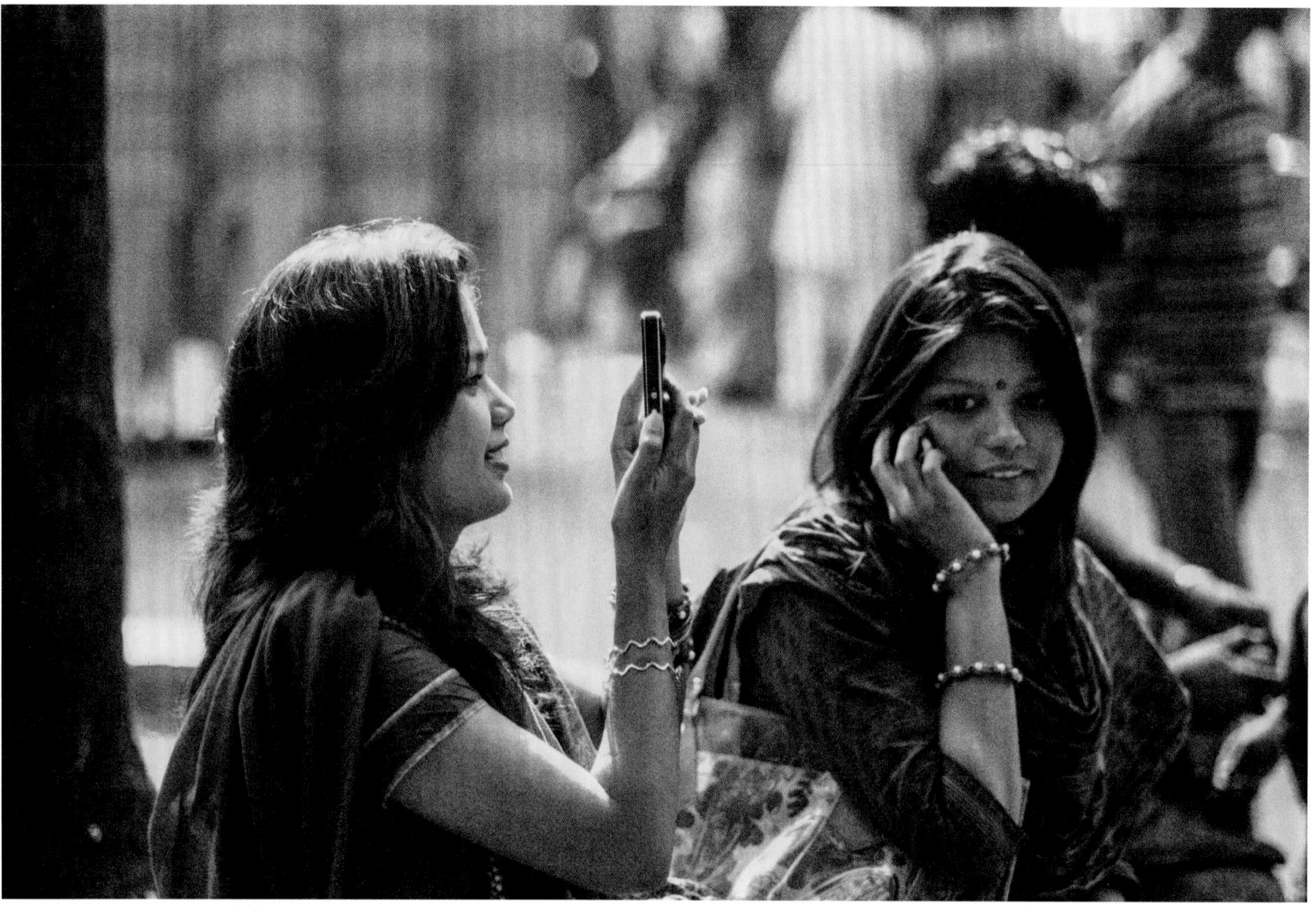

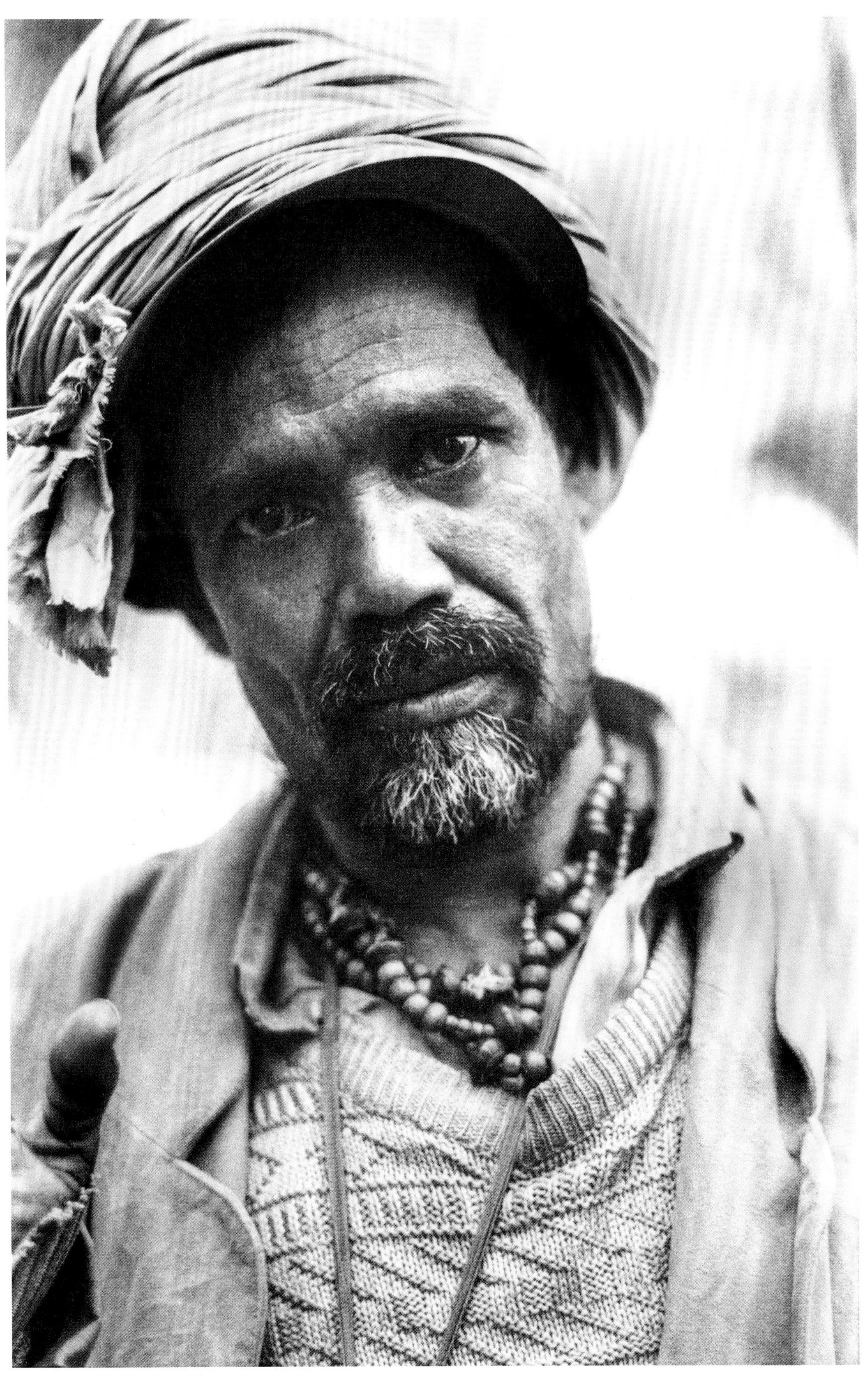

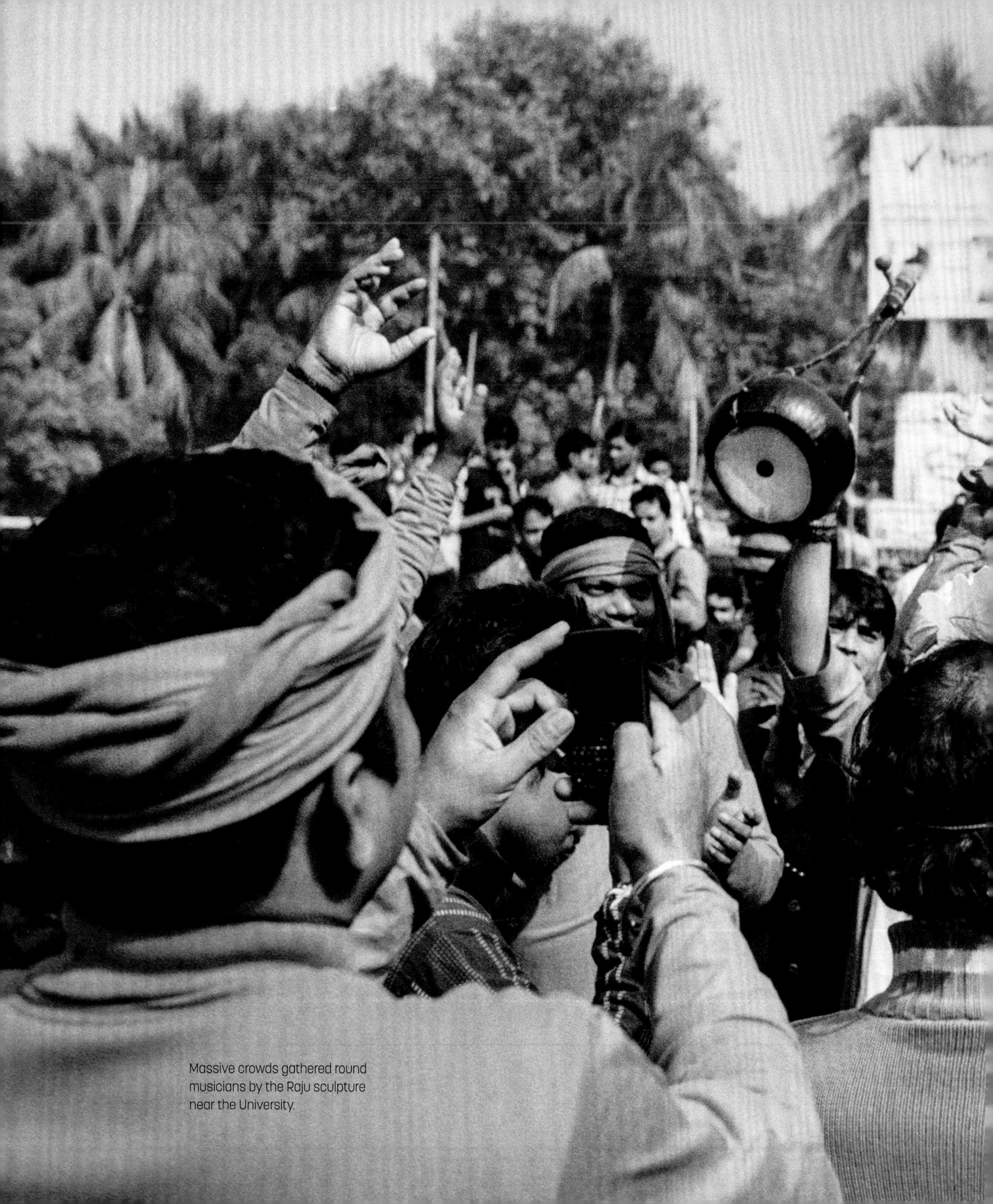

Massive crowds gathered round musicians by the Raju sculpture near the University.

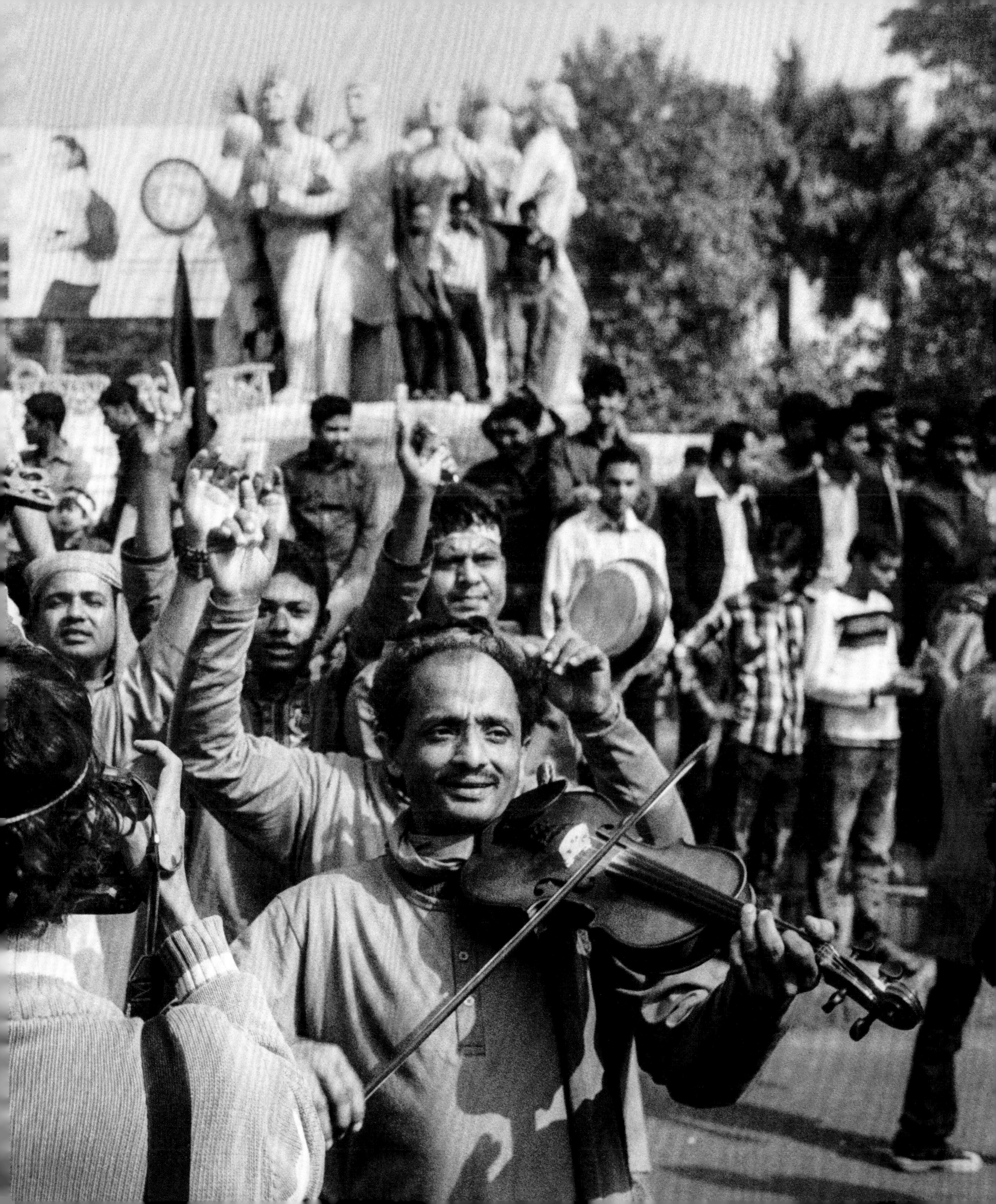

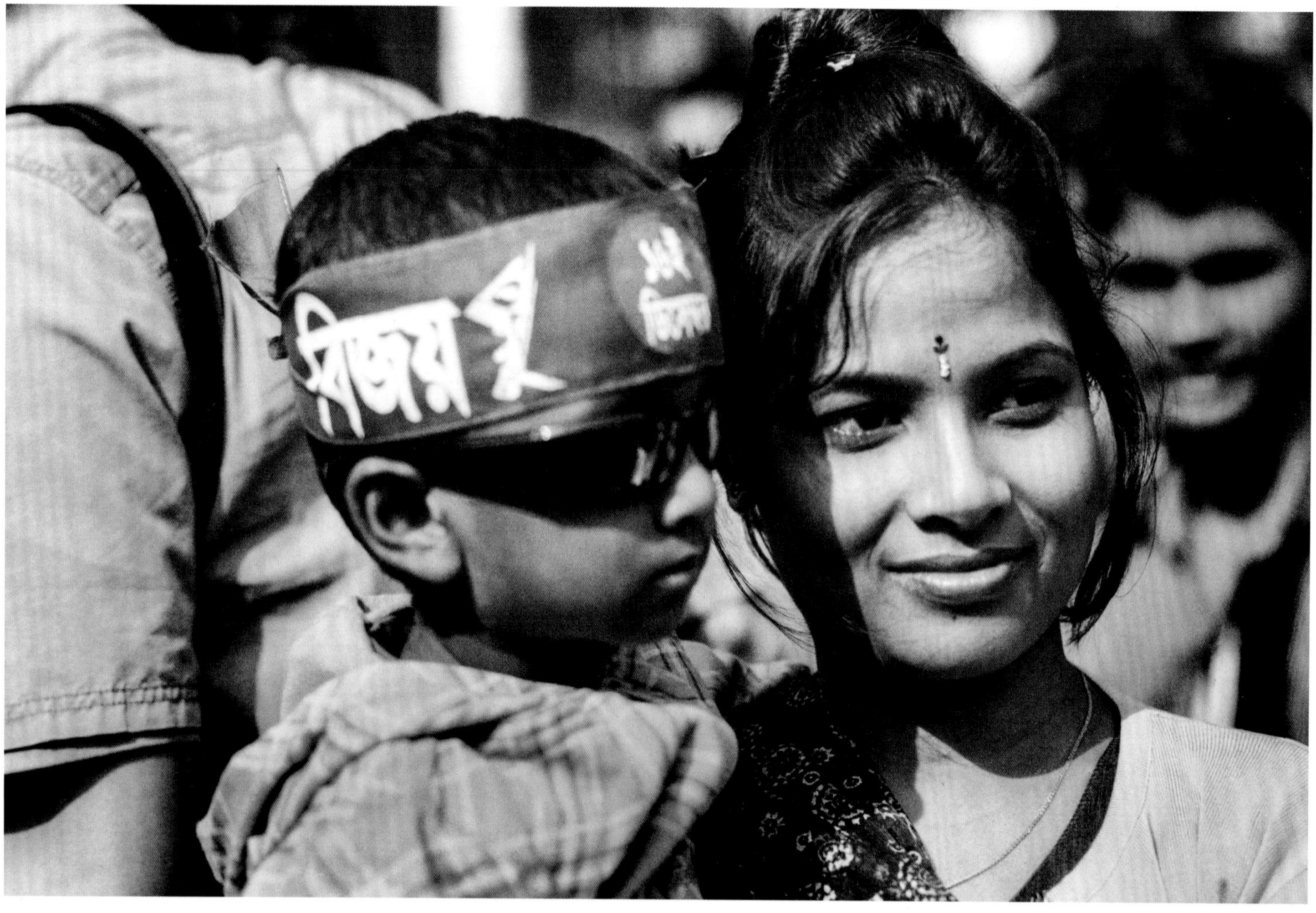
বিজয়

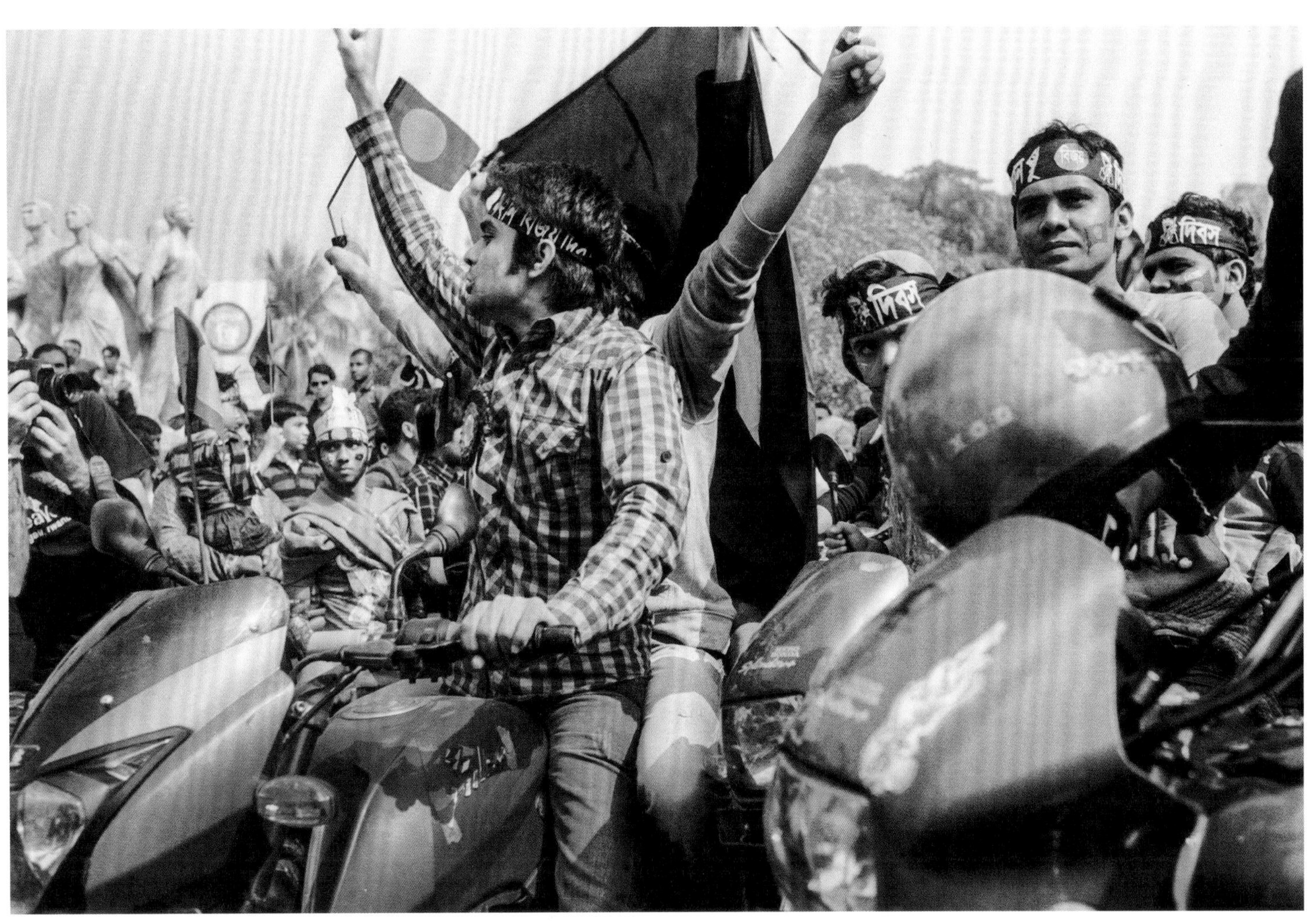

Crowds celebrating Victory Day in front of the statue commemorating Moin Hossain Raju. Raju was a student activist who was shot during a confrontation between police and students in 1992 while protesting against political interference in student politics in Dhaka University. The sculpture depicts a group of students marching in defiance.

Keraniganj Jail, 5 August 2018

On 5 August 2018, as I was climbing a mountain in the Swiss Alps, I received a call from Vincent Hasselbach, an Anglo-German friend who was at that time a student at Pathshala. He told me that thirty minutes before, at 10.00 pm Bangladeshi time, Shahidul Alam had been abducted from his home by plainclothes police.

They gained entry by forcing a female Pathshala student to ask him for help while the police waited outside the door in silence. Shahidul and Rahnuma are available to help students at any hour. On hearing the familiar call for 'Uncle Shahidul' he opened the door. The police grabbed him, beat him, dragged him downstairs, threw him in an unmarked van, destroyed the CCTV cameras and removed the footage.

The reason given for Shahidul's arrest was that he criticised the Bangladeshi government for its brutal repression of student protests in Dhaka during an interview with Al Jazeera earlier that day and, later that evening, in comments on Facebook.

After one night of torture he was brought to court, held on remand and, six days later taken to Keraniganj jail. He was held there for 101 days. He was released on bail on 20 November 2018 following international protests and appeals by human rights groups, Nobel laureates and academics calling for his release. There were mass rallies around the world.

The government's appeal against his release failed.

Shahidul has never been charged.

In 2018, he was selected by *Time* Magazine as Person of the Year, alongside Jamal Khashoggi. The headline read:

'Journalism is under threat. Inside [is] a journalist's dangerous journey from photographer to prisoner'. ■

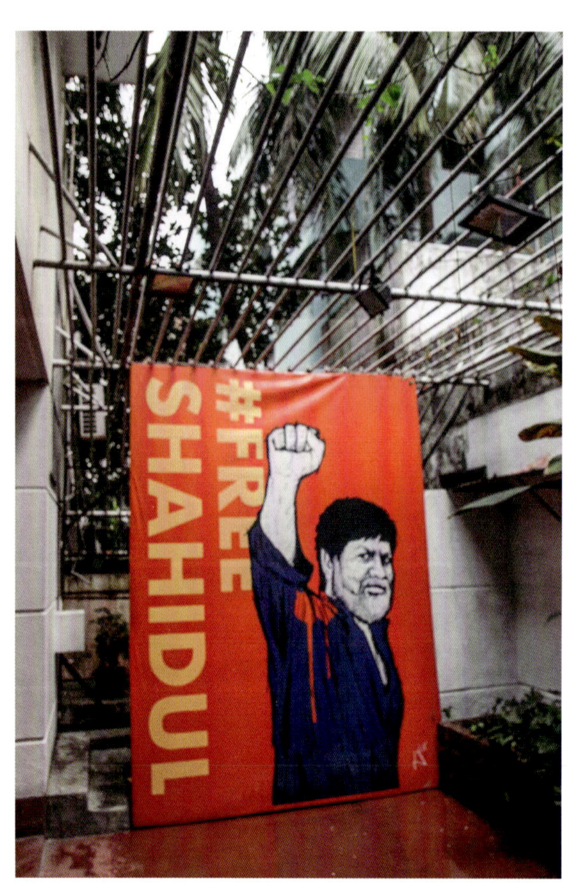

One of the many posters created to raise public awareness of Shahidul's imprisonment; this one was hanging in Drik's offices

Dr Shahidul Alam

Shahidul Alam obtained a PhD in chemistry before taking up photography, concentrating on issues of social justice. He set up the Drik and Majority World agencies, Pathshala South Asian Media Institute and the Chobi Mela festival.

An Honorary Fellow of the Royal Photographic Society and visiting professor at the University of Sunderland, Alam has chaired the World Press Photo jury, among other honours. Alam is also a new media pioneer and introduced email to Bangladesh. His book, *My Journey as a Witness*, has been described by John Morris, the former picture editor of *Life* Magazine, as 'the most important book ever written by a photographer'.

He was Person of the Year for *Time* Magazine in 2018, and appointed as Explorer at Large by the National Geographic Society in 2022, an honour granted to few global changemakers and thought leaders.

Rupert Grey

Rupert is a practising lawyer in London. In the course of a long career he has represented and fought libel actions for and against national papers, politicians, celebrities, photographers, authors, galleries, publishers, bankers and explorers. He was the Senior Partner at Crockers Oswald Hickson, a prominent firm of libel and copyright lawyers, and latterly a partner in Farrer & Co.

Rupert is the founding chair of the Nekton Foundation, an NGO which conducts major research missions in the Western Indian Ocean; he serves on the board of the Mary Rose Museum in Portsmouth, and is General Counsel for the Liverpool Institute for Performing Arts, of which he was a founder in 1990.

In the field of photography he is a founding trustee of the John Kobal Foundation, which holds an important collection of photographs of Hollywood in its prime; he serves on the board of Autograph, a photographic gallery which leads the field in race, identity and human rights, and he is a trustee of the Magnum Foundation, the charitable arm of Magnum Photos. He has for many years been closely associated with Pathshala, a highly regarded school of photography in Bangladesh.

Rupert is primarily an outdoorsman. He started his career as a prospector for copper in the South Pacific, a roughneck on oil-rigs in the Yukon and a deckhand on the oyster boats in the Tasman Sea. After a spell as a photojournalist in the UK, he switched to law at the age of thirty-five.

Armed with his Nikon FM2s and often accompanied by his wife, Jan, and their three daughters, he has travelled on foot and horseback, by dug-out canoe, dog sledge, camel, elephant, bush plane, Land Rover and a vintage Rolls-Royce to the wild places of the earth. His expeditions have led him down rainforest rivers, across oceans and deserts, mountains and the Arctic.

His photographs have been exhibited in several countries and his articles have been widely published.

He has acted in three films: *The Blue Lagoon* (1979), *Yugadistra* (2013), an Assamese production, and the lead part with his wife, Jan, in *Romantic Road* (2017), executive produced by Sharon Stone, now available on Netflix.

Rupert and Jan married in 1977 and live in a remote thatched cottage under the South Downs in Sussex, England, where their principal occupations are planting trees, constructing barns, restoring wagons, and hosting dinner parties and grandchildren.

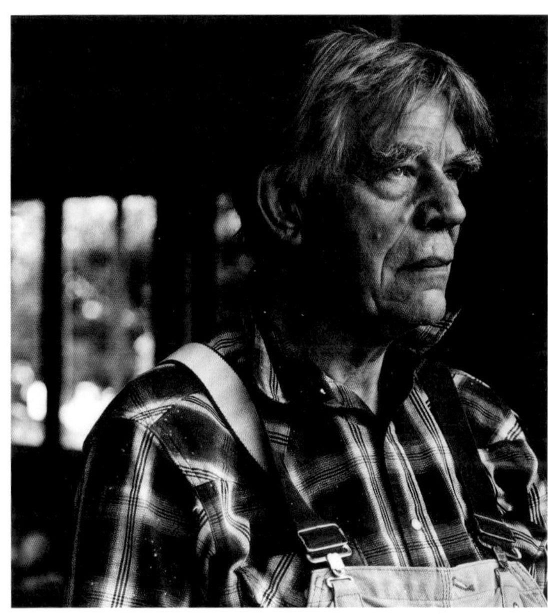

Portrait by Martin Hartley in 2022

January 2023

Acknowledgements

Homage to Bangladesh has five midwives:

- Jan, to whom I have been married for 45 years. Sine qua non.
- Shahidul Alam. During his long fight for embattled democracy and freedom of speech, has altered the landscape of many lives, including mine.
- Clare Blenkinsop and Richard Holloway, professionals in international development and our companions on many expeditions, who led us to the Sundarbans.
- Brett Rogers, then of the British Council and later Director of The Photographers' Gallery, at whose invitation I returned to Dhaka in 2004 to deliver a lecture on copyright.
- The students, teachers and visiting photographers and curators at Pathshala and Chobi Mela, for their determination to hold authority to account despite the dangers, for inspiring talks and countless enlightening conversations. There are too many to name. They sowed the seeds of this book.

I am indebted to many others without whom these photographs would not have been taken, nor the book written:

Katherine, Carmody and Rose, my three clear-thinking and articulate daughters, past whom nothing gets unless it is both true and good.

Oliver McGarvey, film-maker, free-thinker, friend, godson and companion-in-arms. For being the person he is and for producing *Romantic Road*, a widely acclaimed film of our journey across India to Bangladesh in 2013.

Simon Mooney, sports photographer. His critical eye and talent as a photo-editor has been beyond price, as has his patience and his friendship.

Terry Hack and Iris Fernandes of Bayeux in Newman Street, London. Their expertise in all things photographic has been a constant support; their basement is a gathering place for talented photographers.

For their encouragement and invaluable guidance on the business of writing, Michael Holman formerly of the *Financial Times*, Caroline Chapman, friend and author, Nigel Winser of the Royal Geographic Society and Mark Sealy of Autograph.

Rahnuma Ahmed, whose natural habitat is the barricades and with whom conversations, whether in the back of tuk-tuks or round the dinner table with Shahidul and their many friends, are always a joy.

Anna Wang and her team at Photographers 4 Hope, with whom I spent a creative and inspiring week in Dhaka in 2011.

The late Jehangir Alam and his team at Ambrosia in Dhanmondi, whose hospitality is warm and whose well-tended garden is a gathering place for photographers from every nation.

Big Jim (Stokes) and Young Jim (Bright), as they were referred to by the family, both of JSW Engineering. Without them the Rolls (page 116) would not have got to Bangladesh or anywhere near it.

Mr Bhuyan of the border post at Tamabil, who must be the only customs officer in history who, having declared that a car was not permitted to enter his country, made friends with its owners.

Alhaj Md Ghulam Hussain, then Chairman of the National Board of Revenue in Bangladesh who, on hearing of the journey, generously gave us permission to cross the border.

My special thanks and appreciation also to Lucy Duckworth and her team at Unicorn for their expertise, patience and enthusiasm.

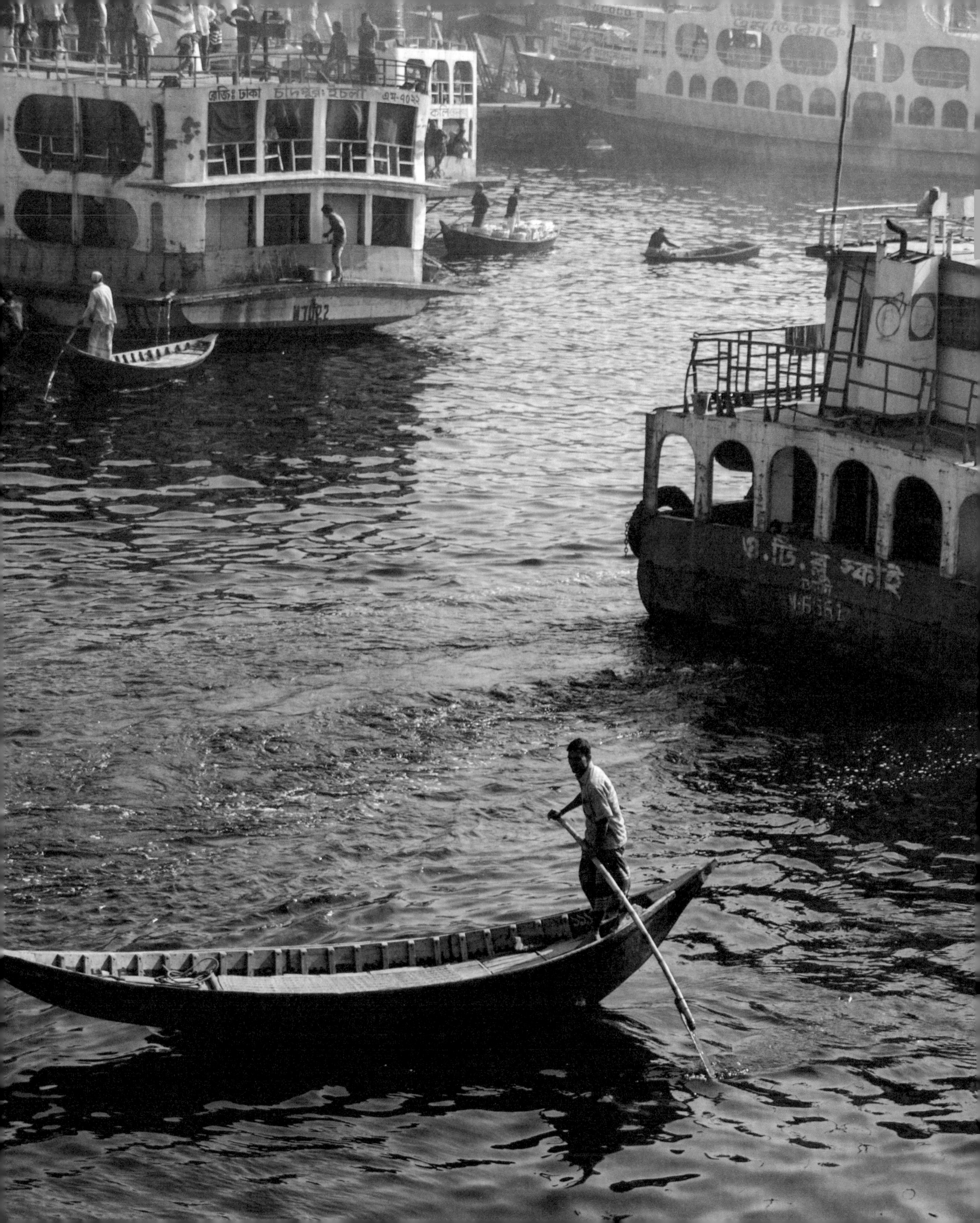
রেজিঃ ঢাকা
এম-৭০২২